Transforming Conflict by Building Relationships

A Manual for Conflict Resolution and Mediation

2nd edition

revised and expanded

by

Patrick J. Ashton, Ph.D.

Department of Sociology
Indiana University Purdue University Fort Wayne
2101 East Coliseum Blvd
Fort Wayne, Indiana 46805-1499
260 481-6669
ashton@ipfw.edu

 The author wishes to thank the following organizations for permission to use their materials in this manual:

Common Ground, Inc.
Community Dispute Resolution Service
Fort Wayne, IN

Mennonite Conciliation Service
21 South 12th Street, P.O. Box 500
Akron, PA 17501-0500
Pages reprinted with permission.

Leif Fearn
Teacher Education
San Diego State University
San Diego, CA 92120

Barbara Daté, Ph.D.
Mediator, Trainer, and Mediation Consultant
Eugene, OR

John Paul Lederach
The Joan B. Kroc Institute of International Peace and Justice Studies at University of Notre Dame
and Eastern Mennonite University
jpbus@aol.com

Published and Distributed by
The Educational Publisher Inc.
www.EduPublisher.com
Columbus, Ohio
ISBN: 1-934849-87-1
ISBN13: 978-1-934849-87-3

To all my fellow mediators,

who seek to increase the peace

by helping people to find mutually satisfying

resolutions to conflicts by building relationships

through empowerment and recognition.

There is no way to peace; peace is the way.

A. J. Muste

Table of Contents

Preface: About this Manual

This manual is designed primarily to accompany a 40-hour college course in conflict resolution and mediation. Conflict resolution is part of the broader field of peace studies. Peace education, say Harris and Synott (2002:4), can be defined as "teaching encounters that draw out from people their desires for peace and provide them with nonviolent alternatives for managing conflicts, as well as the skills for critical analysis of the structural arrangements that legitimate and produce injustice and inequality." In keeping with this charge, there are two major goals for the course: (1) developing practical conflict resolution techniques with wide application in work organizations, families, and the community; and (2) discovering how conflict can be rooted in and shaped by cultural and social structural factors. Having mastered this knowledge and the appropriate techniques, those who successfully complete the course are certified as community mediators. While the training is neither designed nor approved for the development of certified family mediators, its general aim is to produce individuals who can more effectively resolve conflicts in their personal relationships and their families, at work and in their communities, as well as volunteer as community mediators in various nonprofit mediation and dispute resolution centers.

The manual is also designed in a way that allows for self-study. Self-study alone, of course, cannot create successful mediators. Active hands-on practice through roleplays and other simulations guided by trained coaches is necessary. But the person who dedicates themselves to reading the manual and doing the exercises will be rewarded with insights and skills that will enable them to be a more effective resolver and transformer of conflict.

The materials in this manual, as well as the philosophy underlying and animating them, are the intellectual offspring of many who have gone before. I am particularly indebted to those who trained me. Bob Gross, formerly of Education for Conflict Resolution, Inc., has not only developed many valuable materials, but also modeled for me what good mediation training can be. Barbara Daté is the author or the inspiration for many of the exercises in this manual. I owe her a great debt of gratitude for giving me a more complex and subtle understanding of conflict resolution, as well as being a mentor and an excellent role model as a trainer. I also wish to acknowledge the assistance and creative input of those who have helped me teach the course over the years, especially Marsha Banicki Graham, Terri Emrick, Wayne Williams, Shelly Gilliland, Norma Lickey, Terri Jones, and Amanda Doctor.

Community Boards of San Francisco, it is fair to say, is the organizational grandparent of contemporary community-oriented mediation groups. Their materials, which played a large role in my own training, clearly reflect the more than three decades of experience this organization has had in working toward community and individual empowerment. Also of great value to me have been the extensive materials compiled by the Mennonite Conciliation Service in its excellent manual. To me (and many others), it is the "gold standard" of manuals. Nearly every mediation manual I have ever examined has quoted and/or reprinted extensively from the MCS manual. Clearly it is widely respected in the community mediation field.

The philosophy of mediation and conflict resolution that underlies the present manual is fundamentally transformative in orientation. That is, it seeks not merely or even primarily to assist the parties in a dispute to solve their own problems, but rather to empower the parties, provide them with individual recognition, and dignify and heal the relationship between them. This transformative approach was articulated nearly twenty years ago by Robert Baruch Bush and Joseph Folger (1994). Recently they have reflected on the widespread adoption of the model and documentation of its effectiveness and benefits (Bush and Folger 2005). However, I would argue that these authors, like a number of people in the mediation field, have come to interpret transformative mediation as an essentially anarchic approach that leaves the parties to do almost whatever they want, with very little guidance from the mediator, as illustrated by a sample mediation in Bush and Folger's recent edition of their book.

It is my intention to rescue the transformative approach by allowing mediators to be proactive in clarifying issues and finding common ground while maintaining a focus on empowerment and mutual recognition of the parties. Moreover, as a sociologist, I feel compelled to go beyond the almost exclusive focus of most approaches on interpersonal relationships to examine issues of inequality and exploitation produced by the social structure. Real conflict resolution, encompassing meaningful and lasting change, can only come about, I believe, by focusing on both the interpersonal and the structural levels. Sociology as an intellectual discipline has a long history of analyzing conflict and pointing out the positive role it can play in fostering social change and personal growth. I am proud to claim this tradition for my own, and to turn its focus to mediation and conflict resolution as forms of individual and community empowerment.

The manual is divided into six parts. The Introduction establishes the idea of transformative conflict resolution and provides material to launch the course on which the manual is based. Part One defines conflict and investigates its various dimensions. Part Two embarks on an inner journey, in which the reader explores their personal experience of conflict and their personal style and response to conflict. Part Three assists the learner in developing concrete, practical skills for conflict resolution. Part Four explores culture and how it affects conflict and conflict resolution. The paradox of diversity is investigated, in which both individual identity and categorical group membership matter and must be taken into account. Part Five lays out the mediation process—how to do it as well as the rationale for the transformative approach. The Appendixes include resources on ethics, books, training manuals, and conflict resolution and mediation organizations.

In addition to extensive and easily accessible material on transformative conflict resolution and mediation, there are several special features in this manual. First and foremost, there are the hands-on exercises, designated as such:

Exercise

Each of these exercises is designed to reinforce a concept or skill discussed in the text. Ample room is provided so that you can fill in your answers right in this manual.

Another feature consists of practical notes that provide concrete tips, hints, and suggestions about how to be more effective in resolving conflict and conducting mediations. They are designated this way:

Practitioner's Notes

In keeping with this pragmatic approach, a DVD containing several mediation roleplays is included at the back of this manual. Viewing these roleplays will allow you to see experienced mediators at work and to get insights into the process. There is also introduction and commentary on this DVD to explain the mediation process. The points in the manual at which viewing of the DVD is suggested are marked with this symbol:

This manual also aims to situate the skills being learned within the broader context of sociological and conflict resolution theory. Notes to explain how and why conflict and conflict resolution dynamics operate the way they do are designated as such:

Theory

Conflict, conflict resolution, and mediation are all topics on which extensive research has been done. The manual aims to embed the concepts explored here in this larger literature. These notes are identified this way:

Research Note

About the Revised and Expanded Edition

Substantial changes have been made to improve this second edition. Over 40 pages of original material has been added. Fifteen notes on theory have been inserted to provide deeper understanding of course concepts. Five new research notes have also been included. In addition, there is a complete listing at the end of the manual of all the works cited within the text. This both makes the manual more scholarly and permits the reader greater access to the extensive literature on conflict and conflict resolution and the sociological analysis of these phenomena.

The ethical standards in Appendix I have been updated to the latest versions available, and current works have been added to the annotated bibliographies of books and manuals. Nine new exercises have been added to deepen understanding of key concepts. In addition, every website for conflict resolution and mediation organizations in Appendix V has been checked to ensure that it is active and accessible as of this writing.

To enhance ease of use, an index has been added at the back of the manual. This should permit quick access to concepts and exercises.

Introduction: Preparing for Transformative Conflict Resolution

"A consistent and wider emphasis on these dimensions [i.e., empowerment and recognition] would contribute to the transformation of conflict interaction from a negative and destructive social force into a positive and constructive social force – helping individuals to interact with more confidence in themselves and empathy for each other, and helping to transform society as a whole from a truce between enemies into a network of allies."

"In every area, mediation could, with sufficient energy and commitment, help transform the quality of social interaction and, ultimately, social institutions."

– Robert Baruch Bush and Joseph Folger

This section will provide an overview of the transformative approach to conflict resolution and background to help prepare you for the course of study.

Transformative Conflict Resolution: An Overview

How we handle the conflict that inevitably arises in our lives has significant implications for the social organization and quality of life in our society and in our interpersonal relations. There are, of course, multiple and culturally diverse ways of handling this conflict. Some of these mechanisms are formal, with clearly specified statuses and role expectations; others are informal. Americans tend to resolve public disputes in one of four ways: fight, vote, litigate, or appeal to various authorities. The first alternative often results in a cycle of violence, whether physical or symbolic. The other three methods tend to undermine democratic participation and to produce solutions that are ultimately not completely satisfying.

Fear of interpersonal violence has increased dramatically in recent times in part due to the undermining of community in America. Increased mobility, mass consumerism, and a culture of individualism have contributed to a lack of identification with local residential communities, as well as a growing sense of intolerance and unwillingness to engage in dialogue with others. As a result, more and more Americans are inclined to try to resolve conflicts with their fellow community residents by appealing directly to the authorities. This involves calling the police, filing complaints with some formal regulatory authority, or, of course, going to court.

At the same time, however, there is growing dissatisfaction among Americans today with formal mechanisms of dispute resolution. Civil courts have overcrowded dockets, leading to enormous delays in hearing grievances. Moreover, the court system, as well as many other administrative and judicial organizations, relies on a method of dispute resolution that is win/lose. That is, judges and juries apply specific legal principles to decide whose case has the greater merits. Either one party has caused damage or loss to another party or they have not. There will likely be a winner and a loser. This almost inevitably leads to one party—and often both of them—feeling unsatisfied with the outcome. Further, most formal dispute resolution techniques deal only with the specifics of a dispute, and don't address the underlying relationship, or address it only peripherally.

Informal dispute resolution processes, on the other hand, can address the underlying relationship between the parties. But when the parties do not have the skills to empower and recognize each other, this strategy runs the risk of personalizing the dispute, making it mean and hostile, and exacerbating the original conflict. Largely because of this, many of us have learned to deny or avoid conflict, effectively "sweeping it under the rug." Conflict resolution, in this context, becomes "any marked reduction in social conflict" (Schellenberg 1996:9). Johan Galtung, the intellectual father of peace studies, calls this apparent absence of overt conflict *negative peace.* While there are clearly benefits to a reduction in violence, this state of affairs is filled with tension, as violence lurks beneath the surface and threatens to break out at almost any time. *Positive peace,* on the other hand, involves active attempts at preventing violence through constructive conflict resolution based on reconciliation and relationship building (Galtung 1996:1-8).

With regard to mediation, negative peace corresponds to what Bush and Folger (1994) call the Problem-Solving model. While it may solve problems and thereby reduce violence, this model does not empower the parties to solve their own problems. The Transformative Model, on the other hand, focuses on humanizing the parties to one another, building relationships and empowering people to discover their own capacities. As Galtung (1996:70) observes, "there is no viable alternative to creative conflict transformation."

Comparison of Conflict Resolution Processes

Process	Informal Problem-Solving	Negotiation	Mediation	Arbitration	Legislation	Litigation	Avoidance	Extra-Legal Approaches
Description	Dispute resolution thru interpersonal interaction	Consensual process of discussing and adjusting differences	A third party assists disputants in reaching a mutually acceptable agreement	Intervention by a third party to decide how a dispute will be resolved	Dispute resolution thru legal action taken by elected representatives	A formal process of appeal to legitimate authority to solve a dispute	Informal process of denying or running from a dispute	Dispute resolution outside the existing system; non-violent civil disobedience; violence, terrorism
Orientation	Win/Win Win/Lose Lose/Win Lose/Lose	Win/Lose	Win/Win	Win/Lose	Win/Lose	Win/Lose	Lose/Lose Lose/Win	Win/Lose Win/Win
Resolution	Direct or indirect	Direct	Facilitated	Imposed or Advised	Imposed	Imposed	None	Imposed
Agreement	Voluntary Private Non-binding	Voluntary Private Non-binding	Voluntary Private Non-binding	Enforceable Private Binding	Enforceable Public Binding	Enforceable Public Binding	None	Public Non-binding
Representation	Self	Self	Self	Self or attorney	Elected reps Lobbyists	Attorney	None	Self
Decision-maker	Disputants	Disputants	Disputants	Arbitrator	Elected officials	Judge or jury	Self	One set of disputants
Disputants control:	Issues Agreement Follow-thru Resolution Process	Issues Agreement Follow-thru Resolution Process	Issues Agreement Follow-thru	Issues	Issues Other aspects to the extent they can mobilize resources			Issues

Theory *The Third Side* - The foundation of mediating

William Ury is an anthropologist who was one of the founders of the Harvard Negotiation Project, whose mission is "to improve the theory and practice of conflict resolution and negotiation by working on real world conflict intervention, theory building, education and training, and writing and disseminating new ideas" (Harvard Negotiation Project 2011). Ury has studied cultures and conflicts all over the world. Every conflict, he says, "occurs within a community that constitutes the 'third side' of any dispute" (Ury 2000:7).

The Third Side is

- people—from the community
- using a certain kind of power—the power of peers
- from a certain perspective—of common ground
- supporting a certain process—of dialogue and nonviolence
- aiming for a certain product—a triple win

In preindustrial societies the community (the clan, the village) acts as this third side. Though the techniques and the cultural forms vary, all societies seem to have them. The third side existed historically in the United States and other postindustrial societies in the form of organized communities, often ethnic neighbor-hoods. In contemporary society, where most residential areas are characterized by high mobility and social anonymity, the immediate community has largely disappeared as the third side. Its place has been taken by formal organizations like homeowners' associations, police, courts, and various public bureaucracies. Reducing destructive conflict and violence in our neighborhoods requires recovering the community as a third side.

The Three Roles of the Third Side

The motto of the third side, says Ury, is "Contain if necessary, resolve if possible, best of all prevent." (113) At its best, the community prevents many potential conflicts. Those that do break out—or need to break out—are resolved collaboratively if at all possible. Until the conflict can be resolved, or if it is irresolvable, the Third Side can contain the conflict and keep it from being destructive.

Prevent

- **Provider**
  Share resources, knowledge
- **Teacher**
  Teach tolerance, joint problem-solving
- **Bridge-Builder**
  Create ties across boundaries, foster dialogue

Resolve

- **Mediator**
  Facilitate transformative dialogue
- **Arbiter**
  Promote justice
- **Equalizer**
  Balance power; build collaborative democracy
- **Healer**
  LISTEN; facilitate forgiveness and reconciliation

Contain

- **Witness**
  Pay attention; speak out
- **Referee**
  Establish ground rules
- **Peacekeeper**
  Interpose; preempt violence

People who have Power or influence

Skills to fulfill these three roles and accomplish these nine tasks will be taught in this course.

An instructive example of the recovery of community in implementing The Third Side can be seen in modern South Africa. For several centuries the concept of *Ubuntu* animated and informed the indigenous African communities. While the word doesn't translate easily into English (irony intended), it means community in the broadest sense. Its deeper meaning can be found in the Zulu phrase *umuntu ngumuntu ngabantu*—"a person is a person through (other) persons." This traditional perspective was what informed South Africa's Truth and Reconciliation Commission, which worked to heal the country after the fall of apartheid. Bishop Desmond Tutu explains: "A person with *ubuntu* is open and available to others, affirming of others, does not feel threatened that others are able and good, for he or she has a proper self-assurance that comes from knowing that he or she belongs in a greater whole and is diminished when others are humiliated or diminished, when others are tortured or oppressed" (Tutu 2000).

Exercise — *The Third Side in Your Life*

Have you observed The Third Side at work in a dispute? Who fulfilled this role, and how did their actions affect the dynamics of the dispute?

The Third Side Party that I have witnessed in a dispute is the middle person inbetween a three-way friendship. Individuals who are in a conflict between themselves often times have a common friend that will keep the peace between the three of them.

Have you ever played the role of a Third Sider? What was your experience?

Yes, my best friend and her boyfriend always expect me to assist them with their relationship problems therefore if there is a conflict between them they both will call me to "fix" what has been done.

Objectives and Expectations

Course Objectives

The course that accompanies this manual is designed such that a person who successfully completes it will be able to do the following:

1. Analyze and explain conflict and conflict resolution processes.

2. Appropriately use active listening and centered communication techniques.

3. Analyze and explain how power and cultural differences impact conflict resolution and mediation.

4. Explain and apply the transformative mediation process.

5. Mediate a variety of disputes as a community mediator.

This manual is also designed to be useful for those not enrolled in the conflict resolution and mediation course. Reading the material, completing the exercises, and viewing the accompanying DVD will allow an individual to accomplish the first four goals listed above. You would not be prepared to mediate a dispute, however, without extensive roleplay training. In mediation, like most other learning, there is no substitute for active practice with skilled feedback.

Instructor/Trainer Expectations of the Learners

If you want to learn constructive conflict resolution skills, I want to help you do it. In order to ensure maximally effective learning, I expect learners in this course to

✓ Come prepared.
If you have done the reading in advance, the workshop activities will be more accessible and make more sense to you. Your questions will be more focused. Also, you will be able to learn these skills more effectively if you take a moment and center yourself prior to each workshop session. Try to set aside the day's worries and concerns and be present in the moment.

✓ Make an honest effort.
If we all try our best, we enhance everyone's learning – most especially our own.

✓ Challenge yourself.
Often we learn the most when we challenge ourselves to stretch our boundaries. You'll need to get outside your comfort zone to really learn these skills. On the other hand, it is perfectly acceptable to decline to participate in an activity that makes you seriously uncomfortable. You will then become an active observer.

✓ Demonstrate respect for others.
Appreciate the diverse attitudes, beliefs, and experiences of others. Respect their honest efforts, and, when you disagree, remember to separate the person from the

issue. It is acceptable to disagree strongly on an issue, but it is necessary to maintain respect for the person.

Student Expectations of the Instructor/Trainer

What should a student of conflict resolution and mediation expect from an instructor/trainer?

I will:

✓ Take primary responsibility for designing and organizing the course so that students learn conflict resolution and mediation skills.

I've had the time and training to think about this topic, so it's appropriate that I take the lead. Your active participation in shaping the course to meet your needs is expected, however.

✓ Be enthusiastic, knowledgeable, and organized.

Within reason, of course. Research shows that instructor enthusiasm is highly correlated with student learning. And, as you'll see, I'm really excited about sociology and mediation in general and this course in particular. I really want you to learn this material because I believe it's useful and valuable in living your life.

✓ Take responsibility for creating a safe, productive, and fun learning environment.

It is the instructor's job to create a safe, supportive environment in which you can take risks and learn conflict resolution techniques. Everyone is responsible, however, for fostering a sense of community in the class that is tolerant and supportive. Learning to deal productively with conflict is serious, hard work. But we will try to have fun, too, when it is appropriate.

✓ Introduce challenges appropriately.

As we will see, learning conflict resolution skills is a process that proceeds through definite stages. It is the instructor's job to monitor student learning in these stages and to constantly challenge students to stretch themselves without overwhelming or discouraging them.

✓ Provide a variety of learning aids.

I will make every reasonable effort to help every student be successful in this course. If you want to learn about conflict resolution, I want to help you do it, and to certify at the end that you have in fact done so. Different people have different learning styles, and I am committed to providing a variety of ways of accessing and incorporating the material. I will accommodate any disability, if it is at all possible.

✓ Provide direction and consultation on the use of conflict resolution and mediation skills.

I will provide information about practicing as a community mediator and about continuing education opportunities. I am happy to discuss with you almost any issue relating to conflict resolution or mediation.

Exercise — *The Learner's Personal Expectations*

It is appropriate before commencing for each learner to identify their own objectives and expectations. You may want to take some time and reflect on the following statements, then write your answers in the space provided. It will be valuable to return to these expectations during the training and reflect upon how they are met or changed. It is especially useful to reflect upon them when you arrive at the end of the course and do a final self-assessment.

From this course I expect...

To understand why conflict happens and how to resolve this conflict.

From the instructor I expect...

For him to explain/contribute information that in a way I can best grasp the concepts.

From other students I expect...

Contribute to class discussions so that all student may get different perspectives on the course.

From myself I expect...

To speak up in class as well as completing my work so that I know the materials being discussed in class.

Practitioner's Notes *On Journaling*

"There is only one journey. Going inside yourself."
– *Rainer Maria Rilke*

As you move through this course, I recommend that you keep a journal on at least a weekly basis. The journal should be a reflection, both backward and forward, on what you are learning—how it is affecting you, how it relates to what you already know, and how you are incorporating this learning into your life. The way to get the most out of any learning experience is to take responsibility for monitoring your own learning in a conscious way. Journaling is one way to do this. In your journal you may find it helpful to respond to several of the following statements:

I learned ....

I was surprised to discover that ....

I noticed that I ....

I discovered that I ....

I was pleased that I ....

I was frustrated about ....

I want to learn more about ….

Write down questions you have about the work you are doing or the material we're working on. Envision how you will use the insights you have gained and the skills you have developed in the future.

If you think in graphic terms, draw a picture or develop a cognitive map that ties together the concepts and skills and shows the relationships among them.

Your collection of journals will be valuable data to look back over when you do a final self-assessment at the end of the course and anytime in the future when you return to this material.

Exercise *Taking Stock: Where You Begin*

For your first journal, it would be helpful to reflect on where you're at as you begin this training. Try to answer the following questions:

- How do you feel about conflict?
- How does it feel to be in a conflict?
- How do you usually respond to conflict?

You will be answering these questions again in various ways throughout the course, but it's good to establish a baseline now.

Part One: Thinking About Conflict

"Being conscious of how our thinking impacts the outcomes of the peace and reconciliation processes and being flexible, fluid, and willing to change our perspectives, approaches, and paradigms are vital for actualizing peace and reconciliation."

William M. Timpson et al.

"Conflict, like sex, is an essential creative element in human relationships. It is the means to change, the means by which our social values of welfare, security, justice, and opportunities for personal development can be achieved.... The existence of a flow of conflict is the only guarantee that the aspirations of society will be attained. Indeed, conflict, like sex, is to be enjoyed. If such a fundamental and pervasive element in human relations were not enjoyable, there could be no human enjoyment."

John Burton

Conflict is, and always has been, an integral part of human life. Because we are creatures shaped by social learning and possessed of individual free will, we make choices, as individuals and groups, that inevitably bring us into conflict with one another. Moreover, a sociological perspective informs us that, as the societal division of labor grows more complex, statuses and roles proliferate, creating the likelihood of even more interpersonal, organizational, and societal conflict.

In this section of the manual we will explore the nature of conflict, its (surprisingly) positive aspects, and the possibilities of transforming the negatives of conflict into something positive and constructive. We will examine how to analyze conflict as a prelude to dealing constructively with it.

Research Note — *Portraying Conflict and Violence in Human History*

A number of scientists and scientific popularizers have suggested that interpersonal violence is a product of natural selection; it is programmed into our genes. However, in 1989 a distinguished international assembly of natural and social scientists—geneticists, biochemists, anthropologists, psychologists, etc.—summarized the state of scientific knowledge about the bases of war and violence in a document that became known as the Seville Statement. The statement concluded that "it is not scientifically correct to say that war or any other violent behavior is genetically programmed into our human nature," or "that in the course of human evolution there has been a selection for aggressive behavior more than for other kinds of behavior" (Elias and Turpin 1994:66). The statement was later endorsed by the United Nations Educational, Scientific, and Cultural Organization (UNESCO) and many scientific and professional organizations.

Yet as Elise Boulding (2000) argues in *Cultures of Peace: The Hidden Side of History,* our human history is often told from the unsupported, limited, violence-based perspective. We learn about the rise and fall of empires, kings and generals, their armies and wars, and the machinations of individuals and groups to seize or retain power. We rarely, if ever, learn about those who lived peaceful lives and accomplished their goals nonviolently.

Exercise

Think of the stories you have been told about history. What are the basic messages implicit in this narrative?

Have you learned about any examples of people resolving conflicts peacefully and changing the world nonviolently? What are the lessons in these narratives?

If you can't think of any examples, what do you think that means about the history you have learned? Why haven't you learned the history of nonviolent change?

Exercise | *Proverbs about Conflict*

Proverbs are short, pithy statements that sum up important bits of folk wisdom. Every culture has them. (In Mexico, for instance, they are called *dichos*.) Proverbs are passed down from generation to generation precisely because they resonate with people's real experience. Here are some examples of proverbs about conflict:

"The axe forgets; the log does not."
"It takes two to tango."
"Two wrongs do not make a right."
"What goes around comes around."
"You can't make an omelet without breaking eggs."
"When elephants fight, it is the grass that takes a beating."
"The best way to destroy an enemy is to make them a friend."
"Never insult an alligator until after you have crossed the river."
"It's no use crying over spilt milk."
"You reap what you sow."
"Might makes right."

- What proverbs can you think of?

- What truisms do they convey about the nature of conflict?

- What are the implications of these messages for thinking about and dealing with conflict?

Definition of Conflict

2 or more Parties

Conflict: the expressed struggle of interdependent people who perceive incompatible goals, scarce resources, and interference from each other in achieving their goals.

[adapted from Wilmot & Hocker 2005]

my perspective **elements:**
1) expressed struggle
2) interdependence - relationship aspect
3) perceived incompatible goals - one Party has to win
4) perceived scarce resources - if you
5) perceived interference - People are keeping you from what you want

1) While it is possible to speak about latent discord or inherent opposition of interests, conflict as we will view it really has to do with an explicit struggle. That is, conflict is a transaction between individuals, groups, or organizations. The parties actually *act* in opposition to one another. The confrontation may be expressed in what they say or what they do or both. This also implies that conflict is a *process,* with a beginning, middle, and—potentially—an end.

2) Interdependence implies a social relationship. In situations of conflict, there is always a relationship between the parties. While conflict certainly may undermine a social relationship, it may strengthen it as well. Sociologist Georg Simmel (1955) pointed out a century ago that the mere fact of engaging in conflict brings about—except in marginal cases—the common acceptance of implicit or explicit rules governing the conduct of hostilities. It is the existence of a relationship between the parties, then, that allows for the possibility of transformative conflict resolution.

3, 4, 5) Note that it is *perceived* incompatible goals, scarce resources, and interference that lead to conflict. People's perceptions are real to them, whether or not they are supported by objective reality. Sociology emphasizes that, when it comes to human behavior, "A situation defined as real is real in its consequences" (Thomas and Thomas 1928:572). If people believe that their goals are incompatible with those of others, if they suppose that resources are scarce, if they suspect interference from another party or parties, then they will act accordingly. In a conflict situation, then, with regard to interpersonal relationships and interaction, perception is everything. At the same time, we must stress that people's *perceptions* of scarce resources and incompatible goals are often shaped by their real *experience* of injustice, oppression, and exploitation in a society structured on principles of inequality.

Galtung (1996:70-80) portrays this definition in terms of his well-known Conflict Triangle, or A, B, C model. Attitudes correspond to perceptions, resulting in Behaviors that create a Contradiction (expressed struggle). But the existence of a contradiction can also influence attitudes and behaviors. Each of the three components mutually influences the others.

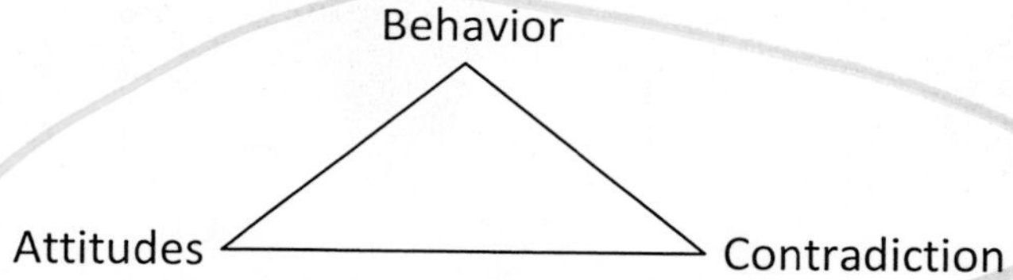

The Significance of Differing Perceptions

Constructive conflict resolution depends upon the ability of the parties to see and acknowledge the validity of differing perceptions of the same phenomenon. Conflict resolution techniques—especially third party interventions such as mediation—must deal with the parties' perceptions. Indeed, the success of mediation turns, not on a search for the "truth" of a situation, nor on a determination of who is right and who is wrong, but rather on a validation of each party's perceptions, which in turn opens the way for finding common ground. At the start of an intervention, whatever the mediator may perceive as objective reality—the "truth" of the matter, the underlying motivations of the parties, the "obvious" solution, etc.—is largely irrelevant. Mediation must begin with where the parties to the dispute are at. At the same time, however, mediation and conflict resolution rely upon a process of facilitating a potential change in the parties' perceptions of what the conflict is about in order to generate a solution. What follows are two exercises in seeing things from different perspectives—one visual and one narrative. Examine them and reflect upon their implications.

Exercise | *Who Do You See in This Picture?*

Study the picture carefully before reading the next page.

Picture designed by psychologist E.G. Boring

Do you see an elderly woman looking down at the lower left corner of the drawing? Her left eye is fully visible, and her right eyelash can be seen on the other side of her nose. Her long pointed chin is partially buried in what seems to be a fur coat.

Or do you see a fashionable young woman peering off into the left back of the frame? Her left ear is visible, along with her strong jawline. Only her left eyelash is visible, and a small part of the outline of her nose. She appears to have a large feather sticking up from the front of her fancy hat.

You may be able to see both women, but not at the same time. This is an artifact of how the brain processes images. Moreover, whichever woman you saw in the picture first is likely to be the woman you will see first whenever you glance again at the picture, even if you can successfully switch to the other view at will.

What does this tell us about conflict? First, that how people see and interpret a conflict is a matter of perception. There is no "right answer;" rather there are multiple "correct" ways of viewing the conflict. Second, people have predilections, predispositions, and accustomed patterns that shape the way they respond to circumstances. Third—and this is the really important insight for transformative conflict resolution—people can learn to see things differently, in spite of these accustomed patterns.

The Maligned Wolf

An alternative fairy tale

The forest was my home. I lived there, and I cared about it. I tried to keep it neat and clean. One sunny day, while I was cleaning up some garbage a thoughtless camper had left behind, I heard footsteps. I leaped behind a tree. When I looked out, I saw a little girl coming down the trail carrying a basket. Right away, I was suspicious of the little girl because she was dressed funny — all in red, with her head covered up as if she didn't want anyone to know who she was. Naturally, I decided to check her out.

I stopped her and asked who she was, where she was going, where she had come from, and so on. She gave me some lame story about going to her grandmother's house with a basket of lunch. She seemed to be a basically honest person, but she was in my forest, and she still looked suspicious with that strange getup of hers. So I decided to teach her a lesson about how serious it is to just walk into the forest unannounced and dressed funny.

I let her go on her way, but I ran ahead and found her grandmother's house. I introduced myself to that nice old woman and explained the problem. She agreed that her granddaughter needed to learn a lesson. So the old woman agreed to stay out of sight until I called her. Actually, she hid under the bed.

When the girl arrived, I invited her into the bedroom, where I was lying in the bed, dressed like the grandmother. The girl came in all rosy-cheeked and right off the bat said something nasty about my big ears. I've been insulted before so I made the best of it by suggesting that my big ears would help me to hear better. Now, what I meant was that I wanted to hear her, and pay close attention to what she was saying. But she made another insulting crack about my bulging eyes. Now you can see how I was beginning to feel about this little girl who put on such a nice front, but was apparently a very nasty person. Still, I've made it a policy to turn the other cheek, so I told her that my big eyes helped me to see her better.

Well, that wasn't the end of it. She went on to make another insulting comment, and this one really got to me. I've got this problem, you see, with having very large teeth, and the little girl made a nasty remark about them, too. I know I should have had better control, but when she made the teeth crack I leaped up from the bed and growled that my large teeth would help me eat her better. Now let's face it. No wolf could ever eat a little girl; everyone knows that. But that crazy girl started running around the house screaming — me chasing after her to calm her down. I'd taken off the grandmother's clothes, but that only seemed to make things worse. All of a sudden the door crashed open, and a big lumberjack was standing there with his axe in hand. He looked at me, and I looked at him, and suddenly it became clear to me that I was in big trouble. There was an open window behind me, so I dove through it and hightailed it out of there.

I'd like to say that was the end of it. But that grandmother character never did tell my side of the story. Before long, the word got around that I was a mean, nasty, dangerous guy. Everyone started avoiding me. I don't know about that little girl with the funny red outfit, but I certainly didn't live happily ever after.

Here is another example of a fairy tale written from an alternative point of view:

The True Story of the Three Little Pigs! by A. Wolf. As told to Jon Scieszka. New York, Viking, 1999.

The wolf gives his version of what happened with the 3 little pigs. Essentially he needed to borrow a cup of sugar and had a bad cold that made him sneeze a lot. In this 10 Year Anniversary edition, A. Wolf gives an update from the slammer.

Exercise

Think of other fairy tales that you might rewrite from a different point of view. How would they be different? What insights can you gain from looking at the story from the point of view of the "villain"?

Exercise *Truth, Mercy, Justice, and Reconciliation*

Write a brief definition of each of the following terms. If you're stuck, there is a resource on the next page.

TRUTH IS:

MERCY IS:

JUSTICE IS: Fairness, to do what is Right

RECONCILIATION IS: To Reconnect a relationship

What is the relationship among these definitions? Are there any commonalities? How might these qualities be reconciled with each other? Can they all be connected or merged without giving up the essence of any of the individual qualities? What would that look like?

SOME DEFINITIONS:

Truth: n. 1. the quality of being in accordance with experience, facts, or reality. 2. conformity to fact or logic. 3. a statement proven to be or accepted as true. 4. freedom from deceit or distortion of fact. 5. sincerity, genuineness, integrity, honesty. 6. fidelity to an original or a standard. 7. according to Christian Science, God.

> Synonyms — truthfulness, veracity, verity, reliability, authenticity, fidelity, actuality, certainty
> Antonyms — untruth, untruthfulness, deceit, deception, inaccuracy, falsity

Mercy: n. 1. compassionate treatment, especially of those under one's power; clemency. 2. a disposition to be kind and forgiving. 3. kindness in excess of what may be expected or demanded by fairness; forbearance. 4. something for which to be thankful; a blessing. 5. alleviation of distress; relief.

> Synonyms — forgiveness, absolution, clemency, amnesty, leniency, indulgence, overlooking, pardon, remission
> Antonyms — unforgiveness, condemnation, severity, cruelty

Justice. n. 1. the quality of being righteous; conformity to moral rightness in action or attitude. 2. freedom from bias; impartiality; fairness; equity. 3. the upholding of what is just, especially fair treatment and due reward in accordance with honor, standards, or law. 4. conformity to truth, fact, or sound reason. 5. Law: a judge.

> Synonyms — fairness, evenhandedness, equitableness, equity, fair-mindedness, impartiality, objectivity, justness, judge, jurist, magistrate
> Antonyms — bias, partiality, prejudice, unfairness

Reconciliation. n. 1. the act of reestablishing a close relationship between. 2. a settlement or resolution of a dispute. 3. the act of acquiescing or bringing oneself to accept a conclusion, outcome, or state of affairs. 4. a state of being compatible or consistent.

> Synonyms — conciliation, rapprochement, appeasement, peacemaking, acclimation, adaptation, adjustment
> Antonyms — provocation, aggravation, separation, denial, disharmony, disagreement, escalation

Peace. n. 1. the absence of war, civil strife, or other hostilities. 2. an agreement or a treaty to end hostilities. 3. freedom from quarrels and disagreement; harmonious relations. 4. public security and order. 5. an undisturbed state of mind; inner contentment; serenity.

> Synonyms — agreement, concord, accord, concert, concurrence, harmony, cooperation, calmness, lull, placidity, quiescence, quiet, repose, rest, serenity, stillness, tranquility, ease
> Antonyms — disturbance, discord, conflict, disagreement, dissension, agitation

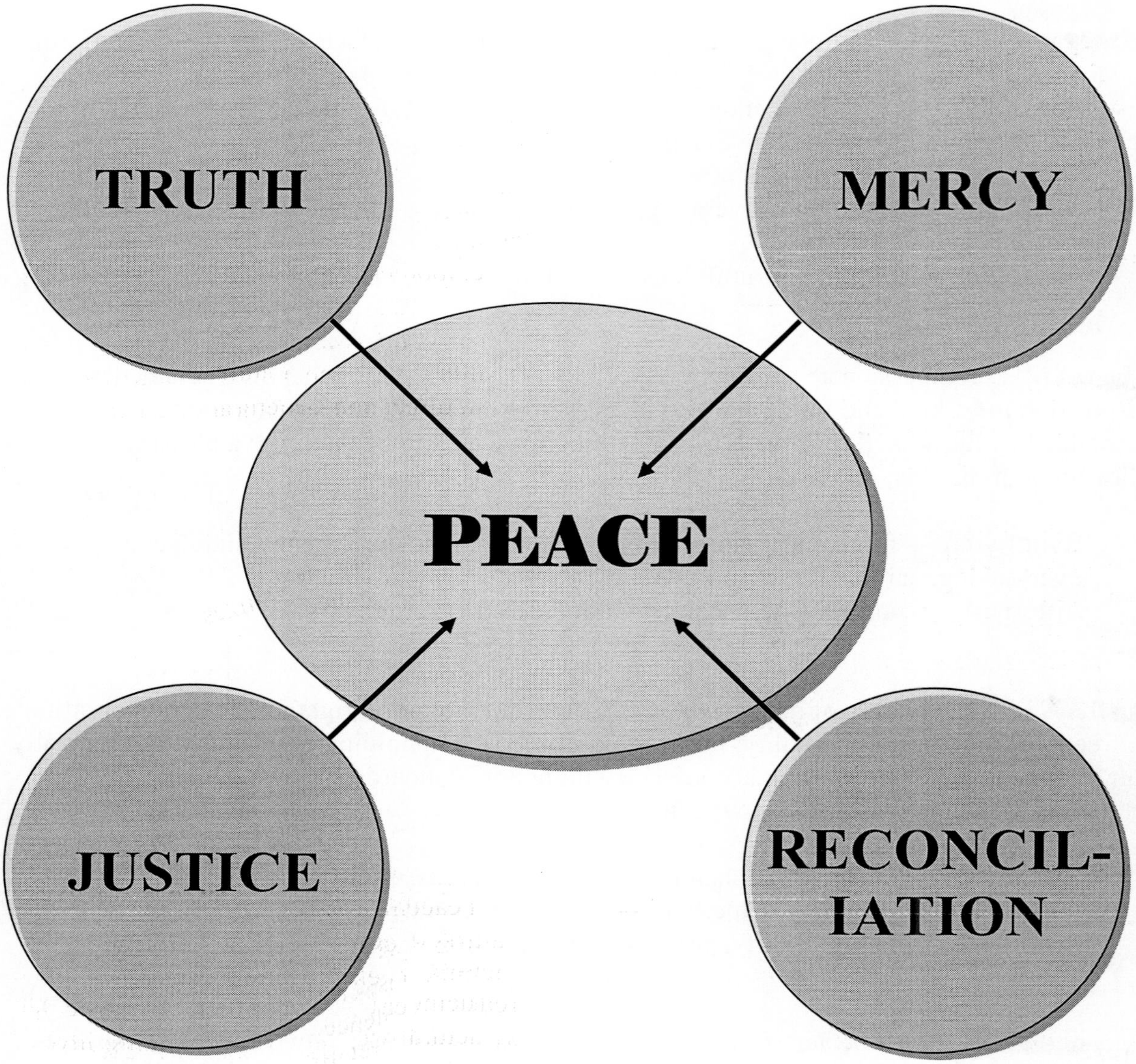

The place where Truth, Mercy, Justice, and Reconciliation meet might be Peace. What would this mean? That is, how would it look? What would it feel like? What would the implications be?

Theory *Theories of Violence and Peace*

Sociologist Johan Galtung is acknowledged as both a founder and an eminent scholar of peace studies. Galtung first distinguishes between negative and positive peace. *Negative peace*, he says, is the absence of violence, whereas *positive peace* is the creation of relationships that promote mutual and individual growth and development (Galtung 1996:24-39). Positive peace represents the ultimate goal because it represents health and the flourishing of human capacities. However, in situations of violence, the first step must be to achieve negative peace.

In order to achieve either negative or positive peace, the sources of violence must be understood. Galtung (1996:1-8), who is partial to the triangle as a heuristic method (recall his Conflict Triangle of attitudes, behavior and contradiction discussed earlier), suggests that there are three forms of violence:

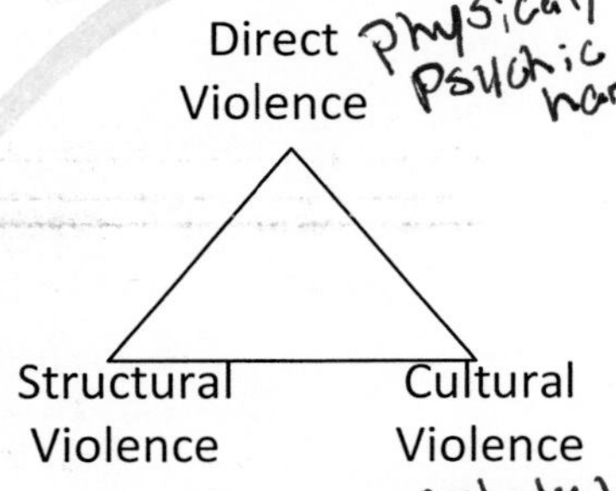

Direct violence involves physical or psychic harm intentionally inflicted on its victims. Structural violence, on the other hand, is indirect; it is a result of societal arrangements that result in repression and/or exploitation. Cultural violence is symbolic; it is embodied in dehumanizing stereotypes expressed in language and promoted by science, law, media, religion, education, etc. Cultural violence, Galtung says, legitimizes both direct and structural violence.

The process of creating peace, then, must take these forms of violence into account. Again using a triangle, Galtung (1996; 2002) lays out three types of action in pursuit of peace.

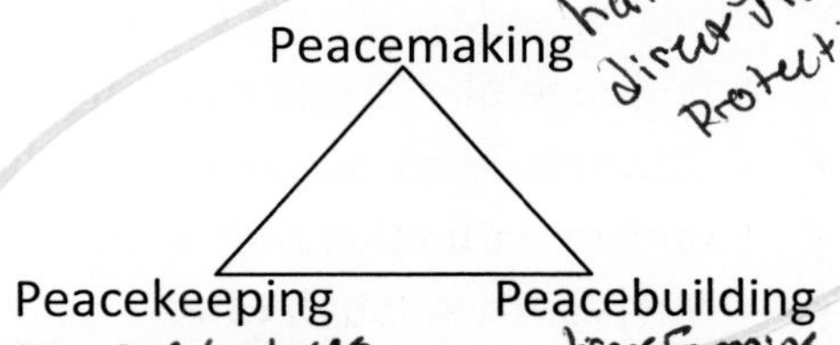

Peacemaking, says Galtung, involves halting direct violence and protecting its victims. Peacekeeping means removing or reducing causes of conflict—in particular, structural violence. Peacebuilding involves transforming relationships between individuals, groups, or nations, building recognition by humanizing them to one another.

Principles of Peace

Constructive conflict resolution is really about creating peace or peacebuilding. Here are four fundamental principles of peace. Can you "C" your way to them?

Exercise

Write a short reflection next to each one about what you could do to implement that component in your life.

Compassion

- ✓ Connection to all people
- ✓ Caring coupled with respect
- ✓ Concern for justice for all
- ✓ Centered
- ✓ Cultivation of openness to experience

Community

- ✓ Cherish and Celebrate Connections to others
- ✓ Challenge biases and develop Cultural Competence
- ✓ Collective work and responsibility
- ✓ Connect with others for social support
- ✓ Conviviality – laugh often and cultivate a sense of humor

Cooperation

- ✓ Common ground – network with others
- ✓ Constructive Conflict resolution; Conciliation
- ✓ Commitment to nonviolence
- ✓ Collaborative problem-solving – fosters Creativity
- ✓ Consensus-based decisionmaking
- ✓ Contribution of everyone is valued

Commitment

- ✓ Clarity of purpose
- ✓ Character – personal integrity
- ✓ Choose to consistently live your values; be the Change you want to see
- ✓ Courage to Confront and Challenge what must be Changed
- ✓ Congruence – authenticity; harmony of means and ends

Adapted by Patrick J. Ashton
from Louise Diamond (2001)

Conflict and Crisis: Latent Possibilities

Conflict is often seen as precipitating a crisis. In English, some of the meanings of crisis include:

- A crucial or decisive point or situation; a turning point.
- An unstable condition, as in political, social, or economic affairs, involving an impending abrupt or decisive change.
- An emotionally stressful event or a traumatic change in a person's life.
- A point in a story or drama when a conflict reaches its highest tension and must be resolved.

Thus in English a crisis is perceived mostly as a negative phenomenon. But consider the Chinese ideogram for the concept of crisis:

危

This character is *weī* (way) which means *danger* or peril.

機

This character is *qī* (jee) which means a crucial or pivotal point, essentially a *turning point.*

Thousands of years of Chinese cultural experience are distilled here into the insight that every situation contains within it both negative and positive possibilities. We can see, then, that a crisis contains the danger of a breakdown—in society, an organization, or a relationship—but also the opportunity for a breakthrough and positive transformation.

So the crisis provoked by a conflict is complex. It would be misleading to prejudge it as a dangerous, negative phenomenon without examining the ways in which it embodies the potential for change, or turning in a new direction.

Functions and Dysfunctions of Conflict

On a societal level, sociologists designate those phenomena that are dangerous, threatening, or disruptive to the social order as *dysfunctions*. Those aspects that uphold, maintain, or contribute to the effective working of the social order are said to be *functional*. But can conflict be functional?

Exercise

Below, list all of the functional and dysfunctional aspects of conflict you can think of.

Functional	Dysfunctional

Here are some functions and dysfunctions of conflict as identified by the research literature. How many were on your list?

DYSFUNCTIONS OF CONFLICT

- disrupts social relations and mutual interdependence
- generates hostility, bad feelings, resentment
- invites defensiveness
- destroys confidence
- forces people to take sides
- undermines effectiveness
- distorts communication
- diverts time and energy
- saps resources
- invites repression, authoritarian responses
- creates further conflict

FUNCTIONS OF CONFLICT

- bonds people together to fight a common enemy; helps to create a group identity
- induces cooperation
- helps define the boundaries of the group
- helps to define roles within the group
- helps to clarify norms, values, and beliefs
- helps to clarify goals and objectives
- helps to clarify needs
- increases understanding of feelings
- brings underlying or suppressed issues out into the open
- clarifies problems
- challenges groupthink
- promotes creative problem solving
- forges a relationship between antagonists that allows for the possibility of resolution
- promotes personal and organizational growth
- acts as a safety valve to reduce frustration and aggression
- maintains or restores equilibrium and the balance of power
- protects minority rights
- creates the opportunity for accomplishing justice

What do you think it means that the list of functional aspects is longer that the list of dysfunctional aspects?

The Dialectics of Conflict: Fire and Rain

As the previous discussion illustrates, conflict is a complex phenomenon. It encompasses within it both positive and negative forces. It can create as well as destroy. Conflict is thus a dialectical phenomenon. By dialectic we refer to a tension of opposites.

The natural world provides many illustrations of this. Consider the rain. On the one hand it is lifegiving—it is vital for the crops, it cleanses the air. On the other hand, rain can be an inconvenience—it washes out ballgames, picnics, parades, and other outdoor activities. Rain can also be destructive in the form of powerful thunderstorms or damaging hail and, ultimately, floods.

Even more powerful is the phenomenon of fire as a metaphor for conflict. While fire is a force of nature, humans have a unique relationship with it. Humans are the only animal species to control fire. And that control is what in large part has made civilization possible. But fire can be hugely destructive, especially when it is out of control. Fire is further apt as a metaphor for conflict because it is a process. It has certain preconditions—tinder, fuel—and a necessary process of development—a spark that catches, smoldering, blazing, going out. Moreover, the process of dealing with conflict can be looked at as a "fire drill." Many of the same actions that are appropriate to a fire drill—stay calm, don't panic, take appropriate action in a direct manner—are also appropriate to conflict resolution. The following page gets us started by looking at fire as a process that can be either constructive or destructive.

"Give me ae spark o' Nature's fire, That's a' the learning I desire.
Robert Burns

"A little fire is quickly trodden out, which, being suffered, rivers cannot quench."
Shakespeare, Henry VI

Destructive Conflict → Social Damage	Fire	Constructive Conflict → Social Change
PEOPLE When social relations or institutional arrangements deny people access to what they need, tension is created. The potential for conflict varies based on the combustibility of the individuals and their situations.	***THE FUEL*** **The raw material for the fire. Some of it is highly combustible; some of it is damp and flame-resistant.**	**PEOPLE** Humans have the potential to challenge one another and to grow. Differing values, opinions, goals, and social situations exist. Awareness, education, and positive communication provide tinder for the fire.
INCIDENT People experience difficulty meeting their needs. Frustration is also created by lack of respect and of centered communication skills. Some frustrations cause a spark that ignites conflict.	***THE SPARK*** **Friction causes sparks to fly. Some land on dry wood and it catches fire.**	**INCIPIENCY** Growing awareness of the tension between the ideal and the real in a community or a relationship. A flash of new insight or a "final straw" can bring the issue to life.
BROODING Tensions and grievances smolder but are unexpressed. The conflict feeds off rumor and gossip. People blame the victim or look for scapegoats.	***SMOLDERING*** **The fuel catches fire and begins to smoke. People might suspect that there is fire.**	**TENTATIVE RESPONSE** People who are passionate about the issue begin to connect with others, based on their shared concern. The issue gains visibility as it heats up.
AGGRAVATION Fear of conflict coupled with real anger and hurt increases sensitivity and results in further provocations. There is an appeal to simplistic explanations and answers. Fear expressed as intolerance.	***FANNING THE FLAMES*** **Some individuals or groups fan the flames, and the flames flicker to life.**	**COALESCENCE** People who are concerned with the issue grow in number. Their mutual encouragement and support gives the issue increased salience. More people are compelled to pay attention.
ESCALATION The situation is intensified by the resurrection of old hurts in the spiral of conflict. Even seemingly innocent acts become pretexts for further hostility. Hateful acts add fuel to the fire.	***STOKING THE FIRE*** **As the fire consumes the fuel, it demands more. The fire is stirred and grows hotter.**	**MOBILIZATION** Response to the issue increases. Energy increases; more people join the movement as the possibility of achieving their aims grows brighter. Organizations are developed and nurtured.
SOCIAL DAMAGE The blazing conflict leaves no one untouched. Some people, groups, and organizations are seriously damaged. Everyone is impoverished.	***THE BLAZE*** **The fire rages into a huge blaze. It will not easily be quenched.**	**EFFECTIVE CHANGE** Aims are achieved as change is accomplished. People celebrate the blazing fire, which is a beacon of light, warmth, and inspiration.

Adapted from MacBeth and Fine, 1995.

Constructive vs. Destructive Conflict

As the metaphor of fire so aptly illustrates, conflict can either be destructive of society, social organizations, and relationships, or it can provoke and produce constructive social change. Any particular conflict, however, may not fall exclusively into one category or another. It may be better to think of constructive and destructive conflict as a continuum. Below is an illustration of that continuum.

Continuum of Constructive and Destructive Conflict

Destructive → ***Constructive***

mutual destruction	intractable standoff	fight or flight	dispute	arbitration/ mediation	problem solving	relationship building

Destructive conflicts:

- position-centered
- focused on personalities
- energy draining
- confine us by narrowing the space we occupy
- latent
- aimed at compromising interdependence
- involved in power preservation and face saving
- rigid and narrow
- involved in a cycle of escalation and avoidance
- seemingly self-sustaining

Constructive conflicts:

- interest-centered
- focused on behaviors
- energy generating
- enlarge the space we occupy
- manifest
- capable of bolstering interdependence
- committed to both parties accomplishing their goals
- flexible and broad-ranging
- involved in a cycle of transformation and healing
- dealt with through conscious effort

We can say then, that the process of intervention in conflicts involves transforming them from destructive into constructive conflicts. How should we understand this transformation process and, as we engage with others, what models do we use for negotiation, bargaining, problem-solving?

Theory | *Conflict Transformation: A Working Definition*

by John Paul Lederach

It is important to clarify what is meant by the term conflict transformation. At essence, transformation refers to change. Transformation as change can be understood in two fundamental ways.

Descriptively, transformation refers to the empirical impact of conflict, in other words to the *effects* that social conflict produces. Here, transformation describes the general changes social conflict creates and the patterns it typically follows.

Prescriptively, transformation implies deliberate intervention to effect change. In this instance transformation refers to the *goals* we have as intervenors as we work with conflict.

Dimensions

At both descriptive and prescriptive levels, transformation is operative in four interdependent dimensions: Personal, relational, structural, and cultural.

1. The **personal** dimension refers to the changes effected in, and desired for the individual. This involves emotional, perceptual, and spiritual aspects of conflict.

   From the descriptive perspective, transformation suggests that individuals are affected by conflict, in both negative and positive ways, for example, in terms of their physical well-being, self esteem, emotional stability, capacity to perceive accurately, and spiritual integrity.

   Prescriptively, transformation represents deliberate intervention to *minimize* the destructive effects of social conflict and *maximize* its potentialities for growth in the person as an individual human being, at physical, emotional, and spiritual levels.

2. The **relational** dimension depicts the changes effected in, and desired for the relationship. Here we take into consideration the areas of relational affectivity and interdependence, and the expressive, communicative and interactive aspects of conflict.

   Descriptively, transformation refers to how the relational patterns of communication and interaction are affected by conflict. It looks beyond the tension around visible issues to the underlying changes produced by conflict in the patterns of how people perceive, and what they desire and pursue in their relationship: how close or distant, or how interdependent they wish to be, what they perceive the other wants, how reactive or proactive they become in the relationship, etc.

   Prescriptively, transformation represents intentional intervention that minimizes poorly functioning communication and maximizes mutual understanding, and that surfaces in an explicit manner the relational fears, hopes and goals of the people involved in terms of affectivity and interdependence.

3. The **structural** dimension highlights underlying causes of conflict, and the patterns and changes it brings about in the social structures. At times understood as the "content" or "substance," structural dimensions focus attention on the areas related to basic human needs, access to resources, and institutional patterns of decision-making.

Transformation at the descriptive level refers to the analysis of social conditions that give rise to conflict and the way that conflict effects in the existing structures and patterns of making decisions.

At a prescriptive level transformation represents the intervention to provide insight into underlying causes and social conditions that create and foster *violent* expressions of conflict, and openly promotes *nonviolent mechanisms* that reduce adversarial confrontation, minimize and ultimately eliminate violence, and foster structures that meet basic human needs (substantive justice) and maximize participation of people in decisions that affect them (procedural justice).

4. The **cultural** dimension refers to the changes produced by conflict in the cultural patterns of a group, and the ways culture affects the development and handling of conflict.

At a descriptive level transformation is interested in how conflict affects and changes cultural patterns of a group, and how those accumulated and shared patterns affect the way people in that setting understand and respond to conflict.

Prescriptively, transformation seeks to understand explicitly the cultural patterns that contribute to the rise of violent expressions of conflict, and to identify, promote, and build on the resources and mechanisms within a cultural setting for constructively responding to and handling conflict.

In summary, conflict transformations represents a comprehensive set of lenses for *describing* the way conflict emerges from, evolves in, and brings about changes in the personal, relational, structural and cultural dimensions, and for *intervening* to promote peaceful change at those levels through nonviolent mechanisms.

Note the parallel and overlap with Johan Galtung's concepts of violence and peace discussed earlier.

Negotiation Paradigms

Our culture teaches us that there are basically two ways to approach bargaining with someone with whom we have a conflict. If obtaining a particular outcome is important to us, then we are encouraged to adopt a "hard" bargaining style in which we announce a position and then do everything we can to get the other person to give in to it. Or, if maintaining the relationship is important to us, we are encouraged to try a "soft," "nice guy" approach. Either way, the negotiation will likely be zero/sum, in which there will be a clear winner and a clear loser. (A simple example of a zero/sum outcome: Imagine that you and a partner are flipping quarters. You agree that if both come up that same, you get the quarters. But if one is heads and the other tails, your partner gets the coins. While there are four possible outcomes—both heads, both tails, heads/tails or tails/heads—each of them is zero/sum: either you get both coins or your partner does. One will win and one will lose.)

The Harvard Negotiation Project, among others, has developed a model of principled negotiation, in which both the outcome and the relationship are important. This is not yet transformative mediation, but it is an improvement over the hard or soft positional bargaining. Collaboration is always preferable to positional bargaining games, and is a useful step when transformative mediation is not possible. The three styles of negotiation are compared on the next page.

Positional Bargaining Games		Collaboration
HARD	**SOFT**	**PRINCIPLED**
Parties are adversaries.	Parties are friends.	Parties are problem-solvers.
Goal is to win.	Goal is to agree.	Goal is to produce a wise outcome efficiently & amicably.
Demand concessions as a condition of the relationship.	Make concessions to cultivate the relationship.	Separate the people from the problem.
Be hard on the problem and the people.	Be soft on the people and the problem.	Be soft on the people and hard on the problem.
Distrust others.	Trust others.	Proceed independent of trust.
Dig into your position.	Change your position easily.	Focus on interests, not positions.
Make threats.	Make offers.	Explore interests.
Mislead re your bottom line.	Disclose your bottom line.	Avoid having a bottom line.
Demand one-sided gains as the price of an agreement.	Accept one-sided losses to reach agreement.	Invent options for mutual gain.
Search for the answer you will accept.	Search for the answer they will accept.	Develop multiple options; decide on them later.
Insist on your position.	Insist on agreement.	Insist on using objective criteria.
Win a contest of wills.	Avoid a contest of wills.	Use objective standards independent of wills.
Apply pressure.	Yield to pressure.	Be open to reason; yield to principle, not pressure.

adapted from Fisher and Ury 1983

Kenneth Boulding (1989) looks at these three paradigms in terms of power. He calls the power of the hard position *threat power* ("Do what I want or I will do what you don't want."). The soft paradigm is based, Boulding says, on *exchange power* ("Do what I want and I will do what you want."). The collaborative model is based on what Boulding calls *integrative power* ("Together we can do something that is better for both of us.")

The principled, collaborative model presented above is not yet transformative mediation because it does not appear to emphasize the importance of the relationship between the parties in a dispute. The dictum that the people should be separated from the problem has been interpreted as a technique for keeping messy emotional issues at bay and focusing on rational problem solving. In the transformative model, however, relationships are not only part of the process, they are its key. In the transformative model, as we will see, it is not either the people or the problem, but both.

Research Note — *Prisoner's Dilemma: The Benefits of Cooperation*

Prisoner's Dilemma is a classic illustration of a non-zero/sum situation in game theory. Most people are familiar with it because the situation is portrayed on innumerable police procedurals in the movies and on television. The hypothetical story is that two people have been arrested and accused of committing a serious crime. The police do not initially have enough evidence to convict them of the serious crime, but do have enough to likely make a lesser charge stick.

The suspects are being held in separate jail cells and are unable to communicate with one another. They are each told that, if they confess to the serious crime, they will receive a hefty but slightly reduced sentence as a reward for their cooperation. But if one of them talks and incriminates their accomplice, the one who talks will be freed without any punishment, while the accomplice will get the maximum sentence for the serious crime.

Here is their dilemma: If both suspects hold out and refuse to talk, they can only be charged with the minor offense. This is their best collective option, a win/win solution. If they both confess and receive a slightly reduced maximum sentence, it is really lose/lose. However, if one of them rats the other out, that one goes free and the accomplice gets the maximum—a win/lose scenario. But they must make their decisions independently of one another because they can't communicate.

Most people assume that the prisoner's will not trust one another—one or both will confess, resulting in either one of the win/lose scenarios, or the lose/lose one. This may indeed be so if there is only one round to the game. But if there are multiple iterations, the possibility of cooperation as a winning strategy emerges.

In *The Evolution of Cooperation,* Robert Axelrod (1984) relates how he invited experts to submit computer programs for a competition involving multiple iterations of the Prisoner's Dilemma game. He received a number of entries, employing strategies from aggressively hostile to cooperative. Each program was tested in pairs against all the others.

The surprise winner was a program submitted by conflict resolution expert Anatol Rapaport. The strategy of this program, called Tit-for-Tat, was simple: it began with cooperation on the first move, then matched its opponent on each subsequent move. The program was generous, forgiving, and predictable. As a result, cooperation emerged in the increasingly consistent choice of win/win strategies. As Ramsbotham et al. (2005:17) observe, "even though 'nasty guys' may seem to do well at first, 'nice guys' come out on top in the end. Natural selection favors cooperation."

So even in competitive environments, under the right conditions, collaborative, win/win solutions are more successful.

Principled or Collaborative Negotiation

"The road from confrontation to cooperation is negotiation."

Collaborative negotiation is principled negotiation.

Successful negotiation should be:

Wise, in that it should produce a wise agreement if agreement is possible.

A wise agreement is one which

- meets the legitimate interests of each side to the extent possible
- resolves conflicting interests fairly
- is durable
- takes community interests into account

Efficient, in that it should use the least amount of time and money that is feasible.

Amicable, in that it should improve or at least not damage the relationship between the parties.

Bargaining over positions violates all three criteria.

Elements of principled negotiation:

People: Separate the people from the problem.

- Positional bargaining entangles the relationship in the problem in a way that endangers it.
- keys to success: perception, emotion, communication

Interests: Focus on interests, not positions.

- Try to reconcile interests, not compromise between positions.
- Shared interests are latent in every negotiation.

Options: Generate a variety of possibilities before deciding what to do.

- obstacles that inhibit this: (1) premature judgment; (2) searching for the single answer; (3) assumption of a fixed pie; and (4) thinking that solving their problem is their problem.
- Make the other side's decision easy if you can.

> **The Power Paradox: The harder you make it for them to say no, the harder you make it for them to say yes.**

Criteria: Insist that the result be based on some objective standard.

- Negotiating as a contest of wills is costly, in both efficiency and amicability.
- Frame the issues as a joint search for objective criteria.

adapted from Fisher and Ury 1983
and Ury 1991

Adversarial vs. Collaborative Modes of Negotiation

DIMENSION OF NEGOTIATION	ADVERSARIAL	COLLABORATIVE
Communication	guarded, secretive, deceptive coercive blaming and fault-finding indirect	open, honest persuasive situation-oriented direct
Attitudes	mistrust and suspicion individualism past-focused aggressive/defensive	trust mutuality future-focused assertive
Process	bargain from positions attack each other use any standard that is convenient consider only options which advance own positions	bargain from interests attack problems develop fair and objective standards invent options for all
Outcomes	win/lose compromise between positions feeling of overpowering or being overpowered battle scars alienation	win/win collaborate to meet mutual needs mutual ownership dignity relationship

The adversarial model looks like this:

The collaborative model looks like this:

In the adversarial model, the parties face off and negotiate over their positions. The problem underlying their dispute remains unspoken, under the table. The parties sit on their individual interests and needs, taking care not to disclose them lest such revelations undermine their bargaining position. As each party seeks a negotiating edge, manipulation and even personal attacks are not ruled out as tactics. In fact, they may be more likely in this setting.

In the collaborative model, the parties separate the person from the problem. The problem itself is on the table as the focus of the discussion. Because the approach is collaborative, the parties can make explicit and share their underlying needs and interests. In the process of doing so, personal insights are gained and the relationship between the parties is built.

In either process, the parties' definition of the situation can lead to a self-fulfilling prophecy. In the adversarial model, their belief that the negotiation is a zero-sum, win/lose scenario can lead the parties to dig in their heels and become more adversarial. Likewise, if the parties believe that a win/win, collaborative process is the only way to a viable solution, they can actually increase their commitment to and use of collaboration.

Theory | *The Self-Fulfilling Prophecy*

The Self-Fulfilling Prophecy is a term coined by the American sociologist Robert Merton (1968). He was very interested in examining the unanticipated consequences of human behavior. Merton asserted that, while all human actions are a result of intentionality and purpose, the outcomes of these behaviors often have additional, unplanned and unintentional effects. The self-fulfilling prophecy is a special case of this.

Building on the insight of earlier American sociologist W.I. Thomas that "a situation defined as real is real in its consequences" (Thomas and Thomas 1928:572), Merton noted that

> The self-fulfilling prophecy is, in the beginning, a *false* definition of the situation evoking a new behavior which makes the original false conception come 'true'. This specious validity of the self-fulfilling prophecy perpetuates a reign of error. For the prophet will cite the actual course of events as proof that he was right from the very beginning (Merton 1968:477).

While Merton defined the self-fulfilling prophecy as a false belief, subsequent work has demonstrated that the phenomenon can work in a positive way, too. That is, people who believe that a positive outcome is possible can actually, through behaviors based on that belief, bring it about.

For instance, an individual who believes in their personal competencies and capabilities for success can actually behave in ways that help to bring about that success. This phenomenon is well-known in sports, education, and business. Similarly, neighbors who believe that "you can fight city hall and win" may act in ways that empower them and foster success.

What does the Self-Fulfilling Prophecy mean for the transformative conflict resolution process? When the parties to a dispute expect the process to be adversarial, they are highly likely to act in ways that conform to that belief, potentially exacerbating the conflict and making a wise, efficient, and amicable resolution more difficult, if not impossible.

On the other hand, when the parties to a dispute believe that they can collaborate on a win/win solution, they are much more likely to act in ways that foster mutual respect and recognition and allow for all parties to meet their needs to the greatest extent possible.

In many conflict resolution processes, and especially in mediation, a third party ("the third side") is crucial in helping to establish a definition of the situation. If that third party advocates, emphasizes, and implements a collaborative process, it is likely that a self-fulfilling prophecy of transformative resolution will predominate.

Part Two: The Inner Journey

"What goes on *between* people cannot be separated from what is going on *within* people. Who we are, deep inside, will determine how well we get along with others, and so, if we want to fix our conflicts, or anyone else's for that matter, we had better get started on ourselves."

– Marc Gopin

"If you cannot remove conflict, why not adjust your thinking about it? Why not try and see conflict as the salt of life, the big energizer, the tickler, the tantalizer, rather than as a bothersome nuisance, as noise in perfect channel, as disturbing ripples in otherwise quiet waters? In short, why not treat conflict as a form of life, particularly since we all know that it is precisely during the period of our lives when we are exposed to a conflict that really challenges us, and that we finally are able to master, that we feel most alive."

– Johan Galtung

"Conflict resolution and transformation teachers, trainers, and third parties who cultivate a rich and reflective inner life will have more creative resources to offer their clients. They will also model creativity. This congruence between a professed value and a way of living is powerful indeed."

– Michelle LeBaron

"Know thyself."

– Pythagoras

"Forgiveness is not an occasional act; it is a permanent attitude."

– Martin Luther King, Jr.

In order to help others resolve conflict, we need to understand ourselves—how we think about and react to conflict, our values, and own personal style. When we have traveled a ways on this inner journey, we can begin to be a guide for others.

Exercise *Word Association*

As quickly as you can, write down the words that come immediately to mind when you hear each of the words in the following list. Don't analyze or process your answers as you think of them; just write them down.

… conflict

… dispute

… dissension

… confrontation

… crisis

Now examine the list of words you wrote. Code the words as negative, positive, neutral, or mixed. How does your list compare to the lists on the next page?

Like many people, you probably have more negative than positive associations with the concept of conflict. Why do you think this is so?

negative terms	*positive terms*
friction	reconciliation
discord	healing
dissonance	change
power	transformation
manipulation	vulnerability
hatred	love
opposition	forgiveness
violence	nonviolence
hostility	harmony
disrespect	respect
attack	mediation
fighting	peacemaking
disagreement	growth
hate	resolution
distrust	understanding
anxiety	help
tension	amicability
frustration	intervention

For most of us, it is because we have had negative personal experiences with conflict that we have come to think of it as negative. We have experienced conflict as frustrating, hurtful, and ultimately unsatisfying. Learning conflict resolution techniques can help us deal more constructively with conflict and produce more satisfying outcomes.

Exercise | *Exploring Attitudes about Conflict*

Mark your opinion on each of the statements below by choosing one of these responses:

STRONGLY AGREE AGREE DISAGREE STRONGLY DISAGREE

1. Conflict is almost always a bad thing.

   SA A D SD

2. If only people tried hard enough, conflict could be avoided.

   SA A D SD

3. Avoiding conflict will generally make it go away.

   SA A D SD

4. Each conflict is unique and personal; you can't really generalize about them.

   SA A D SD

5. Conflicts should be resolved as quickly as possible.

SA A D SD

6. Conflicts are almost always caused by hardheadedness and stupidity.

SA A D SD

7. Conflicts have winners and losers; the goal is to not be on the losing end too often.

SA A D SD

8. Most people would rather stew over a conflict than resolve it.

SA A D SD

9. If people insist on pushing our buttons, they should expect us to get angry with them.

SA A D SD

10. When conflict occurs, everyone loses.

SA A D SD

11. It is always best to be completely honest, candid, and open with people; you should tell others exactly how you feel and why.

SA A D SD

12. Any conflict can be resolved if people would just decide to be nice to one another.

SA A D SD

13. When conflicts occur, someone is to blame.

SA A D SD

14. If I love someone enough, I can prevent conflicts from occurring.

SA A D SD

15. Successful negotiation requires you to always look for an edge over your adversary.

SA A D SD

16. When you're in a conflict, the most important thing is to just try and survive.

SA A D SD

17. The best way to resolve a conflict is to find out who is at fault, get them to admit to it, and determine what they can do to make it right.

SA A D SD

18. Broken relationships can rarely be healed through an intentional reconciliation process; time heals all wounds.

SA A D SD

19. The best way to handle conflict is to just say what you feel and let the chips fall where they may.

SA A D SD

20. When you know you're right, the only thing you can do is dig in your heels and try to wear down your opponent.

SA A D SD

21. When in a conflict, don't get mad, get even.

SA A D SD

22. It is always important to take a stand for justice, regardless of relationships that may be broken as a result.

SA A D SD

Look over your answers. Is there an observable pattern? Do you mostly agree or disagree with the statements?

There are no "correct" answers; the goal is to give you information on your own attitudes toward conflict at this point. As you move through the course, you will discover that the transformative model of conflict resolution would disagree with most of these statements. You may want to come back at the end of the course and take this survey again and see if any of your answers change.

Exercise | *Childhood Messages about Conflict*

Write down, in the form of succinct sentences or phrases, as many messages as you can think of that you received about conflict while growing up. These messages may have been explicit lessons taught by your parents, teachers, or peers, or they may have been generalizations you made based on your experience.

How many of the following ideas appear on your list?

"Fighting never solves anything."
"Turn the other cheek."
"You're older and should know better."
"Bite your tongue!"
"If you don't have something nice to say, don't say anything at all."
"Don't hit kids with glasses or girls."
"An eye for and eye, and a tooth for a tooth."
"Don't pick a fight, but if you're in one, win it."
"Are you a man or a mouse?"
"Are you just going to take it lying down?"
"Don't let people think they can walk all over you."
"Sticks and stones may break my bones, but names will never hurt me."

While the primary socialization process shapes our values, beliefs, and understanding of self, it also forms our attitudes toward conflict. Although childhood lessons about conflict are taught from a variety of viewpoints and for a variety of purposes, the result is generally responses such as avoidance, aggression, or simply giving in. These responses may work in the short run, but, again, they are ultimately unsatisfying because they are unproductive. If we don't examine our childhood messages critically, they are likely to continue to influence our adult behavior – for better or for worse.

Metaphors for Thinking about Conflict

A metaphor is a figure of speech in which a word or phrase that ordinarily designates one thing is used to designate another, thus making an implicit comparison, such as *a sea of troubles.* As Wilmot and Hocker (2005:12-21) note, metaphors structure as well as express our thinking. Many of the metaphors we regularly use are unmarked. Often they are so pervasive in our culture, so much a part of our cultural capital, that we use them without considering what they really imply or how they structure our thinking. Especially with regard to conflict, it can be helpful to surface these metaphors and examine them.

Exercise

Think of a recent or major conflict in which you were involved. In the space below, write down, as graphically as you can, what that experience was like for you. Describe, in graphic terms, the conflict process as it began and developed over time. Describe yourself in the conflict, as well as the other party or parties. Or, if you are more comfortable expressing yourself in art, draw your answer in the space below. In either case, don't spend a lot of time analyzing and planning what you write or draw. Put down what comes to you spontaneously as you think about the conflict. Don't censor your responses; there are no wrong answers here.

Now go back and examine what you have written or drawn. What metaphors do you find? Write those metaphors below. What do these metaphors tell you about the way you perceive and react to conflict?

Here are some other metaphors for conflict. Some have been compiled by Wilmot and Hocker (2005:12-21), and others have been generated by previous students of this course. How does each one affect the way a person reacts to conflict, what they perceive as their possible options, and how does the metaphor enhance or limit the potential for constructive or transformative conflict resolution?

Conflict is War
Your actions are *indefensible.*
I felt *beaten down and defeated.*
Accusations were *hurled back and forth.*
We *shot down* that idea.

Conflict is an Explosion
He's got a *short fuse.*
She really *blew her stack.*
I just needed to *let off steam.*

Conflict is a Trial
The *jury's still out* on that one.
He's got the *best case.*
She *let him off easy* this time.

Conflict is an Act of Nature
We were *caught in an avalanche* of frustration.
This conflict is *snowballing out of control.*
He really *frosts* me.
We seem to be *in the eye of the hurricane.*

Conflict is Animal Behavior
They're *butting heads* again.
He's *as stubborn as a mule.*
Well, don't *tear my head off!*

Conflict is a Game
The *ball's in his court* now.
I'm afraid I've *struck out* here.
It looks like *an end run.*

Conflict is Communication Breakdown
Like *talking with someone from another planet.*
That *doesn't compute.*
It seems like *the lines are down.*

Conflict is Laundry
Let's not *air our dirty laundry* here.
She needs to *come clean.*

Conflict is Geology
I think we're approaching the *fault line.*
He *shifted the terrain* of the argument.
We face a *mountain* of difficulties there.
It's an *uphill battle.*

Conflict is Geometry
You're trying to argue *on a different plane.*
Let's look at it *from a different angle.*
You two are *talking crosswise* to each other.

Conflict is Culinary
You can't *have your cake and eat it too.*
We're just *walking on eggshells.*
Don't *cry over spilt milk.*

Conflict is a Garden
As the twig is bent, so grows the tree.
Let's *plant the seeds* of understanding.
I'm *trying to cultivate* a little good will.
You should *tend your own garden.*

Conflict is a Balancing Act
We're *walking a tightrope* here.
One false move and it's over.
We're *at a delicate stage* of negotiations.

Conflict is a Tide
Don't try to *swim against the tide.*
My energy for this is *at low ebb.*
We may be *going into dangerous waters.*

Conflict is a Mess
Let's not *open that can of worms.*
Let's *get all the garbage out in the open.*
This is a *sticky situation.*

Conflict is a Dance
Quit *dancing around* the issue.
Let's *find our own rhythm.*

After reviewing this list, can you think of other metaphors? What are the implications of these metaphors?

Personal Styles and Conflict

"Everything that irritates us about others can lead us to an understanding of ourselves."
– *Carl Jung*

The study of human differences—at least informally—is probably as old as human societies. Humans seem to have always been interested in what makes individuals different from one another. Among these differences is personal style. A personal style is a predisposition to think, feel, and act in the world according to a certain pattern. The origin of personal styles—sometimes referred to a personality types—is complex. They are a product of the complicated interaction of biological factors like a person's genetic makeup, metabolism, etc. and sociological factors like life experience. For our purposes, the origin of these personal styles is less important than the fact of their existence and the additional fact that they seem to structure our responses to the physical and social worlds. Thus it becomes an important component of self-knowledge to learn what our personal style is and how it affects our choices and our interactions, especially in tension-laden situations of conflict when we tend to fall back on "gut" responses.

While each individual's personal style seems to be fixed early in life, as flexible symbolic creatures we can alter our behavior based on our understanding of our own style as well as that of others. Nowhere is this more beneficial than in situations of conflict. Knowing and understanding internal predispositions can help us to clarify our own predilections and responses, as well as those of others.

Over the years a variety of styles or personality types have been noted and a variety of instruments have been developed to identify these styles. (See Frager 1994 and Appendix III for resources on style identification.) For the purposes of constructive conflict resolution, one of the most useful style identification tools in my judgment is the Friendly Style Profile™ developed by Gilmore and Fraleigh (2004). These authors identify four basic styles:

Accommodating/Harmonizing
Analyzing/Preserving
Achieving/Directing
Affiliating/Perfecting

The graphs below show how the styles are distributed along a number of important continua.

STYLE DIFFERENCE CONTINUA

PACE

achieving/directing   *analyzing/preserving*

fast -- slow

accommodating/harmonizing

--------------------------------- *affiliating/perfecting* ---------------------------------

(variable)

Emotional Intensity

affiliating/perfecting — *analyzing/preserving*

high -- low

achieving/directing — *accommodating/harmonizing*

Purpose

accommodating/harmonizing — *achieving/directing*

person/ relationship -- task

affiliating/perfecting — *analyzing/preserving*

Process

affiliating/perfecting — *achieving/directing*

team/ tandem -- lone ranger

accommodating/harmonizing — *analyzing/preserving*

Goal

analyzing/preserving — *achieving/directing*

avoiding failure -- achieving success

accommodating/harmonizing — *affiliating/perfecting*

Clarifying Thoughts

analyzing/preserving — *affiliating/perfecting*

inside hearers -- outside hearers

accommodating/harmonizing

Parsons/Daté ©1983
Used with permission

Gilmore and Fraleigh point out that each style has unique and significant strengths. Moreover, each style complements and contradicts each of the other styles in particular ways. They also note the kinds of excess to which each style is prone. Now it is time for you to discover your own unique style.

Exercise — *The Friendly Style Profile*

Complete the Friendly Style Profile™ and record your summary scores in the table below.

Your scores:

	Accommodating/ Harmonizing	Analyzing/ Preserving	Achieving/ Directing	Affiliating/ Perfecting
Calm				
Storm				

Examine your scores under **Calm** conditions first. Do you see evidence of a dominant style (3+ points greater than other scores)? Or do you tend to have two dominant styles? In rare cases, you might equally prefer 3 or even all 4 of the styles. Gilmore and Fraleigh (2004) provide an excellent guide for interpreting your particular pattern. They note the basic orientation of each style as well as compatible and contradictory elements between each possible pairing of the four styles.

An advantage of the Friendly Style Profile™ is that it allows the user to identify style tendencies under both calm and storm conditions. This is especially valuable in learning how to manage ourselves and deal constructively with others in situations of conflict. First of all, different conditions are stressful for different styles. What is a healthy challenge for one style may be enormously stressful for another style. So different factors create storm conditions for different styles. Second, the stress of conflict can provoke a person to go into excess in their style. What were formerly strengths, now taken to extremes, become excess and exacerbate the conflict – internally, externally, or both. Third, conflict can produce a storm shift, in which individuals switch to a different dominant style. Examine your **Storm** scores above. Do you see evidence of a **storm shift** (a change of 3+ points from Calm conditions)? Examine Gilmore and Fraleigh's discussion and reflect on how your responses change under conditions of conflict. The authors provide a variety of strategies for managing excess in yourself as well as how to bring out the best in people with other styles.

On the following pages you will find some additional resources on understanding and using styles.

Early Detection of Possible Excess

Below are statements individuals from each style may make when they might be going into excess. Each statement by itself is not an indicator of excess, but if you find yourself saying the things listed under your particular style, it is worth checking yourself to see if you are moving toward excess.

Accommodating/Harmonizing	Analyzing/Preserving
1. Sure… 2. Yes, anything you say… 3. Whatever you want… 4. Certainly. 5. If you want to… 6. What/how do you want to do it? 7. No, I didn't get it done… 8. I tried… 9. I forgot, I didn't have time… 10. Yes, I will do that… 11. OK… 12. OK, I'll do it later… 13. I think it's funny, (even if you don't)… 14. (changes subject) Hey, listen to this… 15. Oh, it's not as bad as you think… 16. It doesn't matter how we do it… 17. I'm not sure what I want… 18. Let's not talk about it any more now… 19. Have you heard this joke? 20. Nonverbals: a. anytime chatting and being overly sociable b. smiling too much c. acting inappropriately silly	1. It won't work… 2. <u>No</u>. 3. I need more information. 4. I can't make a decision now. 5. What, when, who, why, where. 6. I have to think about it. 7. I don't know. 8. I'm not sure. 9. Wait…it's all happening too fast…I need more time. 10. I feel paralyzed. 11. I'm afraid. 12. You're too upset. 13. You don't care about planning ahead. 14. I can't just change my plans just like that. 15. That piece of information just changes everything. 16. That's how it's done/ That's how it's always been done. 17. I've never done that before. 18. I'm just going to do it my way. 19. I just did it my way. 20. It just has to be done this way. 21. What about x, y, z, …? 22. That's impossible. 23. Nonverbals: a. any verbal or nonverbal withdrawal b. silence c. going underground

Achieving/Directing	Affiliating/Perfecting
1. Hurry up!	1. It's not good enough…
2. You're holding me back!	2. It's got to be all or nothing!!!
3. I can't wait forever!	3. This is too hard…
4. I/we have to decide right now!	4. It's/I'm a failure…
5. This is boring/too easy.	5. I've worked hard, so I deserve…
6. This is out of control…	6. It isn't fair…
7. Yes, sure, I'll do it…and that…and that…	7. You don't understand me…
8. Do this…do that…	8. You expect too much of me…
9. We're going to do it my way!	9. You aren't trying hard enough…
10. Let's just try this…	10. You're taking advantage of me…
11. Yes, I think it will work…	11. You don't care about how I feel/what I think…
12. I heard what you said…	12. You haven't done your share…
13. This is how it's just going to be…	13. You haven't met your part of the agreement…
14. Look, I know how to do it!	14. It's my fault/I'm guilty…
15. As soon as I get this done…	15. I only want to do it if I/we do it "right."
16. I just can't deal with that now, until this other task/event/project/program is over…	16. I don't want to do it alone…
17. It's not that complex, it's much more simple…	17. I want help…I need help…
18. I don't know what to do…	18. I can't do it perfectly…
19. Maybe I'm incompetent…	19. You're disappointed in me…
20. Nonverbals: a. any words in a loud voice b. talking fast c. interrupting d. walking or doing anything fast	20. I can't do it; you do it for me…
	21. I should/ought…
	22. You should/ought…
	23. You're being unfair to me…
	24. Any statement that is self-denying or self-critical
	25. Criticism of others
	26. Nonverbals: a. any voice modulations that sound like whining or complaining b. being unassertive c. acting like a doormat

Daté ©1984
Used with permission.

Practitioner's Notes — *Appealing to Others' Strengths*

"Hot-tips" for relating to someone with **Accommodating/Harmonizing**

PACE AND APPROACH
1. Two steps/stages: a) first be friendly, informal and socialize before business; b) then work on the concern/problem/task.
2. Make ritual social overtures (physical, food, chat, touch, walk, bicycle, outdoors, "niceness"!!). Fun!
3. Use humorous appeals (refer to foibles, not flaws).
4. Give encouragement, support ("rally squad").
5. Offer a proactive, benevolent Achieving/Directing posture ("Shelty dog")
DATA NEEDED
6. Let the person know you are pleased.
7. Show how the person fits in or belongs. SMILE!
8. Reassure the person that s/he is liked by you and others.
PROCESS
9. State that you want to hear the person's opinions/preferences even though they may be different from yours.
10. Be willing to try for a compromise.
11. Use a point scale ("On a scale of 1 to 10, …how important is this to you? … or … how much do you want to do this?")
MISCELLANEOUS
12. Allow for "saving face."
13. Provide an opportunity for the person to be in the spotlight to be appreciated.
14. Help them see how failure can be avoided.
15. Initiate choices. (Invite preferences.)
16. Assist or allow the person to get/feel the "lay of the land." (To answer/discern the question "Is it safe yet?")

"Hot-tips" for relating to someone with **Analyzing/Preserving**

PACE AND APPROACH
1. Ritualistically wants time. Use two steps/stages: a) mention a topic and give information; b) give time to get away and think. If pressed for immediate decision, the answer will probably be "No."
2. Give time to reflect and the opportunity to be analytical.
3. Allow for cool-off time.
4. You must approach first.
DATA NEEDED
5. Provide details, use facts, data, policies, procedures.
6. Tie new things to old.
7. Get some additional facts the person will trust.
8. Predictability is essential: plan your calendar in advance together. Don't expect changes in plans to be accepted quickly and easily.
PROCESS
9. Be calm and unemotional, lower tension, minimize emotionality.
10. Be willing to take/offer to do some aspect of the work (e.g., data gathering).
MISCELLANEOUS
11. Discuss criteria desired to evaluate the problem.
12. Be prepared. Do your best to be task-oriented.
13. Describe how the goal/task can be accomplished step by step, thus reducing the risk of failure.

We believe that persons who have a high Analyzing/Preserving score/perspective/orientation are the most misunderstood of the four Styles, and as a result are the most "abused" by our U.S.A. society expectations and relationships.

e.g. "Slow warmer-uppers" and much less "touchy/feely."

"Hot-tips" for relating to someone with **Achieving/Directing**

PACE AND APPROACH
1. Respond quickly (at least acknowledge urgency, even if you cannot solve the problem yet). Speak as briefly and succinctly as possible. 2. Hear the person out: PARAPHRASING IS THE ONLY WAY TO SLOW AND CALM AN ACHIEVING/DIRECTING PERSON!!! 3. Reflect understanding (let the person know you understand his or her purpose/what he or she is trying to accomplish). 4. Move toward the person (touch them lightly). 5. Even if the person looks competent, go ahead and approach.
DATA NEEDED
6. Offer solutions; don't bring up new problems. 7. Suggest alternatives or options, or provide some alternative view of the problem. 8. Clarify your own limitations. 9. State your purpose. 10. State which decisions have been made already, and which are still open for discussion. 11. State that you are doing the best you can. 12. Offer to do an Impact Preview together (as an Achieving/Directing person often over-extends).
PROCESS
13. Speak clearly and firmly. Assert yourself. 14. Respect the person's autonomy. 15. Use a point scale ("On a scale of 1 to 10, how urgent is this?") PRIORITIZE.
MISCELLANEOUS
16. Recognize the person's skills or competencies. 17. Appreciate the person's initiative. 18. Take courage from the knowledge that the Achieving/Directing person's greatest fear is overwhelming and alienating person he/she loves/cares about.

"Hot-tips" for relating to someone with **Affiliating/Perfecting**

PACE AND APPROACH
1. Approach (and touch) the person; you will likely have to approach first. 2. Be accessible, willing to collaborate and to spend additional time. 3. Provide support, encouragement, reassurance. 4. Appeal to ideals, principles, excellence, or the person's sense of fairness.
DATA NEEDED
5. Acknowledge the value of <u>intent</u>, even if the consequences weren't as desired. 6. Affirm the person's worth. 7. Offer <u>concrete</u> and <u>specific</u> assistance. 8. Reassure the person about the relationship; an Affiliating/Perfecting person wants to know there is still an "us" and that the relationship is on solid footing. 9. HEAR THE AFFILIATING/PERFECTING PERSON OUT COMPLETELY! – despite accusations, complaints, moral indignation. Paraphrase everything (the <u>person needs to feel heard and understood in order to calm down</u>). Affiliating/Perfecting people tend to come 180 degrees and see other's point of view <u>after</u> being thoroughly heard out (because that's "fair"). 10. Acknowledge your part in the problem (don't be defensive or the Affiliating/Perfecting person will be off again!). Offer your "confession" – the Affiliating/Perfecting person will come around to offering his/hers because that's "fair." 11. An Affiliating/Perfecting person may seem to be going in circles. Wait and keep paraphrasing. Don't push or defend. S/he will get clear as s/he <u>talks it through</u> out loud. It is the talking it through out loud which helps the confusion reduction process.
PROCESS
12. Keep repeating that you care, that you want to help (be prepared for rejection at first since he or she will likely pull away. Be prepared for him/her to declare it is 100% the other person's fault. <u>Hold out for the second round</u>. 13. Be team-oriented; encourage mutual goal setting. 14. Don't prod for late responses; don't nag.
MISCELLANEOUS
15. Suggest some way the person can "make up" or atone for what they perceive they have done wrong.

Conflict Response Modes

Here are 5 different ways of responding to conflict. While each of us may have a personal preference for one of them over the others, they are also choices—that is, we can choose when to employ one of these strategies over the other possibilities, depending on the importance of the problem and the salience of the relationship to us.

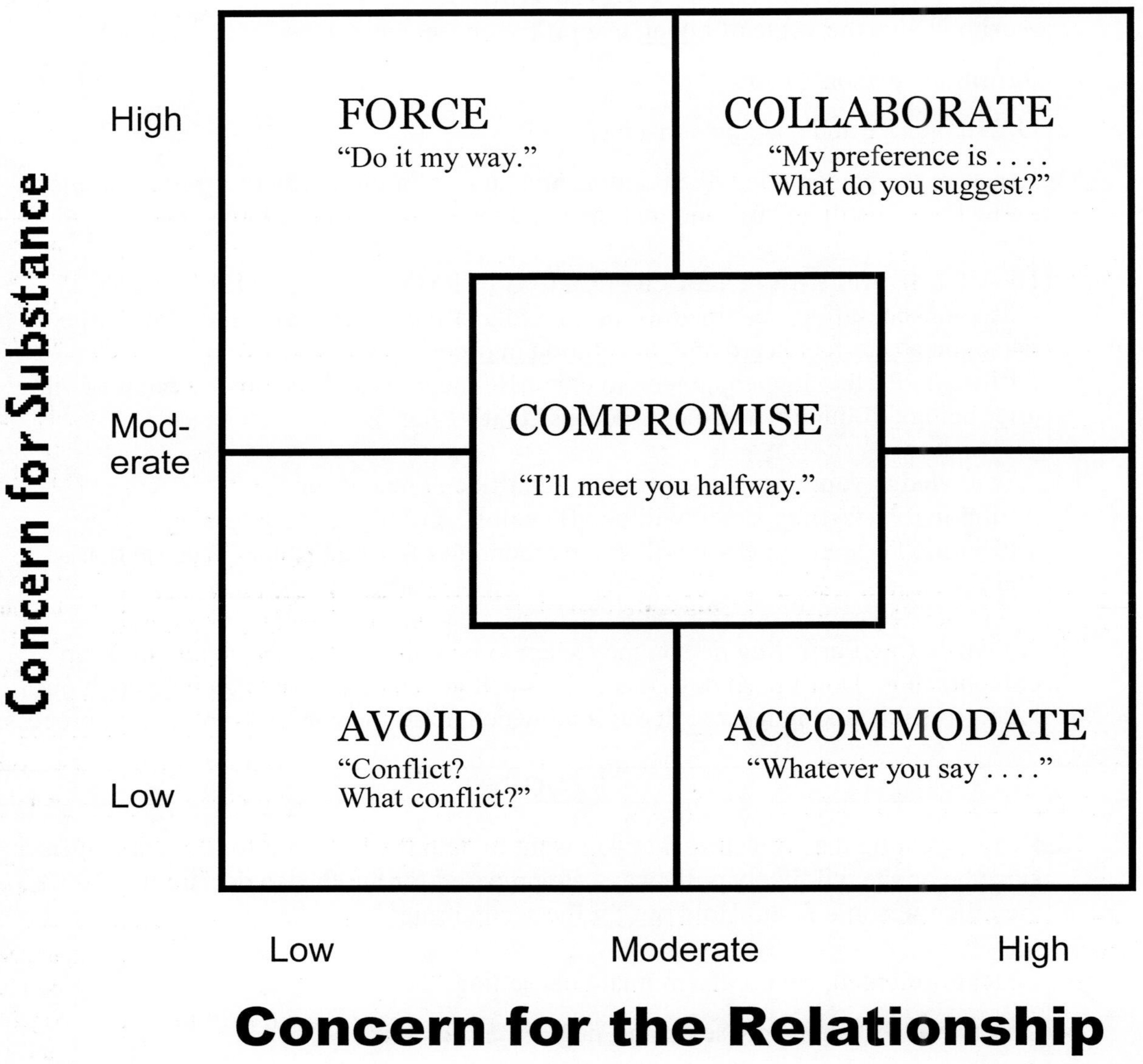

Profiles of the Conflict Response Modes

	FORCE	AVOID	ACCOMMO-DATE	COMPRO-MISE	COLLABO-RATE
Metaphor	"Tiger"	"Turtle"	"Teddy Bear"	"Fox"	"Owl"
Game set	Win/Lose	Lose/Lose	Lose/Win	Win some/ Lose some	Win/Win
Goal	Win without concessions if at all possible	Avoid conflict & confrontation at all costs	Maintain harmony and the relationship above all	Reduce conflict by meeting halfway	Develop the relationship so that both parties can win
Basic Assumption	Conflicting interests can't be reconciled; one or the other must triumph.	Conflict is always bad; you should just take what you can get and cut your losses.	Conflict can lead to unpleasant confrontations that destroy relationships.	Conflict resolution requires give and take on both sides.	Conflict produces a creative, problem-solving situation.
Relationship orientation	Important mainly as an object of control or challenge	Conflict situations are dangerous to it	Most important; maintain it at all costs	Important; maintain it through mutual concessions	Vital; build the relationship through negotiation
Negotiating style	Aggressive; direct, control, or resist; get and maintain the upper hand	Realism; take whatever the other is willing to concede	Make concessions to further the relationship	By splitting the difference each person walks away with something	Explore mutual interests for mutual gains
Strategies	Compete, control, outwit, preempt, coerce, pressure, threaten, intimidate	Deny, ignore, withdraw, flee, delay, yield, relinquish, hope and pray	Agree, give in, yield to pressure, avoid discussing differences	Bargain, split the difference, meet halfway, look for tradeoffs, give in order to get, cajole	Look for common interests, use objective criteria, expand the pie
Prefers others to	Avoid or Accommodate	Avoid or Accommodate	Force or Compromise	Compromise, Accommodate	Collaborate or Compromise
Preference for dialogue	Only as a means to accomplish my ends	Refuse to engage in it	To the extent it avoids conflict & confrontation	Generally uncomfortable with it	Key to the whole process
Orientation to information-gathering	Impatient with it	Not interested due to desire to stay out of the process	Other's information is more important	Within agreed-upon limits	Important to the process and the search for solutions
Leadership character-istics	Competitive; forceful; authoritarian; "take charge"	Passive, timid, focused on "weathering the storm"	Easily swayed, ineffective; group drifts off task	Cautious but open, keeps things moving	Open; emphasizes mutual respect, partnership

Exercise *How Do I Respond to Conflict?*

Think about your personal experience with conflict. Try to come up with at least one example where you have used each of the Conflict Response Modes. Describe the situation and what you did that employed that mode of response. Don't judge or evaluate at this point—just describe.

FORCE

AVOID

ACCOMMODATE

COMPROMISE

COLLABORATE

Each of the conflict response modes has certain costs and benefits, and each is appropriate under certain circumstances, as noted below.

RESPONSE MODE	COSTS: Potential Problems Posed for Conflict Resolution	BENEFITS: Situations Where This Response Might Be Useful
FORCE	Values substance over the relationship and thereby threatens the relationship; creates resentment and jeopardizes future interactions	May be an efficient strategy when speed is vital or fulfilling responsibility requires taking action despite objections
ACCOMMODATE	The one who gives in does not have their issues heard or their needs met; may cause conflict to fester; accommodator's views are eventually not sought or taken seriously	Useful when the issue is of little importance to you but of great importance to them; give in order to get: generate good feelings to draw on at another time; useful when facing a powerful adversary who has the ability to impose severe negative sanctions
AVOID	No one's issues are heard or needs are met; conflict is very likely to fester; a working relationship is not established or maintained; can generate despair, powerlessness, and indifference	Allows time to collect more information or for heated emotions to cool; avoids wasting time on conflicts that are trivial or that are likely to work themselves out; bypasses a confrontation with a powerful adversary who can do you harm
COMPROMISE	Potentially generates a solution which is not really satisfying for either party; they may be able to live with it, but it doesn't satisfy their original goals; makes reducing conflict more important than resolving the problem	Can be useful when parties are stuck and need to move forward, especially in a power struggle when the two parties have relatively equal power; useful when the long-term relationship is more important than resolving the problem
COLLABORATE	May require more time or effort than the parties deem necessary given their relationship and/or the nature of the problem	Valuable when both the relationship and the problem are important, when the parties must maintain an ongoing relationship, or where the conflict is complex and multilayered; likely to produce more creative, compre-hensive, synergistic, mutually satisfying solutions

After reviewing the information above, reflect on your own responses to conflict listed on the previous page. What was effective/ineffective in each of your responses? Would you try to respond differently now?

Practitioner's Notes — *Getting Centered*

Getting centered is key to managing stress well. But it is also crucial to the process of constructively managing our emotions – especially anger. Moreover, when we are centered we can think and perceive more efficiently and communicate with others more effectively. In order to get centered, we must become relaxed and focused. Many spiritual disciplines—from both the West and the East, and from meditation to martial arts—emphasize the importance of relaxing the body in order to improve the mind's focus. For further information on these techniques and how to use them, see the classic Buddhist approach of Hanh (2001) or the more Westernized version in Reilly and Shropshire (2002).

To become centered, we need to slow down and get in touch with our body. Breathing is essential to life, but we are usually unaware that we are doing it. Just focusing on our breathing can slow down our pulse rate, induce relaxation, and promote focus. Further, we can become aware of tension within our body and then release it through deep breathing. Try this:

- Whether sitting or standing, adopt a relaxed, but alert posture. You should be comfortable, but not in a resting state.
- Become aware of your breathing. Don't think of anything else; just concentrate on your breathing. Notice your breath going in and out.
- Become aware of where you are experiencing tension in your body. Take a deep breath. Feel the air filling your lungs. Hold it for a second and then, as you slowly let your breath out, consciously expel the tension as well.
- Take another deep breath. Hold it for a second. As you slowly let the air out of your lungs, imagine that you are also letting go of what happened to you earlier and what you need to do later. Continue to breathe deeply, staying attuned to your breath as it enters and leaves your body. Calmly strive to just be present in the current moment. See what you see. Hear what you hear. Feel what you feel.
- As you become aware of what you are feeling, reflect on how those feelings may influence what you hear and what you say.

This technique should allow you to be in touch with your own feelings, and it should clear your mind to think carefully and lucidly about whatever you need to contemplate. Zen Buddhists call this a state of mindfulness. Michelle LeBaron (2002) calls it mindful receptivity. In this state you can be an effective third party. You can attend to another person with your eyes, facial expression, and posture. You can hear them with your ears, mind, and heart—using both your rational mind and your intuition. You can feel empathy with them. And you can speak with your mind, heart, and body.

Notes on Anger

Assumptions about anger

- Anger is a universal human emotion.
- Anger takes many forms: e.g., fretting, annoyance, irritability, rage.
- Anger is an emotion; aggression is a behavior; hostility is an attitude.
- Anger is rooted in other emotions: fear, insecurity, helplessness or loss of control, a sense of being personally devalued or disrespected.
- The expression of anger is learned behavior. It is not genetic or otherwise predetermined.
- Constructive anger management can be learned as well.
- Angry responses and angry behavior are generally habits.
- Anger is basically an assertion of self. It is a way of saying: "Hey, listen to me!"
- Anger is contagious – and so is calm. We can infect someone else with our anger or our sense of calm.
- Angry behavior is a choice.

> People and events don't make us angry; they trigger perceptions that we use to make ourselves angry.

- Anger becomes a problem when it is felt too intensely, too frequently, or is expressed inappropriately.
- Managing anger makes the individual and the organization more productive.

Positive functions of anger:

- Alerts us and others that something is wrong.
- Relieves frustration.
- Motivates us and provides the energy to deal with injustice.

Negative functions of anger

- Clouds judgment
- Causes misperceptions and distortions in thinking
  - False perception and incorrect attribution of motive
  - Stereotypical thinking

Dimensions of anger: (based on Weisinger 1995)

- **Cognition**: how we think about anger; how we define what makes us angry
- **Physiology**: the biological arousal and responses that anger generates
- **Affect**: how it feels to us to be angry
- **Behavior**: how we act when we are angry
- **Communication**: how we let others know that we are angry

Anger Management

"Nothing can heal anger except compassion." *Thich Nhat Hanh*

Dealing appropriately with our anger means developing an anger management strategy. It should be one based on compassion – for ourselves and others. Here are some crucial assumptions that underlie an effective anger management strategy.

- Everyone can learn effective anger management techniques.
- Contrary to much popular belief and practice, simply venting anger is not usually desirable. Research has found that people who vent their anger aggressively just get better at being angry. (See, e.g., Deutsch and Coleman 2000, p. 249)
- Anger management, in which anger is acknowledged and dealt with constructively, requires self-awareness and self-control.

  ✓ We must acknowledge our humanity and our human frailties.

  This is summed up in the phrase: *Nihil humani a me alienum.* (Nothing human is foreign to me.) Everyone makes mistakes, and everyone sometimes has irrational responses to situations and people.

  ✓ We must embrace our anger in order to transform it.

  Like garbage can be turned into compost, we can turn our anger into positive energy.

  ✓ We must not lash out in order to make others suffer, too.

  We will not suffer less because we make others suffer too. "Misery loves company" is false—making others miserable only spreads sadness and hurt.

Practitioner's Notes

Developing an effective anger management strategy

Based on what we have learned so far, here are some key components of an effective anger management strategy:

✓ Recognize the events, situations, and behavior of other people that trigger anger.

✓ Do not deny your anger, but do not simply vent it. Instead, embrace and understand it.

✓ If necessary, take a timeout by removing yourself from the situation.

Do this for as long as it takes to get yourself under control.

Do not immediately say or do anything to escalate the anger or increase the pain or suffering.

✓ Talk with a friend or other supportive person(s).

You may want to safely release emotion, obtain validation, and/or do a reality check.

✓ Develop workable techniques for dealing with each dimension of anger:

- **Cognition:** Challenge irrational personal beliefs and replace them with more realistic ones through self-talk.

  Acknowledge your own role in creating or escalating the situation.

  Understand that the hurtful behavior of other people is most often an expression of their own pain and suffering.

- **Physiology**: Use deep breathing, muscle relaxation, or meditation. (See *Getting Centered* below.)

  Exercise by taking a walk, running, or working out.

- **Affect**: Acknowledge your own feelings but don't allow them to control your behavior.

  Acknowledge and respect other people's feelings.

- **Behavior**: Develop behavior habits that are assertive, not aggressive. (See *Centered Communication* in the next section of this manual.)

- **Communication**: Develop techniques of centered communication. (See the next section of this manual.)

Exercise *Understanding and Dealing with Your Anger*

The goal of this exercise of for you to gain insight into your own personal experience of anger and to develop effective strategies for dealing with it.

List some of the primary payoffs or apparent gains you have personally experienced by expressing anger:

What are some of the negative consequences of expressing your anger?

List some of the events, situations, and behavior of other people that trigger anger in you (i.e., your personal "red flags.").

Anger cues

Cognitive cues: How do you explain to yourself why you're angry? What reasons do you give for being angry?

Physiological cues: How does your body respond to anger? Where in your body do you tend to lodge your anger and resentment? Look in a mirror when you become angry. How does anger alter your face?

Emotional cues: What other feelings tend to accompany your anger?

Behavioral cues: What do you do when you are angry? (e.g., clench your fists, raise your voice, etc.)

Communication cues: What do you tend to say to other people to let them know you're angry? How do you treat people when you are angry with them?

Personal anger management plan

Based on the information above, what specific strategies can you use to control your anger?

Exercise — *Questions for Interveners*

Here is a set of questions that sum up much of what we have learned on the inner journey. Answer them as honestly as you can.

1. How do you define conflict? What does the concept mean to you? (Reflect on the word association exercise.)

2. What does conflict feel like to you? (Reflect on metaphors for conflict.) How do you respond to conflict situations? (Reflect on your conflict style.)

3. With whom do you tend to have conflicts? (i.e., what categories of people?) What do those conflicts tend to be about? (Reflect on values, beliefs, and personal style.)

4. What types of conflict do you deal with fairly easily? (i.e., dispose of them satisfactorily and relatively quickly)

5. What types of conflict are hard for you to deal with? (i.e., what ones do you avoid or delay dealing with?)

6. What is bad about how people deal with conflict? (i.e., what feels bad/uncomfortable to you?)

7. What, if anything, feels good about conflict?

8. What feels good about conflict resolution?

9. What would you define as a "best case" successful resolution to a conflict?

10. Are there currently any important unresolved conflicts in your life? What are they about? How do they affect you? How would they affect how you would deal with someone else's conflict?

11. When you assist others who are experiencing interpersonal conflict, how would you describe your dominant personal style? (see *Styles of Conflict Management*)

12. What characteristics of parties to a conflict would most affect your ability to be impartial and to treat all sides fairly? (e.g., race, ethnicity, gender, social class, religious preference, sexual orientation, personality, etc.)

13. What, in your opinion, are your most useful skills for intervening in conflict situations?

14. What concrete, practical steps can you take to enhance your effectiveness as an intervener?

Part Three: Skills for Interpersonal Conflict Resolution

Conflict Resolution is sometimes spelled C-O-M-M-U-N-I-C-A-T-I-O-N.
– *Barbara Daté*

R-E-S-P-E-C-T — find out what it means to me!
– *Aretha Franklin*

When it confronts a wall of stone, gentleness overcomes rigidity; the power of water prevails.
– *Tao Te Ching*

All I'm saying is simply this, that all life is interrelated, that somehow we're caught in an inescapable network of mutuality tied in a single garment of destiny. Whatever affects one directly affects all indirectly. For some strange reason, I can never be what I ought to be until you are what you ought to be. You can never be what you ought to be until I am what I ought to be. This is the interrelated structure of reality.
– *Dr. Martin Luther King Jr.*

On the one hand, conflict resolution refers to an *outcome* in which the parties to a dispute reduce or end hostility and antagonism by achieving some mutually satisfactory result. On the other hand, conflict resolution refers to the *process* by which that result is obtained. In this section we will focus on the skills involved in the process of conflict resolution. What skills are needed for effective conflict resolution? Basically there are five:

1) personal insight into one's own orientation to conflict, including experience, biases, and response tendencies;
2) a well-developed set of interpersonal communication skills;
3) a sensitivity to social context and process;
4) an ability to understand and analyze conflict; and
5) knowledge of workable procedures for conflict resolution.

The first skill listed was covered in the previous section. The second and third skills will be discussed in this section, and the third will be elaborated on in the following section. The fourth and fifth skills will be the subject of the final section.

The Process of Skill Learning

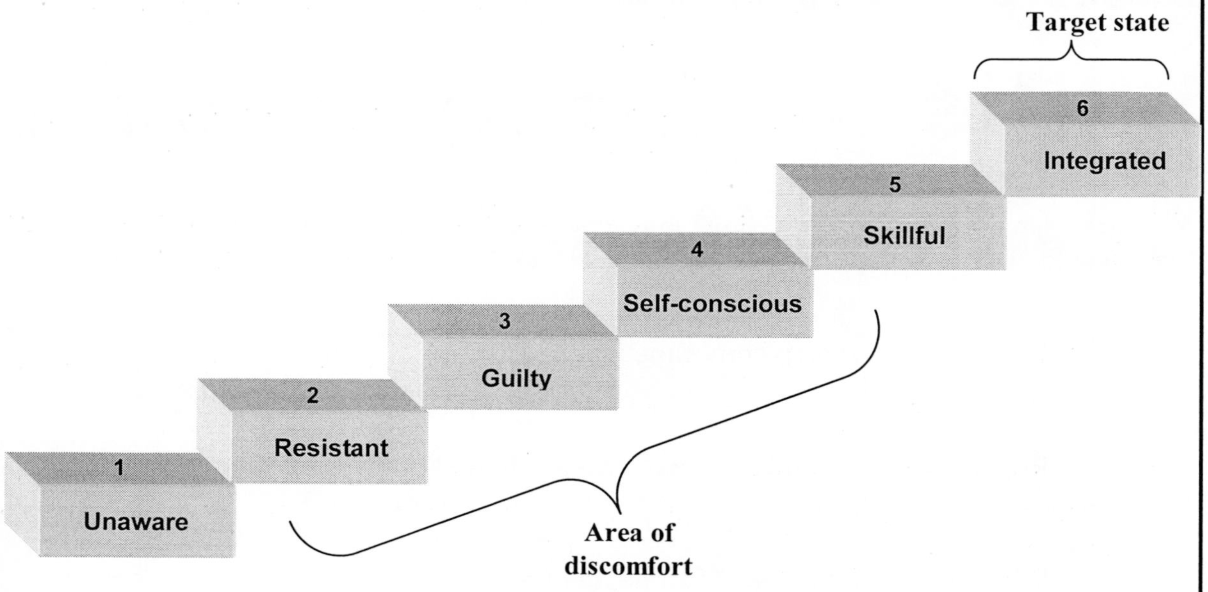

Stages of Skill Learning

By Patrick J. Ashton Adapted from Katz and Lawyer (1994)

Learning conflict resolution skills is a process, with specific stages that learners go through. When you understand this process, you can learn the skills more effectively as you anticipate the emotions and reactions you will have along the way.

You begin by being **unaware** of the specific skills involved. While you of course have standardized personal ways of dealing with conflict, these methods may or may not be effective. In any case, it is likely that the methods you are accustomed to using are not explicitly the ones taught here. As you are introduced to the conflict resolution skills, you may find yourself **resistant** to learning them, or at least to learning them in depth. It is hard work to learn new skills and to reprogram our attitudes and behaviors, and at first it may seem that the payoff is not worth this much effort. As you begin to understand the skills, though, you begin to experience their effectiveness. Now you may feel **guilty** about not knowing about them and not using them in the past. You may feel badly about how you have handled past situations.

As you begin to use the skills, you will have to concentrate and focus in order to use them properly. Undoubtedly you will feel **self-conscious** about using them. You will be aware that you are using them and that others are using them on you. This may lead you to feel that the skills are artificial, or even phony. With continued practice, however, you become more **skillful** in your use of the techniques. Ultimately you want to reach the point where the skills are completely **integrated** into your attitudes and communication patterns, such that you produce them automatically without consciously trying to do so. This is the goal of learning.

A Lesson from the Geese

Every Spring and Fall, we are treated to the sight of large numbers of migrating geese flying overhead. Twice a year, they fly hundreds of miles to their mating or wintering grounds. Have you ever wondered why the geese fly in that familiar "V" formation? It turns out that this is a remarkably efficient way for them to fly long distances. As each bird flaps its wings, it creates an updraft for the bird following behind it and slightly to the side. By flying in "V" formation, the whole flock can travel an average of 71% farther than each bird flying alone.

> **Lesson:** People who share a common direction and sense of community and who work together can go farther and get where they are going faster and easier because they are drawing on one another's energy.

- Whenever a goose falls out of formation, it suddenly feels the drag and resistance of trying to fly alone, and it quickly gets back in formation to take advantage of the lifting power of the bird in front of them.

> **Lesson:** If we have as much sense as a goose, we will stay in formation and solidarity with those who are headed in the direction we want to go.

- When the lead goose — the one who is doing the most work on the point of the "V" — gets tired, it rotates back into the formation and another goose comes forward to fly the point position.

> **Lesson:** With people, as with geese, it only makes sense to take turns doing the hard tasks and to share leadership.

- Why do we hear so much noisy honking when the geese fly over? It's because the geese in formation honk from behind to let those ahead of them know they are still there and to encourage those up front to keep up their speed and effort.

> **Lesson:** It is important that we each participate actively and let our leaders know that we appreciate their efforts. We can do this best by making sure that our honking is encouraging and supportive.

- The geese's long migration is fraught with danger. Hard-to-see power lines, broadcast towers, hunters, and illness brought on by fatigue are some of the primary hazards they face. When a goose gets sick or wounded and falls out of formation, two other geese fall out with that goose and follow it down to lend help and protection. They stay with the fallen goose until it is able to fly again or until it dies. Only then do they launch out on their own, or with another formation, to catch up with their flock.

> **Lesson:** If we have as much sense as the geese, we will stick together in hard times and nurture and protect each other.

source unknown
adapted by Patrick J. Ashton

Interpersonal Skills for Dealing Constructively with Conflict

By the time we are adults, most of us have reasonably good interpersonal communication skills. That is, we are able to successfully negotiate most ordinary everyday interactions. The problem is, in situations of conflict many of these skills seem to desert us. Or perhaps through denial and avoidance of conflict we never learned the skills to communicate about it. That's why it's valuable to explicitly remind ourselves of what these skills are, and to practice and improve our use of them. The following skills are necessary for the kind of communication that leads to constructive, transformative conflict resolution, whether you are a party to the conflict or a third-party intervener. These skills work because they build rapport, lower tension and hostility, create a supportive space for expression, build a bridge of communication, and make possible the search for common ground.

ACTIVE LISTENING SKILLS

Attending

Attending refers to the way we communicate interest and attention to another person. It is how we create a safe, supportive space for them to express themselves. It is a two-way communication, but the listener acts as a witness.

Responding

The most effective form of response that lets someone know that we have really listened to them is paraphrasing. Paraphrasing is the process of dynamic feedback designed to improve the accuracy and effectiveness of communication. It has two important dimensions: **restating** and **reflecting.**

SELF EXPRESSION AND SPEAKING SKILLS

Centered Speaking

Centered communication comes from the heart. First, we must get in touch with our own feelings and gain control over our own bodies. Then, by communicating with other people through **"I" messages,** we take responsibility for our behavior and emotions and convey important information to others without putting them on the defensive.

Agreement Stating

By clearly articulating areas of agreement with another person, we offer moral support and/or common ground as a foundation to continue dialogue.

Preference Stating

When we make a clear statement about our own interests and desires, we can communicate authentically, share choices, and facilitate interaction with another.

Purpose Stating

Purpose stating makes our intentions known to others so that they have clear information about what we are doing and are not inadvertently operating at cross purposes with us.

Posture of Puzzlement

When we are genuinely confused by the statements and/or actions of others, posture of puzzlement lets us respectfully and sincerely convey this confusion to them.

The Importance of Listening

Here are some intriguing statistics about listening from Withers and Lewis (2003, p. 238):

- ✓ Humans have 5 times more capacity to listen than to speak.
- ✓ Looking at communication in the workplace, 53% of our time is spent listening to others; only 47% on all other forms of communication – writing, typing, speaking, etc.
- ✓ In general, when we listen we retain only about 30% of what was said, and later we remember only about ½ of that.

Clearly it behooves us to pay attention to how we listen.

What Does It Mean to Listen?

The Chinese word *tin* means to hear or listen. The ideogram for this verb conveys important information about attending and active listening.

This character aptly illustrates the complexity and the wholeness of deep listening or, as Michelle LeBaron (2002) calls it, "paying exquisite attention to another." When we really listen to someone, we do so with our whole body and our whole being: with our eyes, ears, and heart. The focus is entirely on the other person. At the moment of listening, our own "stuff" doesn't matter; we demonstrate respect for the other person by giving them our undivided attention. To accomplish this, we must become centered and empty ourselves of our own criticisms, judgments, and responses. We must let go of control in order to achieve a stillness that will allow us to be receptive to their message and meanings. Through deep listening, we are creating a space for words to be spoken and feelings to be expressed. Below are some pointers for attending or doing deep listening.

Theory *Ethnomethodology and Conversation Analysis*

Ethnomethodology, a subdiscipline of sociology, was founded by American sociologist Harold Garfinkel (1967). Ethnomethodology—a term Garfinkel invented—means the methods that people use on a daily basis to organize and carry out their everyday lives.

Because humans are conscious social beings, these methods involve figuring things out symbolically and offering accounts or stories that give meaning to our actions. Ethnomethodologists study the accounting practices by which people generate and offer accounts and by which these accounts are either accepted or rejected by others.

Accounts are offered and reacted to through the vehicle of conversations, and thus conversation analysis is a major focus of ethnomethodological research.

Ethnomethodologists assume conversations to be intentional accomplishments of social actors, and to have relatively stable, orderly properties. These conversations include not only words, but hesitations, restarts, silences, cut-offs, noises of various sorts, and the whole range of nonverbal behaviors.

One nonverbal behavior is the gaze. Examining eye contact between subjects in videotaped conversations, Goodwin (1984:230) notes:

> When a speaker gazes at a recipient that recipient should be gazing at him. When speakers gaze at nongazing recipients, and thus locate violations of the rule, they frequently produce phrasal breaks such as restarts and pauses, in their talk. These phrasal breaks both orient to the event as a violation by locating the talk in progress at that point as impaired in some fashion and provide a remedy by functioning as requests for the gaze of the hearer. Thus just after phrasal breaks nongazing recipients frequently begin to move their gaze to the speaker.

Without consciously intending it, the account that is ethnomethodology itself confirms the wisdom embodied in the Chinese word for listen just discussed.

So attending or deep listening is a performance that involves not only hearing the words a speaker is saying, but also developing an appropriate internal mental state and appropriate expressions of body language and verbalizations. Here are some suggestions for doing so successfully.

Practitioner's Notes *How to Listen Deeply*

Internal mental process

DO center yourself by becoming aware of your breathing.

DO stay focused in the moment; there should be nothing else than the now.

DO put aside your own ego and your emotions and concerns about what happened in the past.

DO put aside your sympathy and/or your antipathy for the speaker. They will only get in the way of listening.

DO let go of your need to control or direct the conversation.

DO separate your feelings about the person from what they are saying.

DO keep an open mind; be willing to entertain paradox and ambiguity.

DO try to empathize with the other person. Try to put yourself in their place: what are they trying to say, and why is this important to them?

DO listen for what isn't being said, but might be important.

DO exercise patience; don't rush the process.

DON'T judge or criticize the speaker.

DON'T work on formulating a response while the speaker is talking. Really listen to what they are saying and how they are saying it.

DON'T stereotype or pigeonhole the speaker.

DON'T make assumptions or jump to conclusions.

DON'T try to solve the speaker's problem.

Posture

DO lean forward slightly.

DO maintain a relaxed posture that allows you to listen without resistance.

DON'T lean back or slouch, cross your arms or legs, or keep your body rigid.

Eye contact

DO make frequent eye contact, both while listening and speaking.

DON'T stare or hold the person's gaze for too long at any one time. (It is important to be aware of the variation in cultural norms here.)

DON'T look off into space while the other person is talking; scowl or squint.

Nonverbal communication

DO nod frequently and make appropriate facial gestures to let the person know you are hearing them.

DO respect silences; use stillness to allow the speaker explore their feelings, reflect, reassess and refine their message.

DON'T stare back blankly and unresponsively, or frown.

DON'T fidget, tap your fingers, play with pens, pencils, or paperclips, or jingle your pocket change.

Verbal communication

DO speak clearly with a normal volume.

DO match your tone of voice to the emotional tone of the information you are hearing and wanting to convey.

DON'T speak too rapidly, too softly, or too loudly.

DON'T interrupt the speaker to insert your own message.

DON'T ask questions, except to clarify information or feelings.

DON'T use jargon or language the other person is not likely to understand.

Exercise

Personal notes

What part(s) of attending or deep listening do you find difficult? What would you like to work on? How will you practice these techniques?

Paraphrasing

The purpose of paraphrasing is to convey understanding and caring support to the person speaking. It is most effective when another party has a strong need to express something and you choose to use the time and energy to listen. This recursive process involves a listener capturing either the content or the emotions—or both—of what the speaker is saying and feeding it back to them to be checked for accuracy and/or elaboration and as a validation of their feelings.

The two important dimensions of paraphrasing are **restating** and **reflecting**.

Restating involves repeating, in your own words, what you heard the other person say. The objective is to accurately capture the main idea or content of the speaker's message. It is not about parroting back all the literal details, but rather identifying and restating the heart of their message.

When done correctly, restating can:

- ✓ force you to listen carefully to the speaker.
- ✓ allow the other person to know that you are trying to understand them.
- ✓ avoid frustration and unnecessary, unproductive conflict by clearing up misunderstandings.
- ✓ validate the other person by having someone really listen to them.
- ✓ reduce anger and defensiveness in a person by having someone else take their concerns seriously.
- ✓ allow the speaker to control their message by affording them an opportunity to edit and clarify it.

Reflecting involves mirroring back to the other person the emotions you hear and feel them expressing. The objective is to capture and feed back to the speaker the essence of the emotions they are expressing.

Done properly, reflecting can:

- ✓ create empathy between the speaker and the listener.
- ✓ paradoxically, reduce a person's anger and hostility by giving them permission to feel it.
- ✓ give a person insight into their own behavior by helping them to clarify their emotions.
- ✓ allow a speaker to discuss feelings or an event that they want to share, but find difficult to talk about.
- ✓ generate insights into a conflict by focusing on feelings rather than facts. Conflicts are often more about people's feelings than about any particular set of facts.

Keep in mind that, especially in conflict situations, people are generally much more interested in other people understanding how they feel, rather than getting all the details of the issue at hand. People want their sense of being aggrieved to be validated. Reflecting allows you to do that without agreeing or disagreeing with the facts of the situation.

Practitioner's Notes — *How to Paraphrase*

Focus on the Speaker.
It is helpful to begin your paraphrase with "You…."

Restate and/or Reflect.
Emphasize what you heard them say/feel *so far.* Use synonyms as much as possible, and use a choice of words and a tone of voice that reflects some of the feeling you hear from the other person. Be sincere.

Be Brief.
You should try to be as succinct as possible. If the speaker shares a paragraph of 3 - 5 sentences, your paraphrase should be 3 - 12 words. The shorter the better.

Connecting content and feelings.
Generally you want to paraphrase both the content and the underlying feelings of the speaker's message. You can do this with a compound paraphrase along the lines of the following.

"You feel ______________________ about __________________________."

"You feel ______________________ when __________________________."

"You feel ______________________ that __________________________."

"You're ______________________ because __________________________."

Common Pitfalls of Paraphrasing

- Parroting back their exact words. Pure repetition can seem artificial and lead to frustration.
- Beginning your paraphrases with extraneous phrases like *"What I hear you saying is…." "So you're saying that…."* Focus on the core of the message and leave it at that.
- Inserting your own interpretation of what the other person said or what you think they mean. Let them clarify their own meanings.
- Judging or evaluating what the speaker has said. Don't give the impression that you agree or disagree with what was said, just that you understand it.
- Inserting examples from your own life. It doesn't create empathy, it creates a distraction.
- Asking questions. Contrary to popular belief, asking questions is often unproductive.

The Problem with Questions

Consider the following questions:

What's going on here?

Don't you think this has gone far enough?

What about this don't you understand?

Why do you always do that?

Is this too much to ask?

Are you satisfied?

How many times do I have to tell you?
Don't you know any better than that?
So how do you feel about that?
Why would you say something like that?
Does it bother you to be the only one?
Why don't we all just calm down?
Why can't you see what I'm trying to tell you?
Is it hard for you to admit that you're wrong?
Why didn't you tell me that in the first place?
Don't you think that the right thing to do would be…?

Is this the best you can do?
What's wrong with you?
Do I make you nervous?
Do you trust me?
Was it something I said?
Do you hear me?
What are you going to do now?
Do I make myself clear?
Are you comfortable with this?
What would you do differently?

How do you feel when asked these questions? In your experience, do they advance the conversation and reduce conflict? Or do they throw up roadblocks to communication?

In a mediation session, asking questions instead of paraphrasing the parties can generate some serious roadblocks. In particular, asking questions can:

- be a waste of time because the questions are too broad or general and invite speculation.
  "Why do you think someone would feel that way?"
  "Have you ever heard of anyone doing this before?"

- suggest, rather than reflect, what a person is feeling.
  "What else has he done to make you angry?"
  "So, would it be fair to say that you were pretty upset by this news?"

- put people on the defensive. Questions that begin with *why* are particularly prone to this.
  "Can you prove that?" *"Why do you say that?"*
  "Do you think that's something a reasonable person would say?"
  "Why did you do that?"

- reinforce rather than challenge or undermine expressed prejudice or hostility.
  "So you think all black people are lazy?"

- close off discussion prematurely if the answer is a simple yes or no.
  "So, are you willing to accept this agreement or not?"
  "You're really mad at him, aren't you?"

Common Objections to Paraphrasing

1. **It feels too artificial.**
Most people don't use paraphrasing in their everyday lives (though they'd often be more effective listeners if they did!), so paraphrasing is a new skill. Anytime you learn a new skill, it feels artificial and awkward at first, until you make it an unconscious habit. What's essential is to give it a chance – to practice paraphrasing enough so that it flows naturally.

2. **It feels like I'm interrupting, and interrupting is rude.**
Many of us have been taught that it is rude to talk when someone else is speaking – the polite thing is to wait until the other person finishes and then speak. However, **paraphrasing is *not* interrupting!** Interrupting is when we actually or potentially change the direction of the conversation by inserting our own information. This practice is often perceived as rude. But a paraphrase is all about hearing what the other person is saying and conveying that information to them. Everyone wants to be heard, and it's not rude to let the other person know that you are doing your best to understand what they are saying. If you keep your paraphrases short – 3-5 words, if possible – and put them in between sentences, the conversation will actually be fairly seamless. Just try it – you are likely to be pleasantly surprised.

3. **I'm afraid that my paraphrase will be wrong.**
In a sense, you really can't be wrong. If what you restate is not exactly what the other person thought they said, they will generally be eager to clarify. (e.g., "Not exactly. It's really more like ________.") If the other person hesitates or seems puzzled by your paraphrase, you can always use an I-message to explain yourself: "It's really important to me to understand what you're saying. Did you mean ____________?"

4. **I'm afraid paraphrasing will irritate the other person.**
People are generally so anxious to be heard and understood that they will appreciate almost any sincere effort to help them accomplish this. You're only likely to be irritating if you parrot back everything they say in their exact words or fall into any of the other major pitfalls of paraphrasing mentioned above.

5. **But I really need to ask questions to obtain information.**
Sometimes you do – but probably less frequently than you think you do. In a mediation session, the mediators must remember that it is not about them, but about the disputants. Prior to asking an information question, mediators should ask themselves: Is this something that is important for the other party to know, or is it just something I am curious about? And when further information is necessary, a mediator is generally better off using a preference statement: e.g., "I'd like to know more about…." or "I wonder if you could tell me how you felt when …."

6. **I'm not good at guessing other people's feelings.**
Some of us are better at this than others, but we all can get better. It is a matter of listening carefully for the emotional tone behind a statement, and carefully reflecting that emotion back using appropriate synonyms. See the lists that follow for suggestions, then practice, practice, practice!

7. **I'm afraid that the person I paraphrase will think I agree with what they're saying.** This is more of an imagined than a real concern. When you're actually paraphrasing well, you're letting the other person know that you heard them. Most importantly, when you begin your paraphrase with the word "you," you are leaving ownership of the feelings with the other person. And if you have a good command of synonyms, you don't have to repeat a person's hateful or hurtful language. If you're concerned about being identified with a position or idea you find offensive, after paraphrasing the other person you can always use a posture of puzzlement ("I'm wondering if every left-hander in the world does that?") or a preference statement ("I prefer not to use the word _______.")

8. **I worry that reflecting someone's anger will escalate the conflict.** Paradoxically, it is exactly by acknowledging someone's anger that they calm down. When someone else acknowledges your anger or your right to be angry, it is difficult to stay angry. Paraphrasing is probably the quickest and most effective way to calm an emotional storm. Often the quickest way to escalate a conflict is to deny someone's anger or tell them to calm down.

9. **I worry that paraphrasing may be seen as offensive in some cultural contexts.** People everywhere want to be heard and understood, and paraphrasing may be surprisingly effective even if people are not familiar with it. However, there are cultural contexts in which the practice of paraphrasing as explained above is not appropriate. For instance, in some cultures, a respectful silence is required when another person is talking. If this is the case, then of course the practice of paraphrasing must be modified. But it often doesn't have to be abandoned altogether. For example, you can paraphrase the other person when it is your turn to speak.

Notes on paraphrasing

Synonyms for Use in Paraphrasing

HAPPINESS, JOY	LOVE, AFFECTION	SINCERITY, CONCERN	EFFICACY, POTENCY
amused	affectionate	agreeable	able
at ease	amiable	authentic	adequate
awesome	attractive	big-hearted	assured
blissful	congenial	caring	authoritative
calm	cordial	charitable	bold
cheerful	courteous	comforting	brave
comical	dedicated	conscientious	capable
comfortable	devoted	considerate	competent
contented	easy-going	empathetic	confident
cool	friendly	encouraging	courageous
delighted	giving	fair	daring
ecstatic	good-humored	forgiving	determined
elated	good-natured	genuine	durable
enthusiastic	hospitable	generous	dynamic
excellent	lovable	helpful	effective
excited	loving	honest	efficacious
fantastic	pleasant	interested	energetic
fine	unselfish	kind, kindly	fearless
glad		kind-hearted	firm
good		patient	forceful
gratified		polite	important
great		reasonable	influential
happy		receptive	intense
humorous		reliable	lion-hearted
inspired		respectful	mighty
in high spirits		responsible	powerful
jovial		sensitive	robust
joyful		sympathetic	secure
jubilant		thoughtful	self-confident
marvelous		tolerant	self-reliant
overjoyed		truthful	sharp
pleasant		trustworthy	skillful
serene		understanding	spirited
terrific		warm-hearted	stouthearted
thrilled		well-meaning	strong
triumphant			sure
wonderful			tough

ANGER	HOSTILITY	FEAR	INADEQUACY
agitated	aggressive	afraid	anemic
aggravated	antagonistic	agitated	broken
angry	arrogant	alarmed	broken-down
annoyed	belligerent	anxious	chicken-hearted
bad-tempered	bigoted	apprehensive	cowardly
blunt	biting	bashful	crippled
cantankerous	bullying	desperate	debilitated
cranky	callous	dread	defective
cross	cold-blooded	embarrassed	deficient
disagreeable	combative	fearful	demoralized
enraged	contrary	fidgety	disabled
envious	corrosive	frightened	exhausted
furious	critical	hesitant	exposed
ill-tempered	dictatorial	horrified	feeble
irritated	dogmatic	ill at ease	flimsy
mad	fierce	insecure	fragile
obstinate	hard	intimidated	frail
outraged	cruel	jittery	harmless
perturbed	hard-hearted	jumpy	helpless
resentful	harsh	nervous	impotent
severe	hateful	on edge	inadequate
stern	heartless	overwhelmed	incapable
stormy	hostile	panicky	incompetent
upset	hypercritical	restless	ineffective
	inconsiderate	scared	inept
	insensitive	shaky	inferior
	intolerant	shy	insecure
	malicious	strained	insubstantial
	mean	tense	insufficient
	nasty	terrified	lame
	oppositional	terror-stricken	meek
	oppressive	timid	nerveless
	prejudiced	uncomfortable	paralyzed
	pushy	uneasy	powerless
	reckless	worrying	puny
	rude		small
	ruthless		trivial
	sadistic		unable
	savage		unarmed
	spiteful		uncertain
	unfeeling		unfit
	unmerciful		unimportant
	vengeful		useless
	vicious		vulnerable
	vindictive		weak

FEELING SCORNED		IN DISTRESS	
abandoned	minimized	afflicted	horrible
abused	mistreated	alienated	hurt
alienated	mocked	alone	impaired
annihilated	neglected	anguished	imprisoned
battered	not taken seriously	at the mercy of	in the dumps
belittled	ostracized	awful	lonely
branded	overlooked	awkward	lonesome
cast off	poked fun at	baffled	lost
censured	pooh-poohed	battered	lousy
cheapened	pulled to pieces	below par	low
criticized	put down	bewildered	miserable
crushed	rebuked	blameworthy	moody
debased	rejected	blue	mournful
defamed	reprimanded	burned out	obsolete
defeated	ridiculed	cast off/out	offended
deflated	roasted	confused	out of sorts
degraded	ruined	dejected	pained
demolished	scoffed at	depressed	pathetic
depreciated	scorned	desolate	perplexed
derided	shamed	despaired	pitiful
despised	slighted	despondent	plaything of
destroyed	thought nothing of	discouraged	puppet of
diminished	underestimated	disgusted	puzzled
discarded	underrated	disliked	regretful
discredited		dismal	ridiculous
disdained		displeased	rotten
disgraced		dissatisfied	run down
disparaged		distrustful	sad
disrespected		disturbed	sickened
dissed		done for	silly
downtrodden		doubtful	strained
excluded		downcast	stranded
hated		downhearted	swamped
humiliated		estranged	tearful
ignored		foolish	terrible
jeered		forlorn	tormented
jilted		forsaken	touchy
kaput		futile	unhappy
lampooned		gloomy	unloved
laughed at		glum	unpopular
left out		grieving	unsatisfied
libeled		grim	unsure
loathed		helpless	valueless
made light of		hindered	worthless
maligned		hopeless	wrecked

Paraphrasing: Some Examples

What follows are several interactions with before and after scenarios. Note the difference that paraphrasing, with appropriate restating and/or reflecting, makes in the tone and outcome of the interaction.

Situation #1: a worker and a supervisor at a construction site

BEFORE

Carpenter: I have just had enough of your "know it all" attitude. When you came over yesterday and started correcting my work on building that house, I just wanted to throw all my tools in your face and walk off the job. Who put you in charge and gave you instant wisdom about construction? I know what I'm doing.	
Supervisor: You didn't look like you knew what you were doing! You were putting the nails in the wrong place. All I did was give you a little advice. As for who put me in charge, the project director did, and you're just going to have to take some direction on this job.	criticism defense command
C: Advice?! You took the hammer away from me and said, "You're doing this wrong. You have to do it *this* way!" You've been on a power trip ever since you got here. I know what I'm doing, and I'm not going to take "advice" from you when it's wrong.	accusation
S: You don't seem to be able to take *any* advice. I'm just trying to make sure this job gets done right.	criticism defense
C: Done *your* way. You never take anyone else's ideas, or think that there might be a better way to do things.	
S: If you've got an idea, why don't you say so? Do you expect me to read your mind? Nobody has suggested different ways to go about the project, so I've had to go ahead and do it.	criticism sarcasm defense
C: You don't give anybody any room to suggest ideas. You just barge in and say "This is the way we're going to do it." I have just about had enough.	
S: I can't believe you haven't brought up any of this before when you felt this way. You've waited this long and now expect big changes in me and the project. Why didn't you show any guts before?	criticism
C: You just don't understand anyone else's feelings. This is tearing me apart and you don't even care. I don't want to talk anymore right now, but this discussion isn't over.	accusation implied threat

AFTER

C: I have just had enough of your "know it all" attitude. When you came over yesterday and started correcting my work on building that house, I just wanted to throw all my tools in your face and walk off the job. Whoever put you in charge and gave you instant wisdom about construction? I know what I'm doing.

S: You were really angry because I tried to give you advice yesterday. — paraphrase

C: Advice?! You took the hammer away from me and said, "You're doing this wrong. You have to put the nails in *this* way!" You just love to throw your weight around. I know what I'm doing, and I'm not going to take "advice" from you when it's wrong. — accusation

S: You think I'm on a power trip. — paraphrase

C: Yes, I felt pretty humiliated. You never asked *why* I was doing it that way; I thought it would reinforce the frame. You never ask anyone for their opinions about the project. — criticism

S: You think I ignore other people's ideas. — paraphrase

C: Well, I'm not sure you ignore them. You just don't give anybody a chance to give any ideas. I guess what I'm asking for is some way for us to get together and share ideas. And I wanted to tell you how upset I was yesterday. — clarification

S: I'm glad you felt able to do that. I'm sorry I came across to forcefully yesterday. I guess sometimes I forget that I can overpower people. It really would be helpful to set up some time for everyone to share ideas on the project. I'd really like it if you felt comfortable setting up the meeting and the agenda. — compliment, apology, preference statement

C: Sure. I'll check with everyone else and get back to you.

Situation #2: The Chair and the department secretary

BEFORE

Chair:	I'm sorry to say that I'm unhappy with your work lately. It's been sloppy and full of mistakes. It's just not up to the standards that we have in this department.	
Sec:	I can't believe I'm hearing this! First you complain that I'm too slow and not efficient enough, and then when I speed up you have more to complain about! This is ridiculous!	defense
Chair:	I just don't see what the problem is! Can't you do a good job and do it quickly too? I don't think that is too demanding. If you keep slacking off then I'm afraid you'll just have to look for work elsewhere.	threat
Sec:	I don't think that I have to sit here and listen to this! I know that I am a good worker; I always come to work early and I'm here every day. If you can't see that, then maybe you don't deserve me!	counter attack
Chair:	Fine! If you have a hard time taking orders, I'm sure we can find someone else to replace you! There are plenty of people out there who aren't afraid to work! And don't expect us to give you a good reference, either! Then you'll have trouble finding any job!	lecture threat
Sec:	FINE! I'm leaving now. Good riddance!	

AFTER

Chair:	I'm sorry to say that I'm unhappy with your work lately. It's been sloppy and full of mistakes. It's just not up to the standards that we have in this department.	
Sec:	You feel that my work has been unacceptable.	paraphrase
Chair:	Exactly. I've been concerned about the quality of your work. For the first two months you were conscientious and did such good work. But in the last two weeks it's been different…sloppy, with lots of mistakes. I know you are able to do better because we've seen it. I'd like to know what the problem is so that I can assist you in finding ways to improve.	preference statement
Sec:	You are puzzled by the recent change and want to help.	paraphrase
Chair:	Yes, and as I said, I would be interested in hearing your reasons for this rather sudden change. It's not like you to not care about producing high	

quality work. Maybe we can sit down and talk about what's bothering you.

Sec: You're very concerned about me. — paraphrase

Chair: Yes, I am. It's hard to find good help, so I'd like to problem-solve with you. It's easier to keep good help than to train a new person. It is cost effective and also I like you a lot and would like to keep you on.

Sec: You're eager to get this worked out. — paraphrase

Chair: Yes, exactly. I'd be willing to work on this right now if you have time.

Sec: That would be great. I have felt so alone. It means a lot to me that you are willing to listen. What has happened is that I had to move out of my basement apartment because it flooded. Most of our stuff was ruined. For the past two weeks we've been staying at my sister's and sleeping on the floor. I can't find anything and I'm just so worried about everything. I've barely been able to find my clothes to get dressed and get to work.

Chair: You're stressed out. — paraphrase

Sec: Right. Not only that, but they don't know how long it will be before they can clean up the sewage, so we think we need to try and find another apartment. So after work each day I've been out apartment hunting. I'm exhausted and stressed out. I can hardly think.

Chair: Wow! You're really frazzled. — paraphrase

Sec: Yes. It's really caused me to almost shut down. As you know I usually am not like this at all. I feel terrible about this—I'm really embarrassed and sorry if my work hasn't been up to snuff. I really like working here, and I want things to work out. I'm sure I will be better eventually, as soon as I have a home back. — apology

Chair: You are confident that you'll get back to normal. I am too. And also I know someone who has a nice apartment for rent beginning Sunday. If you'd like I'd be glad to give you her number. Maybe you'll find something soon. In the meantime I won't bug you. Working slower for now is fine. We'll hang in with you. — paraphrase

Sec: Thanks. This means a lot to me. I'd like the phone number; I'm hopeful to find a place soon. I'll also work at preventing mistakes.

Scenario originally developed by Daté, McNab, and Monkman, ©1997.
Adapted by Patrick J. Ashton

Exercise *Practice Paraphrasing*

Imagine someone saying each of the following to you. First, write a paraphrase that reflects the primary feelings being expressed. Then write a paraphrase that restates the content and connects it with the feelings. Examples are given for the first one, but see if you can construct your own paraphrases for this one, too.

1. Today just isn't my day! Just about everything has gone wrong. I agreed to pick up the materials we need for the presentation this afternoon — but I drove right by the store and forgot to stop until 15 minutes later, so I drove back but couldn't find a parking space right away. I was in such a rush that I bought the wrong item, which I discovered when I got to campus. So I had to go back and exchange it. But when I got there the only clerk was busy and I had to wait another 15 minutes. I've been running around all morning and I feel that I haven't accomplished a thing.

   Feelings: *You're frazzled.*

   Content and Feelings: *You're frustrated because you don't seem to have accomplished much this morning.*

2. They must be out of their minds! My great-grandparents built this farm from nothing. They worked hard and built it up to what it is today. And now they want to rezone the area and ruin it with commercial development! It threatens everything my family has worked for.

   Feelings: Frustrated -Sad

   Both: Take down the family farm and make it into Commerial development

3. I just can't believe it! It hardly seems possible that this could happen at a university! The founders of this university must be rolling over in their graves! To think that this could happen here! I wonder if there's any hope for us.

   Feelings: Hopeless + Confussed

   Both: Something happend on campus therefore the University is shocked

4. I'm about ready to quit this committee. We've been working so hard for so long. Every time we suggest an idea, Dr. E finds something wrong with it. I think I'd best resign now, before I get even more upset.

   Feelings: Burnt out

   Both: No appriction for your hard work

5. I don't know how you ever got to be department chair! Chairs are supposed to fix problems, not make them worse! Since you always take her side, I can never get my point across. Didn't they teach you how to listen?

Feelings: Frustration

Both: Individual is taking Sides therefore not being heard

6. You are some kind of worthless friend! I tell you a really important personal secret, and the next thing I know my business is all over the street. Don't expect me to trust you ever again.

Feelings: Betrayed

Both: Spreading Secrets.

7. At our last meeting attendance was less than usual. While this made it real challenging to get anything done, we managed to get quite a bit of work done anyway. We identified task groups which spent about an hour planning and organizing. Because so many more people are here today, we should probably hear reports from each of the task groups, even though it may seem like a waste of time to those who were at the last meeting.

Feelings: Annoyed

Both: Waste of time due to lack of attendence

8. My husband doesn't understand me at all! I've been trying so hard to finish my degree, and all the while he seems to be oblivious of how difficult it is for me. He thinks that, since I don't work outside the home, I must have a lot of leisure time for taking care of the children, the household, and being a wife to him. Right now I just need some support. I just can't keep this up any longer!

Feelings: DeFeated

Both: Over Worked & frustrated because of a lack of support

9. I don't understand. It seems like the course should be about what the bulletin says it's about. The prof should have to teach us what we have to know, not just what interests them. I feel like I'm getting ripped off in this course.

Feelings: Cheated

Both: Not getting what you wanted out of the course

10. The filing system that was in place previously is not very helpful and as a consequence I have been having trouble retrieving any of the files that the department chair has been requesting. I know that I could respond better if I could organize the files the way I know they should be arranged.

Feelings: Frustrated / Annoyed

Both: Files are not organized therefore work cannot get done

11. I'm really tired of you kids fighting all the time over who's going to watch what TV show. If you keep this up I'm going to cut off all of your TV privileges until you learn to get along. I've told you in the past to figure out some way to cooperate, but you just won't listen.

Feelings: Aggervated

Both: Children are not listening

12. Well, since I got a C in that class, I guess I can pretty much kiss any chance of getting into graduate school goodbye. My chances look pretty bleak. I know my parents and the rest of the family will be so disappointed. They'll probably disown me.

Feelings: Hopeless / Defeated

Both: Did not perform the way you wanted to

13. My friend R is so negative! With her, the glass is always half empty. She manages to find the worst aspect of every situation. I like her, but I find it hard to be around her much because she really brings me down.

Feelings: Burnt out

Both: Always feels negative therefore She is done

14. Why are you such a rotten neighbor? You don't take care of your yard, you don't bag your trash so that it blows all over my property, and your dog uses my yard as his personal outhouse. I'd be happier if you just moved away.

Feelings: Frustrated / Pissed

Both: Your yard is getting destroyed due to your neighboor

Originally conceived by Barbara Daté. Adapted and modified by Patrick J. Ashton.

Exercise

Practice in Paraphrasing Feelings: The Jilted Spouse Roleplay

The roleplay below involves a married couple on the verge of splitting up. There are many underlying unresolved issues that can only be discovered through active listening and paraphrasing. Designate one partner as the spouse and one as the listener. While the spouse tells their story, the listener should concentrate exclusively on active listening and paraphrasing. Resist the temptation to interject your own personal experience.

Background: The Spouse's Perspective

You and your spouse of nine years are on the verge of splitting up. You have no children. You both have worked, but your spouse has been unemployed for about a year. Your finances are strained.

You are a welter of confused feelings and reluctant to delve into them even with this sympathetic listener. When people seem to sense that you are under strain and ask you how things are going, you generally acknowledge the financial issues, but not problems with the marriage itself.

Actually, you resent your spouse's unemployment and seeming lack of diligence in finding another job. While you work hard, your spouse fritters the day away with friends. You are also frustrated because the financial problems are making it impossible to even think about one of your long-cherished dreams—opening your own business.

It will be a little harder to talk about another frustration: your spouse's unwillingness to have children. In fact, you fear that time may run out before you can fulfill a desire even more intense than opening a business—to have two or three children. You just love kids and watch your friends' children longingly.

You will be reluctant to talk about the third, most painful, problem. You have recently discovered that your spouse had an affair three years ago. When your spouse confessed, you declared complete forgiveness. Yet you are still full of bitter resentment, shame and embarrassment for both your spouse and yourself about this episode, although you won't admit it unless your listener is exceptionally adept.

All in all, you say that you still love your spouse, but you currently find his/her company barely tolerable. You are secretly almost hoping that the marriage will dissolve, because you long for the freedom to pursue a business and a family with children. You do not yet recognize how little effort you have made to understand your spouse and re-open communication. You don't want to bother with the hard work of reconciliation.

Practitioner's Notes — *Centered Communication: Speaking*

Centered communication comes from the heart, or the center of our being. By providing information from our own center we invite others to share from their center as well. Centered speaking involves using "I messages." These "I messages" are used to provide important information about myself to another person about

- ✓ my emotions.
- ✓ my needs.
- ✓ the impact of their actions on me.
- ✓ my views and preferences.
- ✓ my intentions/purposes/goals.

Examples:

"I feel ___________ when you ___________."
"I get frustrated when you _____________ because I _______________."
"What I'm concerned about is _______________."
"What I need here is ______________."
"What I would like to see happen is _______________."
"What I'm trying to do here is ________________."

Centered speaking is most effective when it:

- is rooted in the here-and-now — i.e., it expresses the feelings I'm having right now.
- avoids blaming of accusing the other.
- talks about specific events and behaviors, not "general problems."
- is honest.
- commands, not demands, respect for my feelings.
- takes responsibility for my own feelings.
- recognizes that I can only change me, not you.

OBSTACLES TO CENTERED COMMUNICATION

- ➢ **Advising:** "What you should do is…." "Well, if I were you…."
- ➢ **Commanding**: "You had better…." "It's time you faced facts."
- ➢ **Diagnosing**: "Your problem is that you…." "The real problem here is that…."
- ➢ **Minimizing**: "It can't be all that bad." "Things will look different in the morning."
- ➢ **Judging**: "That was really stupid." "You're being too sensitive. Lighten up."
- ➢ **Lecturing**: "How many times do I have to tell you…?" "Don't you realize what you're doing?"
- ➢ **Preaching:** "You ought to know better than to…!" "Well, you're just going to have to…."
- ➢ **Threatening:** "If you do that, I'll…." "You had better, or else…." "I'm warning you…."
- ➢ **Diverting:** "Forget about it. It's not worth it." "Look on the bright side."

Techniques of Centered Communication

Here are the basic techniques of centered communication. Practice them until they become a routine part of your communication interaction.

Agreement Stating

Purpose: to offer moral support and/or common ground as a foundation to continue dialogue.
Definition: a statement of what you agree with, perhaps as a preface to expressing your own opinion.
Process: Use the following stems:

"I agree…."
"Yes, I can see that…."
"To me, there's no doubt that…."
"You're right…."
"You've got a good point when you say that…."
"I can go along with you when you say…"

Preference Stating

Purpose: to be open and vulnerable and to signal willingness to share choices.
Definition: a statement expressing clearly your wishes and desires
Process: Use the following stems:

"I prefer…."
"I would rather…."
"I would like…."
"It may not be possible, but I would like…."
"It would be helpful to me if…."
"My preference would be…."

Purpose Stating

Purpose: to make your intentions clear to others.
Definition: a statement clearly expressing your intentions.
Process: Use the following stems:

"My purpose is…."
"I'm hoping to…."
"What I'm trying to do here is…."
"My intention is to…."

Posture of Puzzlement

Purpose: to respectfully express confusion about another's behavior.
Definition: a statement expressing confusion and inviting clarification
Process: Use the following stems:

"I'm puzzled by what you mean by that."
"I'm baffled by what's happening here."
"I'm confused about what you're trying to tell me. You said X but did Y. Please help me understand."

Developed by Barbara Daté
Used with permission.

Agreement Stating: An Example

Here is a situation that demonstrates agreement stating. Note the differences in the before and after scenarios.

Situation: a student called into a professor's office

BEFORE

Professor: You were sleeping during my lecture yesterday. If you don't stay awake in my class, you'll never learn the material. If you don't pass the exam at the end of the semester, I'm afraid you'll fail this class and you won't graduate.

Student: Don't worry about it! I'll pass the exam. I know that I pay more attention than most of the students in that class. And I'm always in class.

Professor: Well, you may be in class, but if you're sleeping through it, you probably won't pass. Good intentions won't get you a grade, and they won't get you a job if you flunk out of college.

AFTER

Professor: You were sleeping during my lecture yesterday. If you don't stay awake in my class, you'll never learn the material. If you don't pass the exam at the end of the semester, I'm afraid you'll fail this class and you won't graduate.

Student: I agree that it's important for me to pass this class. You think it's important that we stay awake to learn the material; I agree with you there, too. The fact is that I'm working two jobs to pay for my schooling, and I often have to come to class with little sleep. I do my best to stay awake.

Professor: I can see that you take your education seriously. It's unfortunate that you have to work so many hours as well as go to school. Perhaps you could shorten your work hours just until you graduate. If not, you might try sitting in front of the room and asking a lot of questions to stay involved in the class.

Scenario originally developed by Barbara Daté.
Adapted by Patrick J. Ashton.

Exercise *Practice Agreement Stating*

Imagine someone says each of the following to you. Write your statement of agreement on the line below.

1. Everything about this place is screwed up! We need some competent management people in here to run things properly!

   ____

2. This new computer program is really difficult. I don't think I will ever learn how to use it.

   ____

3. There are books and papers strewn all over the house. It's a real mess! I'd be really embarrassed if anyone dropped in to visit right now.

   ____

4. The [fill in appropriate political party] are sure making a mess of things in this country.

   ____

5. We've spent so much time arguing about this trivial matter that it looks like we won't get to the important agenda items.

   ____

6. It sure seems like someone has got something to hide when criteria for awarding merit raises are not made explicit and shared with everyone.

   ____

7. We have to oppose the proposed change in zoning if we want to preserve the character of the neighborhood. Anyone with a brain in their head should be against it.

   ____

Preference Stating: An Example

Situation: friends discussing plans

BEFORE

A: Do you want to go to a movie tonight?

B: I don't know. Do you want to go?

A: What do you want to do?

B: If you want to go to a movie, I'd go with you.

A: Do you want to go?

B: Well, OK, let's go. What movie do you want to see?

A: Well, actually, there's no movie I really want to see. I think I'd rather just stay home and watch TV.

B: What? You were the one who asked *me* if *I* wanted to go to a movie! And yes, now I really want to go. So why won't you go?

A: I'm really too tired to go. Would you mind going by yourself?

AFTER

A: I'm really tired today. I realize that I had said I would go to a movie with you tonight, but I would rather just watch some mindless TV—it takes less energy! Unless you're really dying to now, I'd rather go some other time. I'd like to know how badly you want to go tonight.

B: Actually, I have been looking forward to seeing one of the popular new releases, but I think I can stand to wait. Maybe we could go tomorrow instead.

A: Sure. You're such a good friend. I'm glad it's OK that I changed my mind. How about the early show tomorrow?

B: It's a deal!

Exercise *Practice Preference Stating*

Imagine you find yourself in each of the following situations. Write your preference statement on the line below.

1. You know that the committee chair is going to ask you to take minutes at the next meeting. You know that you're much better at typing the minutes up afterward than you are at taking them during the meeting.

   ____

2. Your co-worker has asked if you could help her tomorrow with the new computer program that she is having difficulty with. You have deadlines to meet by tomorrow and could help her the day after.

   ____

3. After a meeting, you are with some co-workers who are deciding where to go to eat dinner. One person suggests the new Thai restaurant. You dislike spicy food because it gives you indigestion.

   ____

4. A friend calls you up late at night and wants to chat on the telephone. You need to be up early in the morning.

   ____

5. Members of a committee you are on are trying to decide when to meet next. Your schedule is very tight, especially early in the week.

   ____

6. A co-worker has asked you to fill in for them next Monday night. You have already planned to go to dinner with a friend that night, but you could change your plans if you really have to.

   ____

7. Nearly every Friday night, a group of your friends gets together and goes to a bar or club. Most of the places allow smoking, and you invariably wake up the next morning with a headache and clothes that reek. You're tired of the hassle, but you enjoy your friends and don't want them to dump you or leave you out.

   ____

Purpose Stating: Some Examples

Example #1: 2 siblings in the living room

BEFORE

A: Where's the scissors?

B: I don't know. Go look in the desk drawer. Leave me alone. I'm busy.

A: Where's the paper?

B: I don't know. I told you to leave me alone. I'm busy, can't you see? I don't know where the paper is. You must have left it somewhere.

A: Where's the crayons?

B: Can't you understand plain English? I told you I was busy!!! Paper, crayons, scissors—I'm not your secretary. Get lost!!!!!

AFTER

A: I need your help. I want to make a surprise birthday card for Mom. I'm trying to do it secretly so she won't guess I'm doing something special for her. I looked for the scissors, paper, and crayons and I can't find them.

B: Well, I'm sort of busy, but I can see that you can't go and ask Mom. I think I saw the scissors and crayons on the dining room table. I think the paper may be in the desk. If you can't find everything, come back and I'll help you look.

Example #2: two college friends talk about the upcoming break

BEFORE

Lee: This town is sure going to be empty over Spring Break. Everyone's leaving except me, it seems.

Sam: Well, I know many people are going South.

Lee: So when are you taking off?

Sam: Oh I'll leave on Friday.

Lee: And you'll be back on Tuesday?

Sam: No, I'm taking the week off. I'll be back the following Sunday.

Lee: Is everyone else in your house taking the same time off?

Sam: No. I think Jim's leaving earlier than I am, for instance.

Lee: Well, I mean, for that whole week, is your house empty? Will everyone be gone?

Sam: (agitated) Lee, what are you going to do? Rob our house?

Lee: No! I was just wondering if I could borrow your house's VCR while everyone was gone!

AFTER

Lee: Sam, I'm trying to figure out how to entertain myself over the Break since everyone but me will be leaving town, it seems. I was wondering if I could borrow your VCR while you are gone.

Sam: I'll have to check with the other people in the house, but I'm sure we can work something out. We also have a bunch of videos that you can use if you want.

Lee: That'll be great! Thanks a lot!

Exercise *Practice Purpose Stating*

Imagine you find yourself in each of the following situations. Write your purpose statement on the line below.

1. You are working on a project when a colleague calls and wants you to come to their office and talk. You are in the middle of a difficult part of the project, but you're on a roll and want to finish the current section.

   ____

2. You think that you might have left your notebook under your desk after your previous class. When you return to the classroom to look for it, another class is underway. You are unsuccessful in trying to slip into the classroom unnoticed. The professor and some of the students are clearly uncomfortable with your presence in the room.

   ____

3. You are planning to have a potluck dinner with your extended family members next Saturday. You want to phone everyone and coordinate what they will bring.

   ____

4. You are in the library looking for an important envelope you inadvertently stuck in one of the many books you were browsing through. In an effort to find the letter, you have taken about fifteen books off the shelves and piled them on a nearby reading table. A librarian walks by and comments, "What are you trying to do? Make more work for librarians???"...

   ____

5. It's 10 p.m. on a Friday night and you're at a friend's apartment listening to music. Suddenly you remember some important mail that you received earlier in the day and are afraid that you might have misplaced it. As you get up to go see if it is in your car, one of your friends says, "Hey, party pooper! Where are you going so soon?"

   ____

6. You are working with two others on a group project. It is due in less than an hour. But the sections your colleagues wrote and just gave you to paste into your master document seem to have a lot of grammatical and spelling errors. As you are going through the document line by line, your colleagues tell you to remember the deadline and just send it off.

   ____

Exercises developed by McNab, Monkman, & Daté ©1983, 1997.
Adapted by Patrick J. Ashton.

Posture of Puzzlement: Some Examples

Example #1: at the drinking fountain

BEFORE

11th grade bully: Hey, jerk! We don't like 9th graders hanging around here!

9th grader: Well, I just wanted to use the drinking fountain.

11th grader: Sorry creep. Only juniors and seniors can drink here.

9th grader: You don't own this place!

11th grader: (shoves the 9th grader) Yeah? Says who? Move it or lose it.

AFTER

11th grade bully: Hey, jerk! We don't like 9th graders hanging around here!

9th grader: I'm puzzled by your saying that. — Posture of Puzzlement

11th grader: We don't like 9th graders, can't you hear?!

9th grader: I wonder how you can dislike a whole category of people. — Posture of Puzzlement

11th grader: Well, uh….

9th grader: I'd sure like it if we could get along with each other, so everyone can use this drinking fountain. — Preference Statement

11th grader: I wasn't thirsty anyway. (Exits.)

Example #2: two children getting off the school bus

BEFORE

Bully: I am going to beat you to a pulp at recess.

Child: I'll tell the teacher if you do.

Bully: Sissy! You're in for it now! Get lost! I'll see you at recess.

AFTER

Bully: I am going to beat you to a pulp at recess.

Child: I'm really puzzled why you're planning to do that. — Posture of Puzzlement

Bully: I'm going to beat you up. You're a little wimp. And a sissy.

Child: I'm baffled about how you drew that conclusion, given that you don't really know me. — Posture of Puzzlement

Bully: Well, uh….

Child: I'd sure like it if we could just get along together.
I'd prefer you not make snap judgments about people. — Preference Statements

Bully: Well, uh, see you around.

Scenarios developed by Barbara Daté.
Adapted by Patrick J. Ashton.

Exercise *Practice Posture of Puzzlement*

Imagine someone says each of the following to you. Write your posture of puzzlement statement on the line below.

1. You go back to your office late at night to retrieve a document you're working on. You notice that the custodial staff is moving the furniture out of your office.

   ____

2. You arrive at your classroom to find several students rearranging the desks to face in the opposite direction.

   ____

3. Several weeks into the term, you notice one particular student who never brings a notebook to class or ever attempts to write anything down.

   ____

4. You bought your daughter a new dress that she wanted for a birthday party. You notice that she is wearing a different dress to the party.

   ____

5. One of your children is pulling the snowblower out of the garage — in the middle of summer!

   ____

6. A colleague, visibly upset, says to you: "I called you last week and set up a meeting for today. And then you missed it!" You know that you were out of town at a conference all of last week.

   ____

Exercises originally developed by McNab, Monkman, & Daté ©1997.
Adapted by Patrick J. Ashton.

Practitioner's Notes *Dealing with an Angry Person*

> "To understand and transform anger, we must learn the practice of compassionate listening and using loving speech."
>
> *Thich Nhat Hanh*

An angry person can be frightening and upsetting. Of course they may be deliberately using anger as a weapon to unsettle you. Or they may be entirely caught up in their own feelings of being hurt, wronged, or disrespected. When a person expresses strong anger or hostility toward you, here are some ways you can de-escalate the level of emotion.

- ✓ **DON'T TELL AN ANGRY PERSON TO CALM DOWN!** This is worst thing you can do – it is equivalent to pouring gasoline on a fire! An angry person thinks they have been wronged and that they have a right to be angry. Denying them this perceived right will only make them angrier.

- ✓ **Stay calm and listen.** Rising to meet their anger will only escalate the situation. Don't try to explain or defend yourself, or point out where the angry person is mistaken. Take some deep breaths and try to relax and focus. Listen carefully and compassionately to what they are saying, and speak in a voice significantly quieter than the angry person. As Thich Nhat Hanh notes, "Listening with compassion can help the other person to suffer less."

- ✓ **Paraphrase.** This is the most effective thing you can do with an intensely angry person. First of all, it lets them know that you are hearing their concerns. Being heard deflates their "emotional balloon" and de-escalates the anger. An angry person feels justified in their anger. When their reasons for being angry are heard, it removes much of the emotional need to be angry. Second, when you are paraphrasing, the angry person's story is the only thing being discussed, and it is extremely difficult for someone to argue with their own story. Third, the process of active listening – while it should not be deliberately designed to do so – actually slows the angry person down. This de-escalates their anger, as it is difficult to maintain an intense emotional state for long. Finally, the process of restating and reflecting forces the angry person to actually hear what they are saying, and they may decide that they are overreacting.

- ✓ **Validate the angry person's feelings.** Validation does not mean agreement with the angry person's point of view, reasoning, or specific arguments. It simply means acknowledging that you understand that they are angry, and why they are angry. You are acknowledging their suffering in order to transform it.

- ✓ **Try to reframe the issue in more neutral terms**. Keep the focus on the problem. Ignore personal attacks and provocations if at all possible. People can't fundamentally change who they are, but they can change their behavior. Focus on the parts of the problem that can be changed.

- ✓ **Point out new information.** Anger is often generated by misunderstandings. When you point out information that you are hearing for the first time, you acknowledge a problem without making it personal. You also provide a way for the angry person to save face.

✓ **Don't respond until the other person is ready to hear you.** Wait until you have significantly deflated the angry person's emotional balloon. If the person resorts to an angry position again, resume your active listening.

Exercise *Responding to Manipulation Using Centered Communication*

Normal social life requires a fair amount of give-and-take. We learn that sometimes you have to give a little to get a little (or a lot). But sometimes we just can't go along with what another person is requesting of us—it's inconvenient, violates our morals or ethics, we don't find it appropriate, or we just don't feel like doing it. Whatever our rationale, when we don't agree to the request, the other person often resorts to manipulation. They attempt to push our buttons in order to make us feel obligated or just wear us down. The outcomes of these types of interactions are usually unsatisfactory. They either turn ugly, or someone winds up doing something they didn't want to do, just to avoid further conflict. The key to dealing with manipulation tricks is to use the techniques of centered communication.

Directions. Find a partner and decide who will go first in the role of the manipulator. The manipulator's task is to get the other person to do something they don't want to do. The manipulator should "pull out all the stops"—within appropriate moral and ethical guidelines—in trying to manipulate the other person. The second person's job is resist being manipulated through the use of centered communication techniques. Choose one of the scenarios below or make up one of your own. Then switch roles.

Scenarios

You want to borrow something (a car, money, a tool, etc.) from a friend that they don't want to lend to you.

You want a friend to fill in for you at work.

You are a supervisor asking an employee to volunteer for additional work on the weekend.

You want a friend to go out for a social activity and they don't want to go.

You want to get a fellow club or church member to make an announcement that you both know will make many members unhappy.

You want someone else to answer the phone and talk to someone you don't want to talk to.

You want to get a friend to babysit your kids on short notice.

You have a long car trip to go on, and you want your friend to do the driving and you want to go in their car.

Outcomes. What did this exercise feel like? How was it different or similar to your usual experience of situations like this? Did the use of centered communication allow you to resist manipulation? If you did, how did it change the dynamics of the interaction?

ImpACT Preview

ImpACT Preview is a technique that allows you to plan a confrontation with another person or persons in order to achieve a constructive end that accomplishes its purpose while enhancing the relationship. An ImpACT Preview is easiest to think of as a play in six acts, with a cast that may include two or more people of any age. What follows is a typical process for an ImpACT Preview.

ACT I VISUALIZING A FUTURE EVENT (Setting the Stage)

Get a picture in your mind of what is about to happen. Talk through your picture of what might happen, *who* will be there, *when* the event will take place, *how long* it will last, and *what* people will be doing. Be as specific as you can.

Visualizing an impending situation, or seeing it in your "mind's eye," is a skill of its own and is an essential ingredient in the makeup of a caring and competent person. Without visualizing we cannot plan ahead and thus are left at the mercy of the situation. Visualizing is a major tool for remaining calm and carrying out your purposes.

ACT II IDENTIFYING INDIVIDUAL DIFFERENCES

Assess your own personal style strengths and excesses that contribute to your holding back from or proactively using your skills to prevent or resolve dysfunctional conflict. Remind yourself of those capabilities and skills you have to offer in this situation.

Discern what individual differences seem apparent in the other person(s). Remind yourself about what you can do to appeal to the other person's strengths and help them to keep centered.

ACT III IDENTIFYING PURPOSES THAT ARE HELPFUL, COOPERATIVE, AND CARING

Clarify your purpose. Make a clear purpose statement or statements; e.g., you are hoping to

- face a difficult relationship problem and work it out harmoniously
- participate in a collaborative, successful endeavor
- assist others in resolving a dispute
- talk about a difficult topic with a positive outcome
- nurture, cooperate, share in an interpersonal interaction
- give constructive feedback

ACT IV BRAINSTORMING OPTIONS AND CHOOSING

Define a list of possibilities by brainstorming. Remember that when brainstorming, *any* idea is okay. Once you have generated a dozen or so items, choose a few ideas that might achieve your purpose(s).

ACT V THE BEHAVIOR REHEARSAL (Visualizing a Positive Outcome)

In almost any interpersonal difficulty, it is useful to assume that the problem is probably due to lack of skill. It is not enough to help identify *what* you need to do because you have no assurance that you know *how* to carry out your plan. You need to practice some of the requisite skills, which in this case are primarily verbal.

Act out this part of the situation so that you can actually experience speaking your lines. You will literally rehearse your purposeful behavior. Rehearse the lines four or five times together until you feel comfortable about using them. If you are unable to do a behavior rehearsal, do a complete covert rehearsal in your head.

ACT VI THE IMPACT REVIEW

Understanding that this situation is part of your "daily struggle," plan to review the outcome after the event so you can evaluate what went well or what to do differently next time. It is important to be especially cautious in this kind of review, to prevent yourself or others from feeling embarrassed or hurt if the actual outcome was undesirable.

Exercise — *ImpACT Preview Worksheet*

Use this worksheet as a guide to construct your own Impact Preview.

ACT I VISUALIZING A FUTURE EVENT (Setting the Stage)

ACT II IDENTIFYING INDIVIDUAL DIFFERENCES

ACT III IDENTIFYING PURPOSES THAT ARE HELPFUL, COOPERATIVE, AND CARING

ACT IV BRAINSTORMING OPTIONS AND CHOOSING

ACT V THE BEHAVIOR REHEARSAL (Visualizing a Positive Outcome)

ACT VI THE IMPACT REVIEW

Exercise *Practice in Confronting Another*

Using the principles of confrontation and the worksheet above as a guide, develop your own ImpACT Preview for each of the following situations.

Conflict with a friend

_________, your friend, is taking a class with you. The instructor requires a group project and presentation which makes up the majority of the grade for the course. Everyone in the group will receive the same grade. At first you were excited to have your friend in your group. Now, however, you find yourself doing almost all of the work, and you're starting to resent it. Your friend is very personable, and is well-liked by everyone in the group. But when you stop to think about it, it seems like your friend is using their popularity to get out of doing any significant work for the project. You really need and want a good grade in this course, and as a result you will do whatever needs to get done to ensure a quality group project. You resent, however, the fact that everyone else will get a good grade based on your work. It seems particularly unfair that your friend seems to be taking advantage of you here. You are unsure of how to handle this, because __________ is a good friend and you don't want to alienate them.

Conflict with a neighbor

Your neighbor __________ recently went through a painful and messy divorce. In order to regain financial footing, __________ is working long hours and is rarely home. That would be OK, except for __________'s dog. You think the dog, a shepherd/collie mix, is cute. Before __________'s divorce you and __________ used to play with the dog, and you grew quite attached to it. At night, when __________ is still not home from work, you can hear the dog whining pitifully next door, and it breaks your heart. Furthermore, when __________ comes home late at night, __________ is too tired to take the dog for a walk, just letting the dog out the back door. Apparently running over to see if you're home (you are, but you're fast asleep), the dog winds up pooping in your yard. What's worse, __________ has apparently fallen asleep and the dog winds up barking to be let in for what seems like a long time. Frequently you are awakened by the barking.

Conflict with a co-worker

There have been cutbacks and downsizing at your workplace. For the past three months you have had to share an administrative assistant with __________. You have accommodated yourself to the new situation, figuring out what sorts of things you can do for yourself and prioritizing what you need to give to the administrative. Your co-worker, __________, however, hates the new system. Basically __________ has coped by not changing working styles at all. As a result, the administrative assistant is constantly swamped with __________'s demands and can't always get to your work. As a result, some of your work has been late, and you fear it is going to reflect badly on you. You're starting to resent __________, but you know that you have to continue to work together.

Practitioner's Notes

Joint Problem-Solving in Situations of Conflict: What Can You Do?

Prepare

- ✓ Figure out your interests.
- ✓ Figure out their interests.
- ✓ Think about your options and try to expand your alternatives.
- ✓ Identify your BATNA (Best Alternative To a Negotiated Agreement).
  - This is better than a bottom line, which limits creativity in the search for an acceptable solution.
  - It empowers you to negotiate with a clear focus on the process.
- ✓ Identify objective standards that could be applied.
- ✓ Generate some possible proposals.

Think creatively: What might be some win-win solutions?

Don't React: GO TO THE BALCONY

- ✓ Look at the situation as if it is an unfolding play and you are in the audience.
- ✓ Don't be taken in by emotional provocations: don't strike back, give in, or walk out.
- ✓ Tune in to your own emotional reaction and where it is coming from.
- ✓ Slow down, pause, or take a break.
- ✓ Step back, go to the balcony to get some perspective on the situation.
- ✓ Stay focused on your goal.

Don't get mad and don't get even, but get what you want.

Don't Argue: STEP TO THEIR SIDE

- ✓ Use active listening to let the other person know they're heard and understood.
- ✓ Acknowledge their right to their own opinion.
- ✓ Validate their feelings.
- ✓ Agree with them whenever you can.
- ✓ Use "I messages" to express your views.
- ✓ Don't defend your ideas; invite criticism and advice.

Don't attack their position, look behind it.

Don't Reject: REFRAME

- ✓ Recast an attack on you as an attack on the problem.
- ✓ Let the problem be their teacher.
- ✓ Use silence appropriately and creatively.
- ✓ Recognize and acknowledge unfair tactics, then engage in principled negotiation about the negotiation process itself.

> **"To change the game, change the frame."**

Don't Push: BUILD THEM A GOLDEN BRIDGE

- ✓ Involve the other person in building and shaping the agreement.
- ✓ Be generous with credit for a solution.
- ✓ Make sure that the other person's (spoken and unspoken) needs are met by the agreement.
- ✓ Help the other person to save face.
- ✓ Take all the time necessary to craft a wise agreement: go slow to go fast.

> **The Power Paradox: The harder you make it for them to say NO,**
> **the harder you make it for them to say YES.**

Don't Escalate: USE POWER TO EDUCATE

- ✓ Help them to consider realistically the alternatives to a negotiated agreement.
- ✓ If appropriate, share your BATNA. Help the other person to discover their own.
- ✓ Don't back the other person into a corner; always leave them a way out.
- ✓ Use negotiation jujitsu — don't resist their force, but sidestep, deflect, and channel it constructively.
- ✓ Use third parties to promote principled negotiation.
- ✓ Aim to forge a mutually satisfactory, lasting agreement, not to win a victory.

> **"Use power to bring them to their senses, not to their knees."**

adapted from Fisher and Ury 1983 and Ury 1991

Conflict and Power

Assumptions about power:

1. The word power comes from the Latin *potere* meaning "to be able."
2. Power is the ability to take action effectively. This often involves controlling or influencing events. This is "power to."
3. Power sometimes involves getting someone else to do something, in spite of their opposition. This is "power over."
4. Power is neither a "thing" nor an individual characteristic; it is a relationship.
5. Power can be exercised through collaborative democratic action. This is "power with."
6. Power is not a fixed or finite resource. It is fluid and can be expanded or reduced.
7. Power is related to dependency; the more someone tries to control someone else, the more dependent on them they become.
8. Dependency and fear can be minimized or maximized by either party.
9. Conflicts over power are more difficult to resolve than conflicts over issues that do not affect the distribution of power.
10. Everyone has access to some kind of power (power "currencies"), though most people are unaware of it or may choose not to use some forms of power.
11. Forms of power:
    - Credibility or claims to special knowledge
    - Control of resources
    - Emotional/intimacy power
    - Network or relational power – derived from links to others
    - Community power – legitimately conferred and exercised by the collective
    - Personality/personal skills power – negotiation, charisma, presence
    - Violence and the threat of violence
    - Legal power
    - Moral authority

Practitioner's Notes — *Guidelines for Using Power*

Guidelines for those who exercise power in positions of formal authority:

- Be aware that subordinates may not be inclined to tell you the whole truth. You will have to draw out important information and feelings through the atmosphere you create and the techniques you use.

- As a leader, it is vitally important for you to "walk the talk." People will pay more attention to what you do than what you say. And if there is a discrepancy between what you do and what you say, it will undermine trust.

- Use power wisely and judiciously. Collaborate when possible. Take responsibility for directing when necessary.

- Find ways to empower subordinates.

Guidelines for those who do not have formal authority and who exercise less power:

- Realize that you deserve respect as a person; reserve the right to protest abuse, contempt, and disrespect.

- Pick your battles wisely. Creating conflict over everything will diminish the significance and impact of any particular conflict.

- Keep the focus on the problem, not on the person. In situations of unequal power, you will always lose a personality clash.

- Find your own currencies of power.

Strategies for balancing power:

- Make the power imbalance transparent by calling attention to it.
- Make clear the mutual dependency of the parties.
- Provide modeling, training, coaching, and support to help the less powerful.
- Reframe the issues in ways that minimize the power disparity.
- Set and observe clear boundaries on the process; make rules and procedures explicit.
- Design the process to allow all parties to fully and appropriately express themselves. This may require dispensing with an arbitrary and formal equality in speaking times, etc.
- Allow a support person to be present during a confrontation.

Exercise | *The Experience of Power*

Directions: Pair up with a partner. Take turns telling your partner about each of the following situations. The listening partner should focus on paraphrasing and active listening, without adding any new information.

Discuss with your partner:

- a time when someone had power over you and you felt unable to do anything about it.
- a time when someone had power over you and you stood up to them.
- a time when you had power and used it well.

When each partner has had a turn discussing each situation, process the exercise by discussing the following questions:

- How did it feel to talk about these issues?

- How did it feel to be listened to?

- How did you feel as you listened to these stories?

- What have you learned about power?

- What have you learned about yourself?

CENTRAL HIGH Case Study: Problems at School

By Carolyn Schrock-Shenk

Tiandra Wilson's school experience has not been a good one. Her elementary school years were spent in the Bronx, where, because of overcrowding and under-funding, she got lost in the system. Though she could barely read or write, she got passed along from one grade to another. One of her older brothers, Craig, had gotten frustrated and quit school after his sophomore year. Her other brother, Oscar, made it through high school but was struggling in his first year of college, angry at the lack of preparation his high school had given him. Tiandra's response to school was to skip it often, choosing instead to hang around with out-of-school friends.

At the beginning of Tiandra's first year of high school, her mother, Betty Jo, took stock of Tiandra's situation and with Oscar's encouragement, decided to move to more rural Lancaster, Pennsylvania, where several relatives lived. Tiandra wasn't excited about the move, but she did not resist it. The two moved to a Lancaster suburb that was reportedly in a top-quality school system. There were only a few other African Americans among the Anglos in that particular neighborhood. Tiandra was enrolled in the local school and was immediately placed in a remedial reading and tutoring program. The principal had talked with them both, clarifying the program's expectations and the school's expectations generally. At one point he noted that "there aren't many of your kind" and later made it clear that he "wanted no trouble." The interaction troubled Betty Jo, but she didn't pursue it, not wanting to make waves.

Several weeks into the school year, Tiandra got off the bus in an extremely foul mood. After much coaxing, she told her mother about the two white boys who were heckling her on the bus; touching her hair and calling her velcro-head, mimicking her way of talking and even using the "n" word several times under their breath. Tiandra said she refused to respond and stared out the window with folded arms throughout the entire incident. She seemed ready to explode as she told the story. Betty Jo and Tiandra discussed what to do but could not come up with a response that felt both right and safe.

Nothing happened for several days. Then on Thursday, Betty Jo was called into the principal's office soon after the morning bus ride to school. The vice-principal, Mr. Waters, who was also Anglo, was there as well. As was Tiandra, sullen and angry. "Your daughter," said Mr. Clark, "has been expelled for hitting." Betty Jo asked for details of the story. Mr. Clark said several boys on the bus were teasing Tiandra "a bit." "Boys will be boys you know," and, "It was all in good fun, of course." At that point, Betty Jo exploded. She said many things in the course of that explosion, including a mention of a law suit charging discrimination. It may not have been wise, but at least it got Mr. Clark's attention. He and Mr. Waters finally got Betty Jo and Tiandra out of the office and promised they would "see what we can do."

You are a local mediator who successfully mediated a recent, well-publicized dispute. At noon on Thursday when you walked into your house for some lunch, the phone was ringing. It was Mr. Clark. He explained the situation and said he definitely wanted to avoid a lawsuit. He practically begged you to serve as a mediator between the school and the Wilsons. "We really need your help," he said. "We want to put this situation behind us." You said you'd need to think about it and would get back to him.

DISCUSSION QUESTIONS

1. What are the power sources or currencies for Tiandra? For Betty Jo? For Mr. Clark?
2. Is there an imbalance of power? If so, what are some ways that power could be more balanced?
3. Would you mediate? Why or why not?
4. Would other strategies be more appropriate in this situation? If so, what strategies?

Exercise

How Do You Feel Right Now? A Visual Representation

Imagine that one of these children represents how you feel at this point in your training. Which one would it be, and why?

You can also use this picture with parties during the mediation process to "check in" on how they are feeling. This is particularly valuable if you get stuck, and/or if one or more parties has difficulty articulating their feelings.

Part Four: Culture, Diversity, and Conflict Resolution

> Culture is a tool kit of symbols, stories, rituals, and world views, which people may use in varying configurations to solve different kinds of problems.
>
> – *Ann Swidler*

> One of the messages Sam [Samuel L. Jackson] wanted to get out in *A Time to Kill* was just how separate his character's life was from that of Matthew McConaughey's character. In one scene he tells Matthew, 'We're not friends. You go to work, you're nice to me, I'm nice to you, but you've never even been to my house.' I think most white and black relationships in this country are like that. A white person can't be my friend if he doesn't come to my house, hang out with my kid, something like that. We go to dinner, we go to work together, but if it ends there, we're not friends. We're just co-workers, or maybe associates. And if black people and white people are working together, it's usually on white people's terms.
>
> – *Charles Barkley*

In this section we will examine culture in order to understand how it affects the origin and dynamics of conflict.

Theory *About Culture and Values*

Culture consists of the shared knowledge, rules, values, customs, beliefs, language, and material objects that are passed from one generation to the next in human groups and societies. Culture makes possible the adaptation of humans to their physical and social environment. Culture is therefore a human creation, and all humans everywhere have and participate in it. Anthropologist Marvin Harris (1990:64) puts it this way:

> Cultural artifacts, practices, rules, and relationships constitute the largest part of our environment. Humans cannot eat, breathe, defecate, mate, reproduce, sit, move about, sleep, or lie down with-out following or expressing some aspect of their society's culture. Our cultures grow, expand, evolve. It's their nature. Cultural reality comes from, but rises above ordinary organic reality, just as organic reality comes from, but rises above, its chemical and physical substrates.

Because culture is based on symbols, which are inherently arbitrary, culture must be learned. On the other hand, like the air that we breathe, culture is largely taken for granted. Cultural assumptions are usually so complete-ly accepted within the group that there is little need to be state, question, or defend them.

Our culture influences what we see, hear, and feel and how we process what we see, hear, and feel. Culture is the lens through which we see and understand the natural and social worlds. There are no cultural absolutes—responses are "right" or "wrong" only within the context of a particular culture. One group is not inherently better or worse than another—only different.

Cultural differences are created by nationality, ethnicity, occupation, religion, politics, geography, social class, lifestyle, and so forth. Everyone is to some degree ethnocentric, in that each culture thinks its own ways are superior. We all have biases and prejudices, which show up in our interactions. People are not necessarily evil for being biased or prejudiced; usually they are ignorant. Discrimination and hostility toward other cultural groups is based on stereotypes created by fear, which is usually a projection of our own insecurities.

To overcome ethnocentrism (which means judging other cultures by the standard of our own cultural values), we must engage in cultural relativism, which is judging each culture in its own terms—i.e., relative to itself. To overcome bias, we must challenge our prejudices and stereotypes by educating ourselves about other cultures. Discussing biases and prejudices is risky, however, because it is easy to be misunderstood due to different cultural understandings.

Intercultural problems may occur when a person from one culture is suddenly thrust into another culture that is markedly different, or when a person from one culture tries to communicate with someone from another culture. This is called culture shock.

Values are based on deeply-held beliefs. Our values determine our hierarchy of choices. We compare people, events, and groups based on our values. Discussing values is difficult because people (1) are emotionally attached to their beliefs and values, and (2) often "talk past one another" because their values rest on different assumptions. This is why we are taught never to discuss religion or politics on social occasions.

Culture influences people's style of communication. In every culture, people communicate because they want to be understood. In every culture, people respond to respect and disrespect. We can increase our effectiveness as intercultural communicators.

Values

"The moment of self-reflection is about confronting yourself and who it is that you want to be."

– Marc Gopin

Knowing our own personal values is not only an important aspect of being centered, but it is also important to our self-awareness in conflict situations and our understanding of the potential for constructive conflict resolution. Deep and potentially intractable conflicts are often about opposing values—or at least the perception of opposing values. Knowing our own values is crucial to setting priorities. What conflicts are worth having, and which ones are not? Here is an exercise to help you clarify your values.

Exercise *Identifying Your Values*

What people, ideas, or values would you be willing to die for?

In the eulogy at your funeral, what would you want people to say you stood for? What would they say your life was all about?

Your challenge is to live your life now in such a way that people will indeed be able to say these things about you when you are no longer here.

Exercise | *A Cross-Cultural Negotiation*

Different cultures, as we have seen, have different norms and values. Often these differences can create barriers to effective communication as well as misunderstandings that feed cultural stereotypes. Consider the following negotiation. Read about the situation, but at first only read the background for the character to which you have been assigned.

The Situation

Terry Archibold has advertised a lake cottage for rent on the Internet. The Marigolds, from Gold Country, are planning to fly to Bold Country and would like to rent a lake cottage while visiting friends at a nearby town. Archibold's web page reads:

Bold Country
Lake cottage for rent
Reasonable price, holds up to six comfortably,
lake view, rowboat
Must rent by the week.
Most dates available May through September.
Call (444) 444-4444 and ask for Terry.

The Marigold family decides to place the call, and Mr(s). Marigold leaves a message on Archibold's voicemail. Archibold returns the call, and they negotiate over the phone.

Terry Archibold's Background

You are a member of the Bold culture. As such, you believe and value the following:

- It is important to get to the point quickly and strike a deal.
- While it is important to focus on the bottom line, it is also necessary to maintain a friendly, joking manner and get on a first-name basis right off the bat.
- The best response to stress in negotiations is to be more assertive, including talking louder and faster, before things get out of hand. It is important to lay it on the line and tell it like it is in order to stay in top form.

With regard to the terms preferred, the quoted price is always given as $700, but deals are typically closed for $500 - $650 per week. Anything over $475 is gravy, since $475 per week meets expenses for the cottage. An advance deposit of 50% in Bold Country funds is non-negotiable.

Mr(s). Marigold's Background

You are a member of the Gold culture. As such, you believe and value the following:

- It is important to maintain formality in language and tone, referring to Terry Archibold as "Mr. or Mrs. Archibold," because using first names with a stranger implies inappropriate familiarity and disrespect.

- Direct, open conflict is to be avoided since it would interfere with the appearance that you are having an enjoyable conversation with a person worthy of respect. If there is a disagreement, the main topic needs to be avoided. It is better to focus on minor matters such as the climate, the surroundings, floor plan, neighbors, etc.

- If there is stress, two acceptable ways to reduce the level of tension are silence and laughing. If the other person is disrespectful and loses control, becoming loud and boisterous, it is important to consistently maintain a quiet manner.

- It is crucial to ask for time to decide, because no decisions can be made without first consulting the family. To do otherwise would deny them their rightful respect.

With regard to the terms preferred, it is expected that Bold Country residents will dicker over the price, and that stated prices are merely starting points for negotiation. Your family has budgeted $500 for the week, but has agreed to pay up to $600 in rent if necessary.

Roleplay authored by Janet Mitchell-Dix. Modified by Patrick J. Ashton

Personal and Social Identity

Each of us has a unique personal identity that consists of our internalized self-concept and our social identity. Our self-concept is our symbolically-constructed understanding of who we are—our likes and dislikes, our personality, style, and understanding of our biography. We share different parts of our self-concept with different people, but we never share it all—it is generally private information. Our social identity comes from the statuses we occupy and the groups to which we belong.

When we encounter others, and they encounter us, each of our identities is like an iceberg. As is well-known (and the Titanic discovered), most of an iceberg is under the surface of the water. What we can see from the surface is only a small part of the reality. So too with identities. What we know about someone else is only a few surface characteristics—there is much about their personality, self-concept, and even social identity that we do not know. So we need to be careful about making judgments about people based on this limited information.

Theory — *Status and Role*

In sociological terms, a status is a socially defined position in the social structure of a society. (The word comes from the Latin *stare*, to stand. Literally, where does someone stand in the social structure?) Although in popular usage the word sometimes is meant to connote prestige, or high status ("That neighborhood has a lot of status."), status as used by social scientists is neutral—any given status can be ranked high or low or not ranked at all.

Statuses exist independent of individuals. There are two ways an individual can come to occupy a status: it can be conferred involuntarily upon a person (e.g., age, race, height, eye color, sibling, disabled) or an individual can do something to achieve that status (e.g., parent, student, friend, employee). The first is called *ascribed status*, and the latter *achieved status*. A *status symbol* is some material object that, because of its cultural definition, gives a clue to one or more of a person's statuses. Again, a given status symbol may or may not be associated with prestge.

Individuals occupy multiple statuses simultaneously. The complete list of a person's statuses at any given time is their *status set*. The more complex the society, the larger the status set of individuals within it. This status set, combined with significant group memberships, constitutes an individual's *social identity*.

Usually one status is more prominent at any given time in terms either of how an individual defines themselves, or how society defines them. This is called a *master status*. When an individual occupies two or more statuses whose rankings are significantly incongruent, this is called *status inconsistency*—a very young manager, for instance, or a well-educated immigrant who speaks English with a heavy foreign accent.

A *role* consists of the behavioral expectations associated with a position. It is the "job description" of a status. Of course no status is so simple as to have only one behavioral expectation associated with it. In fact, each status has a bundle of roles, or a *role set*, associated with it. So we occupy multiple statuses, each with multiple roles attached. Inevitably, the expectations associated with one status come into conflict with those of another status. We simply don't have the time and energy to do everything. This is called *role conflict.*

We will have occasion to apply these concepts later when we discuss the mediation process. But now we want to examine the part they play in conferring social identity.

Exercise — *Who Am I? An Identity Exercise*

Understanding our own identity first is crucial to bridging cultural differences with others. As quickly as you can, write an answer in *each* box below in response to the question: Who Am I? There are no "right" or "wrong" answers. Whatever you respond is right for you.

1.	Kind
2.	Quiet

3.	Quirky
4.	Love my family
5.	Student Athlete
6.	Motivated
7.	Passionate
8.	Day Dreamer
9.	Book smart
10.	Christian
11.	Republican
12.	Female
13.	
14.	
15.	
16.	
17.	
18.	
19.	
20.	

Now review your answers. What role does culture play in how you define yourself? How many of your answers are statuses? Which ones are ascribed and which achieved? Did you list your master status? Why or why not? What is the relative mix of self-concept and social identity?

The Paradox of Diversity

Every human being is a unique individual. Although we share much in common, no one else—in history or prehistory—has ever lived our particular life, or has our particular constellation of physical and personality characteristics and outlook on life. This is something to be recognized and celebrated.

On the other hand, we belong to multiple social groups and categories with which we share important characteristics. These collective social identities are important because they affect not only the way we understand our own self-concept, but more importantly the way that other people perceive and interact with us.

So the paradox is that, while we want to treat people as individuals and celebrate the wide range of diverse individual characteristics, at the same time we must pay attention to group characteristics because they clearly affect a person's life chances and the way that they move through the world. To emphasize one side of the paradox over the other is to miss important information and to misunderstand and perhaps to mistreat individuals. Overemphasizing group membership can result in stereotyping; overemphasizing individual identity can cause us to miss the role of unearned privilege or oppression.

Stereotyping

A stereotype is a distorted, usually exaggerated view of some group characteristic and the automatic assumption that each and every member of the group possesses this characteristic. So, rather than treating a person as an individual, stereotyping imposes a categorical definition upon them. In a social sense, stereotyping causes us to miss important individual characteristics.

Let's look at this graphically. Take an individual characteristic—height, for instance. Typically in a relatively large population this variable will be distributed normally. That is to say that it will take the shape of a bell curve. The mean, or average, will be in the middle, at the high point of the curve, as illustrated here.

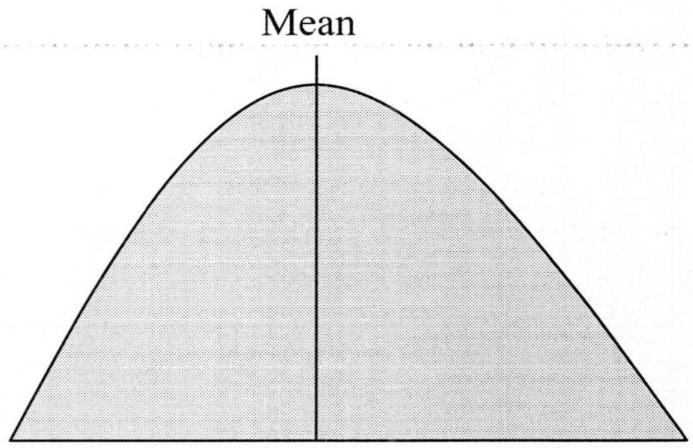

Let's say we measured the height of men and women separately. What we have is two overlapping distributions. And of course the means, or averages, are different. One way the process of stereotyping works is to emphasize the difference of means, rather than look at individuals. Averages are a mathematical phenomenon; individuals are a human one. Focusing on average differences misses the individual characteristics. Moreover, knowing the mean differences would not allow one to predict the height of any given individual.

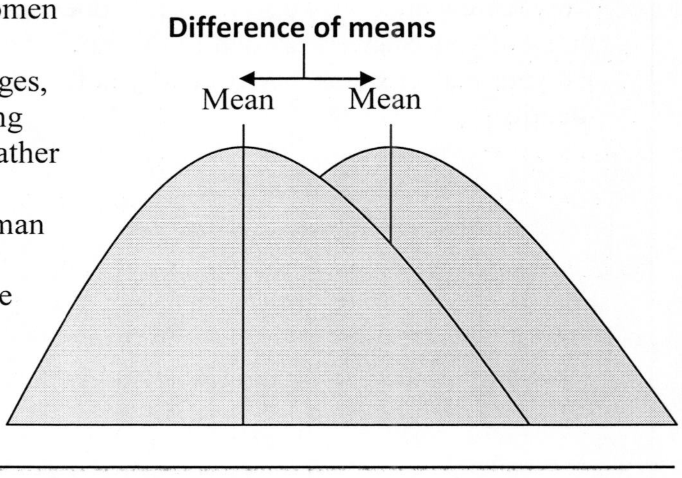

This stereotyping by group categorization misses other things as well. By focusing on the extremes of difference, stereotypes ignore the extensive similarities among group members. In fact, people tend to be more similar than different, except at the extremes. When we focus exclusively on the extremes, we miss the commonalities.

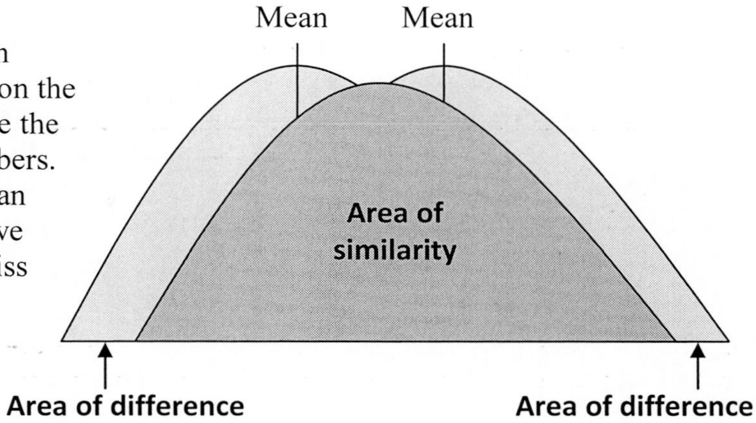

In addition, there is always greater variation within a group than there is between groups. Men, for instance, are more different from one another than they are from women. Likewise, Whites have more internal variation within their own category than they do differences from Blacks, and vice-versa.

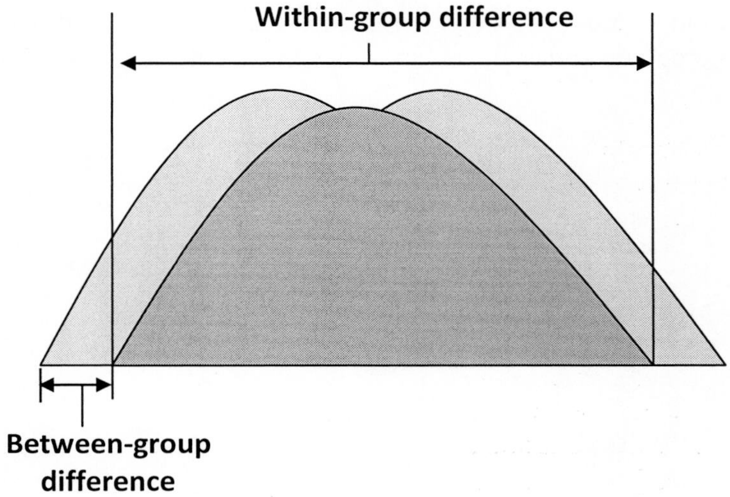

So stereotyping masks both individual differences and similarities across groups and categories. The lesson to be learned here is to treat people as individuals, not as categories.

On the other hand, these social categories do matter because they affect the way that people are treated in society, and their life chances. Membership in a particular category often confers unearned privilege or social oppression on an individual, regardless of their individual moral character or actions.

To the extent that they share common experiences, groups and categories of people tend to develop common meaning systems that interpret that experience. These meaning systems are called cultures. But not all cultures are equally valued in a society. Some cultures are seen as the standard; these are dominant cultures. Holding the status of a person in a dominant culture confers unearned privilege. Unearned privilege can be defined as social advantages systematically conferred upon a person—whether they want them or not—solely because of their belonging to a particular social category. The nature of unearned privilege is that it is largely invisible to those who hold it. They simply assume that their experience is true of everyone else.

Other cultures are seen as lesser or even deviant. These are subordinate cultures, or minority groups. A minority group is a category of people who, because of certain physical or cultural characteristics, are singled out for differential and unequal treatment and who therefore regard themselves as objects of collective discrimination. People whose identities are associated with these categories experience exclusion and oppression. Often this is subtly embodied in the language used. But it also takes the form of discrimination, which is the act of singling out an individual for unequal and injurious treatment based on their membership in a particular social category or their possession of certain characteristics. When the discrimination is systematic and embodied in institutional practices, it is called institutionalized prejudice and discrimination—a set of societal arrangements that systematically restricts the life chances and choices of a particular category of people.

Exercise *Dominant and Subordinate Cultures*

Reflect on the phenomenon of dominant and subordinate cultures in American society. See how many statuses you can list in each category. Note: this is not your personal ranking, but how you perceive American society ranks these cultures. I have given you some suggestions to get started.

Dominant Culture	Subordinate Culture
male	*female*
temporarily able-bodied	*handicapped*

Everyone's social identity is some combination of dominant and subordinate statuses. That is, everyone is differentially enabled and disabled. Reflect on how this applies to you.

Two important caveats: This is not to say that everyone is equally privileged and oppressed. Clearly, some statuses confer privilege or oppression that is so socially powerful that it significantly impacts a person's experiences and life chances. Second, all conflicts involving people of differing cultural statuses are not necessarily cultural conflicts.

Theory — *The Veil and Double-Consciousness*

William Edward Burghardt Du Bois was a pioneering American sociologist and civil rights activist in the first two-thirds of the 20th century. Du Bois was the first African American to receive a Ph.D. from Harvard. He taught at Wilberforce, Penn, and Atlanta universities. Du Bois was a leader in founding the NAACP and edited its magazine, *The Crisis,* for two decades. Du Bois was an early Pan-Africanist, and became a citizen of Ghana—the first independent African nation—near the end of his long life.

W.E.B. Du Bois was a prolific writer; he wrote several dozen books and hundreds of essays. Among the most prominent is his autobiographical study *The Souls of Black Folk* (1903/1995) in which he presciently identified the color line as the major problem of the 20th century. *The Souls of Black Folk* is filled with rich insights into African American culture and the state of African American society. Among its most important sociological insights are the concepts of double consciousness and the veil.

As a minority group in American society, said Du Bois, African Americans face persistent stereotypes and active hostility and discrimination. The result is that each African American inhabits

> a world which yields him no true self-consciousness, but only lets him see himself through the revelation of the other world. It is a peculiar sensation, this double-consciousness, this sense of always looking at one's self through the eyes of others, of measuring one's soul by the tape of a world that looks on in amused contempt and pity. One ever feels his two-ness,—an American, a Negro; two warring souls, two thoughts, two unreconciled strivings; two warring ideals in one dark body, whose dogged strength alone keeps it from being torn asunder (Du Bois 1903/1995).

Interestingly, Frederick Douglass, the great abolitionist activist, had made the same point 60 years earlier in a speech to the Rochester, New York Anti-Slavery Society (Douglass 1852).

Du Bois also argued that, as a discriminated-against minority group, African Americans essentially lived behind a veil. On the one hand, this means that the dominant group cannot see them clearly. This is what we have referred to earlier as the unearned privilege of the dominant group—not to have to notice or pay attention to nuances of Black people and Black culture. On the other hand, the veil causes African Americans to see American society in a substantially different way than Whites. It is the same society, but the experience of stereotyping and discrimination means that African Americans experience and see it differently from Whites. Whites can only begin to understand if they try to look at themselves and their society from the other side of the veil.

Although W.E.B. Du Bois was referring specifically to African Americans, the concepts of double consciousness and the veil can apply to any culturally subordinate group. The dynamics will be similar, and this is important for analyzing conflict and promoting transformative conflict resolution.

Theory *Prejudice and Discrimination*

Prejudice is a preconceived judgment or opinion, usually based on limited information and accompanied by strong emotion. Everyone has prejudices, but a key part of the process of education and personal growth is being willing to challenge those prejudices. This is made especially difficult, of course, by the emotional attachment we have to those judgments. It is also why conflicts involving prejudices can escalate quickly.

Discrimination is the act of singling out an individual for unequal and injurious treatment based on their membership in a particular social category or their possession of certain characteristics. As such, it is much more harmful because it blocks a person from access to opportunities and resources.

Sociologist Robert Merton (1976:189-216) suggested that we can gain insight into the interplay of prejudice and discrimination by looking at them in a 2x2 typology.

Merton's Typology

Discriminates?

Prejudiced?	Discriminates? Yes	Discriminates? No
Yes	Prejudiced Discriminator	Prejudiced Nondiscriminator
No	Unprejudiced Discriminator	Unprejudiced Nondiscriminator

It is easy to dismiss people in the upper left quadrant as ignorant haters, who are inclined not only to dislike individuals from subordinate groups, but to actively discriminate against them. Likewise, it is easy to admire people in the lower right quadrant, who work to overcome their prejudices and treat each individual fairly.

But what of people in the upper right quadrant? They are prejudiced, but they don't discriminate. These people, says Merton, are generally social cowards. They would prefer to discriminate against subordinate groups, but they are afraid of personal, legal, social, economic, or political consequences. So they don't discriminate.

That leaves the lower left quadrant. Here we find people who are not prejudiced, but still engage in discrimination. How is this possible? When discrimination is built into the institutions and traditional cultural mechanisms of a society, then anyone who follows and fails to challenge them is in fact discriminating and perpetuating discrimination. This is a hard insight for members of dominant group cultures to understand, especially in highly individualistic American society. Dominant-group people will say, "*I'm* not prejudiced. Some of my best friends are ____________." Or "*I* didn't oppress these people in the past. I wasn't part of that." While there is certainly truth in these statements, what they overlook is the impact of *behavior.* One may have a healthy and open attitude, but if the effect of one's behavior is discriminatory, how is that outcome any different from the behavior of the haters? In both cases the outcome is denial of access to resources or opportunities. In fact, say members of subordinate groups, the haters are easier to deal with because at least they are predictable in their intention to discriminate. People in the lower left quadrant, however, say one thing but in fact do another.

Merton's insight teaches us that, whenever we are in a dominant group situation, we need to examine not only our attitudes, but our behaviors and their impact on subordinate groups. Try this out in the exercise below.

Exercise | *Experiencing Prejudice and Discrimination*

Situation: You are a member of a white family living in an all-white suburban neighborhood. Your oldest child is a boy who is 23; he applied for a job in the city fire department, but didn't receive one. He was told by one supervisor that they "had to give the job to a minority." Your other children include a girl who is 17 years old, a boy 13, and a girl who is 8. Your neighbors two houses away put their house up for sale. After it had been on the market about 8 months, a rumor went around the neighborhood that your neighbors were considering selling the house to an African American family. One neighbor called an "emergency" meeting about it, but you were unable to attend. About 6 weeks later, the house did indeed sell to a black family. They have two boys—17 and 12—and a girl who is 9. Their children attend the same schools as your children. They ride school buses that pick them up and drop them off at the addition entrance. Your 17-year-old doesn't ride the bus; you participate in a carpool with 2 other families in the neighborhood to get her back and forth to high school.

Task: With regard to the events described above, define the attitude of a person or persons in each of these categories and describe the actions they might take.

Prejudiced Discriminator

Attitude: Don't want the African American family to move in

Actions: Calls a neighborhood meeting

Unprejudiced Discriminator

Attitude: Does not care but follows the status quote

Actions: Does not go to meeting however stills avoid

Prejudiced Nondiscriminator

Attitude:

Actions:

Unprejudiced Nondiscriminator

Attitude:

Actions:

Practitioner's Notes

Coming to Grips with Privilege and Oppression

It can be disorienting, frustrating, and even maddening to learn about cultural domination and subordination, unearned privilege, and the interrelationship of prejudice and discrimination. As we struggle to figure out our personal responsibility and course of action, we may well go through stages similar to the stages of grief put forth by Dr. Elisabeth Kübler-Ross in her pathbreaking work *On Death and Dying.* Kübler-Ross (1969) originally applied these stages to people suffering from terminal illness, and later to any form of catastrophic personal loss. The disorientation we feel, the loss of personal security as we challenge deeply-held prejudices, can be understood as part of the five-stage process laid out by Kübler-Ross. It should be noted that the stages are not strictly chronological. While there is a logical sequence, in the actual living of it, we tend to jump around, move forward and back, and even feel emotions from several stages at once.

Denial. This is the first stage. When we first hear stories of systematic oppression and discrimination, we frequently react initially with denial. "This can't be true—not in America, the land of opportunity." "Surely things are not as bad as they seem. They must be exaggerating." "This is just one person's experience. The problem can't possibly be that extensive and pervasive." Denial provides a temporary equilibrium in an unsettling situation. But it's hard to forget what we have learned—especially when we can't escape frequent reminders of the issue.

Anger. As we begin to overcome denial and contemplate the extent of the inequities, it is natural to become angry. "Why me/us? It's not fair!" "How can this happen to me/us?" "The people that are to blame for this have to pay!" "I'm mad as hell about this!" Our anger may lead us to blame the victims for the problem, or we may demand vengeance from the oppressors. Neither of these is particularly productive of problem-solving, and after the initial rush of emotion subsides, there is the potential of a lapse into apathy.

Guilt/Shame/Bargaining. As we study the issue of oppression and privilege further, we begin to come to grips with our own culpability and involvement in the problem. We reinterpret some of our past actions as hostile, we are embarrassed by our expressed ignorance and failure to challenge injustice, we feel inadequate to the challenge of personal growth and transformation. "I feel so bad to be a __________ person. They must hate me." "If I can just tell one person I'm sorry and get forgiveness, then I'll feel better." "I will work on my personal attitude; that's all I can do." "Maybe if I do just this one thing...."

Depression. At some point we may well become overwhelmed with the enormity of what needs to change and just feel like giving up. "People are just the way they are. They'll never change." "It just makes me so sad, why bother with anything?" "I'm just one person after all. What can I really do?" "What's the point in trying to change or fix anything? The problems seem so overwhelming...." The guilty knowledge one has of the problem, combined with apathy, worsens the dissonance and the depression.

Acceptance. In particular, this means acceptance of responsibility. "I can—and will—make a difference." "I will accept my share of the responsibility for the problem—and for creating the solution." This final stage brings a certain peace, but at the same time motivates us to sustained action to end oppression and to reject unearned privilege.

Exercise *Coming to Grips: A Personal Assessment*

As you reflect on the issue of privilege and oppression, where would you currently place yourself in terms of Kübler-Ross' stages? Why? What are you doing to move through to Acceptance of Responsibility?

Four Generations of Americans

The symbolic events and references of various age groups can differ significantly.

Generation	Traditionalists 1900-45	Boomers 1946-64	Gen Xers 1965-80	Millennials 1981-99
Size	75 million	80 million	46 million	76 million
Values	*Loyal* Faith in institutions and traditional hierarchy; unquestioning patriotism	*Optimistic, Competitive* Belief that the world can be made better, that problems can be fixed, need to challenge authority	*Skeptical* They witnessed every institution sullied and called into question	*Realistic, Collaborative* Pragmatic, but confident and empowered to act; appreciation for, and expectation of diversity
Defining Events	WWI, the Roaring Twenties, Prohibition, Great Depression, the New Deal, WWII, Korean War, theGI Bill, suburbanization	Civil Rights, feminist, anti-war, & environmental movements, Peace Corps, Vietnam, Elvis and the Beatles on Ed Sullivan, Detroit, Newark, Watts, & other urban riots, assassinations: JFK ('63),	lowered expectations, 3x divorce rate, crack, AIDS, latchkey kids, drunk drivers, *Challenger* disaster, Rodney King beating and aftermath, *Star Wars*	Hip hop, Gulf War, Columbine, 9/11, War on Terror,Raised by highly communicative, participation-oriented Boomers
Things	Flappers, roadsters, rumble seats, Coca-Cola, drive-ins, Carhops, The organization Man, "78s"'	Television, bell bottoms, mood rings, Brooks Brothers suits, Rolex watches, fast food, LSD, marijuana, disco, Twister,"45s,"	Cable TV, MTV, VCRs, video arcades, cassettes, fax machines, microwave ovens, pagers, personal computers, the Internet	Personal computers, cell phones, home video games, CDs, DVDs, MP3s, instant messaging, tattoos and body piercing, Ecstasy
Places	Pearl Harbor, Normandy, Midway, Iwo Jima, Hiroshima, Korea, the Bay of Pigs, Victory gardens, bread lines	Camelot, Watergate Hotel, Hanoi Hilton, My Lai, Kent State, Chappaquiddick, San Francisco, Woodstock, Chicago, suburbs, Selma, Memphis, communes, the moon, the Berlin Wall, Mayberry	Chernobyl, ex-Soviet Union, Somalia, Lockerbie, Scotland, Starbucks, the World Wide Web, the Persian Gulf, Gilligan's Island, Sesame Street	Chat rooms, cyberspace, outer space, Oklahoma City, NYC, 90210, Dawson's Creek, Napster, Afghanistan and Iraq
Influential People	Joe DiMaggio, Joe Louis, Alfred Hitchcock, the Rat Pack, John Wayne, Bob Hope, Elizabeth Taylor, Betty Grable, Duke Ellington, Ella Fitzgerald, Charles Lindbergh, FDR, Joe McCarthy, Dr. Spock	Martin Luther King, Jr., Rosa Parks, JFK, RFK, LBJ, Richard Nixon, "Deep Throat," Walter Cronkite, Eldridge Cleaver, H. Rap Brown, Gloria Steinem, McEnroe and Connors, Evert and Navratilova, Captain Kangaroo, Beaver Cleaver, BarbraStreisand, Kingston Trio, Beatles, Monkees, Stones, Beach Boys, Bob Dylan, Janis Joplin, Jimi Hendrix, James Brown, Captain Kirk, John Belushi, Manson family, Black Panthers, Village People	The Brat Pack, Bill Gates, Bill Clinton, Monica Lewinsky, Newt Gingrich, Clarence Thomas, Beavis and Butthead, Quentin Tarentino, Madonna, supermodels, Dilbert, O.J. Simpson, Dennis Rodman, Michael Jordan, Scooby Doo, Michael Jackson, Bon Jovi	Prince William, Chelsea Clinton, 2Pac, Ricky Martin, Barney, Britney Spears, Backstreet Boys, Buffy, Tinky Winky, Leonardo DiCaprio, Marilyn Manson, Kurt Cobain and Courtney Love, Felicity, Cartman, Mark McGwire and Sammy Sosa, Venus and Serena Williams, Tiger Woods, Snoop Dogg, Eminem, Harry Potter

Cuspers are those who find themselves between the two generations. They can play important bridging roles.

Adapted by Patrick J. Ashton from Lancaster and Stillman 2002.

Practitioner's Notes *Dealing with Different Age Groups*

Age can be an important cultural difference. People have different priorities and interests at different life stages. Moreover, the events and popular culture during the time we "come of age" provide important and unique cultural referents and touchstones. Like all cultural differences, however, one must be careful not to stereotype. What follows are generalizations, meant to sensitize us to potential issues that can cause misperception, miscommunication, and misunderstanding.

Tips for Dealing with Youth

- Like everyone else, young people want respect. Give it to them, and ask for it in return. Be careful not to automatically interpret as rude what may be normal kid behaviors.
- Avoid using jargon or words that they might not understand, but don't patronize them, speak in a condescending tone, or "dumb it down."
- Most youth are sensitive to authority. Don't lecture, sermonize, or stand on authority. Don't ask questions in a way that makes it seem like you are putting them on the spot. Resist the urge to try to teach them something in mediation.
- Young people generally have shorter attention spans. Get to the point quickly and don't belabor it.
- Don't strain to be hip or cool or "with it" in an attempt to build rapport. Young people will see right through this strategy and it will alienate them.

Tips for Dealing with the Elderly

- Elderly persons may have more trouble hearing and may be more sensitive to distractions. Speak slowly and clearly, but don't patronize.
- Some elderly people may not understand the specialized language of mediation, but may be too embarrassed to ask. Make sure you check understandings with them in a respectful way.
- Elderly persons may have trouble sitting for long periods of time. Schedule breaks appropriately.

Exercise 20 Questions: How much do you know about the Hidden Rules of Social Class?

Some sociologists have suggested the each social class possesses taken-for-granted knowledge (or CLASSified information) needed to survive in that social class and that this knowledge is largely hidden from the other social classes. Below are three questionnaires of 20 questions each. For each of the three questionnaires, place a check mark in front of each item that you know how to do—right now, today, at this very minute. Be honest. If you are the least bit unsure, do not check the item. For questions that apply to children: if you don't have children, use yourself and your siblings as a reference group.
Questionnaires adapted from Payne (1995).

Surviving in Poverty

____ 1. I know which churches and sections of town have the best rummage sales.
____ 2. I know where the nearest food bank is and when it is open.
____ 3. I know which grocery stores and restaurant garbage bins can be accessed for thrown- away food.
____ 4. I know how to get someone out of jail.
____ 5. I know how to physically fight and can defend myself physically if necessary.
____ 6. I know how a person can get a gun even if they have a police record.
____ 7. I know how to keep my clothes from being stolen at the laundromat.
____ 8. I know what problems to look for in a used car.
____ 9. I know how to live without a checking account.
____ 10. I know how to get by without electricity and without a phone.
____ 11. I know how to use a knife as scissors.
____ 12. I can entertain a group of friends with my personality and my stories.
____ 13. I know what to do when I don't have the money to pay my bills.
____ 14. I know how to move my residence in less than a day.
____ 15. I know how to feed 3 people for 5 days on $25.
____ 16. I know how to get and use food stamps.
____ 17. I know where the free medical clinics are, when they are open, and what time you have to arrive to be seen that day.
____ 18. I am very good at trading and bartering.
____ 19. I know how to get around without a car.
____ 20. I know what day of the month welfare and social security checks are deposited.

Functioning in the Middle Class

____ 1. I know how to get my children signed up for Little League, soccer, piano lessons, etc.
____ 2. I know how to properly set a table.
____ 3. I know which stores are most likely to carry the clothing brands my family wears.
____ 4. My children know the best name brands in clothing.
____ 5. I know how to order in a nice restaurant.

____ 6. I know how to use a credit card, checking account, and savings account.
____ 7. I know how to use an ATM card, and I know where the nearest ATM machines are.
____ 8. The children in my family expect to go to college.
____ 9. I understand term life insurance, disability insurance, house and flood insurance.
____ 10. I know how to get the best interest rates on a mortgage or new car loan.
____ 11. I understand what a pension annuity is and how it works.
____ 12. I understand the difference among the principal, interest, and escrow statements on my house payment.
____ 13. I know how to help my children with their homework.
____ 14. If my children have a problem at school, I do not hesitate to contact the teacher or principal.
____ 15. I know how to decorate the house for different holidays.
____ 16. I know how to get a library card and how to check out books at the public library.
____ 17. I know how to use the different tools in the garage or basement workbench.
____ 18. I know where to go and register to vote and where my local polling place is.
____ 19. I repair items in my house immediately when they break or know a repair service and call it.
____ 20. I know how to use at least three of the following: personal computer, telephone answering machine, cell phone, dvd player, cable box, iPod.

Functioning in the Upper Class

____ 1. I can read a menu in French, English, and another language.
____ 2. I have several favorite restaurants in different parts of the country or in different countries.
____ 3. I know how and where to hire an interior decorator to identify the appropriate themes and items with which to decorate my residence.
____ 4. I know how and where to hire domestic help, including maids, caterers, and gardeners.
____ 5. I can name my regular financial advisor, lawyer, and accountant.
____ 6. I have at least two residences which are staffed and maintained.
____ 7. I know how to ensure confidentiality and loyalty from my domestic staff.
____ 8. I have at least two people who serve as "screens" that keep people from me whom I do not wish to see.
____ 9. I frequently vacation in foreign countries.
____ 10. When I fly, it's in my own private plane, the company plane, or first-class commercial.
____ 11. I belong to at least two exclusive, members-only private clubs.
____ 12. I know how to enroll my children in the preferred private schools.
____ 13. I know how to host parties that "key" people (i.e., the socially, politically, and/or economically powerful) attend.
____ 14. I am on the boards of at least two charities.
____ 15. I know the hidden rules of the Junior League, the country club, and other private organizations.
____ 16. I have the personal cell phone numbers and/or private email addresses of at least a

dozen well-known people.

____ 17. I am familiar with the operation of personal security systems and devices.

____ 18. I have a favorite artist whom I support by buying his or her original work (not mass market).

____ 19. I know how to read a corporate financial statement, an investment prospectus, and the stock reports in the daily paper.

____ 20. I can easily converse about the "best" wines, art, designers, resorts, etc. My clothing, personal items, and residential furnishings have the labels of the most exclusive designers.

How many boxes did you check in each section of the questionnaire?

____ Surviving in Poverty
____ Functioning in the Middle Class
____ Functioning in the Upper Class

On which questionnaire did you have the most check marks? On which one did you have the least? Were you surprised by the outcome? Did any of the information surprise you? How did you feel when doing the exercise? How do you account for your reaction, in sociological terms?

Analyze the type of taken-for-granted information found in each questionnaire:

- what is the knowledge about?

- how and where does one learn it?

- how do you gain access to the people and places where it can be learned?

What conclusions can you draw about the nature of hidden knowledge necessary to be successful in each social class?

Research Note: The Hidden Injuries of Class

In the late 1960s, Richard Sennett and Jonathan Cobb (1972) studied ethnic immigrant communities in Boston. These mostly first- and second-generation immigrants were overwhelmingly blue-collar workers, doing jobs classified as unskilled or semiskilled.

In-depth interviews with the men revealed a crisis of self-respect. The workers perceived a cultural hierarchy in America in which they, as less-educated blue-collar workers could never measure up. Moreover, they felt that the native-born (i.e., children and grandchildren of earlier immigrants) middle class had the power to judge them. And they constantly fell short.

This feeling of inadequacy drove the subjects of Sennett and Cobb's study to try to achieve the American Dream. Yet even when they achieved material success, they still felt inadequate. Now they felt like imposters on the middle-class landscape; at any moment they could be exposed as interlopers. Thus, regardless of their material success these men were plagued by self-doubts.

Sennett and Cobb conclude that the hidden injuries of the American class system are the deep and persistent feelings of inadequacy and loss of self-esteem felt by working- and lower-middle-class people.

In conflict situations, these hidden injuries can manifest themselves as defensiveness. Empowering people who have this orientation is crucial to transformative conflict resolution.

Exercise *Diversity Experience Inventory*

Rank your experience with diversity (of any kind) in each of the following areas according to the following scale:

1 = no experience at all **2** = some experience **3** = a lot of experience

Area of Experience	**IN THE PAST**	**NOW**
Immediate Family		
Extended Family		
Neighborhood		
Religious Community		
Elementary School		X
Middle School		X
High School		X
College		
Civic and Voluntary Groups		
Work experience		
Personal Friendships		
Total Score		

If you don't have a score higher than 15 in the right-hand column, you probably aren't working enough on ensuring that there is diversity in your life. All of us, of course, can do better. Ask yourself: What am I doing right now – concretely and specifically – to become the person I want to be?

Practitioner's Notes — *Skills for Respecting and Supporting Diversity*

Research shows that these are the skills that promote tolerance and acceptance of differences.

Skills

- Learn reconciliation skills to deal constructively with conflict, disagreement, and difference.
  - ✓ Learn to really listen by developing attending and paraphrasing skills.
  - ✓ Learn and practice centered speaking.
  - ✓ Do not assume that you know what someone else is perceiving or thinking.

- Learn to respect and appreciate differences.
  - ✓ Deprogram stereotypical thinking.
  - ✓ Develop cultural relativism.
  - ✓ Be open to experience.
  - ✓ Know about and consciously choose one's own heritage/culture.
  - ✓ Actively learn the "stories" of other cultures.
  - ✓ Develop empathy, not sympathy, for those who experience oppression.
  - ✓ Cultivate personal relationships across social boundaries.

- Develop a strong self-concept.
  - ✓ Identify basic values.
  - ✓ Cultivate sincerity and authenticity.
  - ✓ Cultivate curiosity, creativity, critical thinking, and a willingness to take risks.
  - ✓ Develop empathy; integrate thinking and feeling.
  - ✓ Develop self-respect and respect for others; tolerance and acceptance.
  - ✓ Develop trust in one's own intuition and competency.

- Participate in community.
  - ✓ Develop strong community norms of tolerance and acceptance.
  - ✓ Take personal responsibility for letting people know where you stand.
  - ✓ Develop community institutions that promote diversity.
  - ✓ Create a shared vision of a good society and participate in groups that work to make it possible.

How To Socialize Children To Be Helpers And Interveners

Research on those who actively helped Jews and other persecuted people during the Holocaust and on bystanders who intervene to help a person in crisis indicates that they have childhoods characterized by similar experiences. In short, they were raised according to the following guidelines:

- Nurture, support, and love children unconditionally with no threatened love withdrawal.
- Nurture self-esteem and independence by explaining, listening, and giving choices.
- Provide role models of helping behavior and standing up for one's values.
- Teach empathy and acceptance, respect for differences.
- Educate children about other cultures, emphasizing commonalities as well as differences.

Part Five: The Mediation Process

By taking a step toward each other, the parties can find a place where *us* and *them* become *we*.

— *Mark Gerzon*

"All too often in families, in organizations, and in communities, when well-intentioned people find themselves struggling with difficult and contentious issues, there is a simple but powerful explanation: they haven't created the shared expectations — the ground rules — for working out their differences. And even when they do work out their differences, they often do so in ways that leave them frustrated, alienated from one another, resentful, and in dread of their next confrontation.

— *E. Franklin Dukes, Marina A. Piscolish, and John B. Stephens*

"The deepest hunger in life is a secret that is revealed only when a person is willing to unlock a hidden part of the self.... Transformation means radical change of form, the way a caterpillar transforms into a butterfly. In human terms, it means turning fear, aggression, doubt, insecurity, hatred, and emptiness into their opposites."

Deepak Chopra

"If given the choice, choose what makes your life larger rather than smaller."

Clarissa Pinkola Estés

"Never in this world can hatred be stilled by hatred; it will be stilled only by non-hatred; this is the law eternal."

Buddha

At this point, we have learned how to understand and analyze conflict; we have explored centrally important interpersonal communication skills, acquired personal insight into our own orientation to conflict, and developed a sensitivity to social context and processes. What remains is to gain a thorough working knowledge of the mediation process. In this section we will explore the "nuts and bolts" of mediation as well as contextual issues such as ethics and confidentiality. We will also examine when mediation is not appropriate.

Theory | *Repressive vs. Restitutive Law*

Emile Durkheim (1858-1917) was one of the founders of the discipline of sociology. In fact, he was the first person to hold an academic appointment as Professor of Sociology. Durkheim lived at a time when the Industrial Revolution was continuing to transform Europe. He wanted to develop a science of society that could explain how social order and solidarity were maintained in the face of increasing differentiation, complexity, and individualism.

To explain this transformation, Durkheim (1964) developed the concepts of mechanical and organic solidarity. Mechanical solidarity is characteristic of preindustrial societies, where there is relatively little division of labor. Here people engage in similar activities and have similar responsibilities. They have generalized knowledge about all important statuses and roles. In this situation, solidarity is automatic, or mechanical.

In modern industrial society, there is a complex division of labor in which people perform specific, limited tasks with limited knowledge. Paradoxically, their very specialization makes them dependent upon one another for survival. No one can get by without the input of many others, because any particular individual lacks the whole skill set. In this situation, said Durkheim, solidarity emerges from this complex interdependence. It is thus organic.

Durkheim further observed that a society bound together by mechanical solidarity was also characterized by repressive law. The extensive similarity in knowledge and skills leads to a strong common morality that is both unitary and extensive. Thus someone who violates this morality by doing wrong is not just guilty of a specific offense, but of an affront to the whole society. Punishment is harsh and severe, extending from corporal punishment to death, expulsion, or shunning (social death). Even minor offenses cannot be overlooked, because they threaten the entire social order.

On the other hand, a society bound together by organic solidarity, said Durkheim, is characterized by restitutive law. First of all, the complexity and diversity of such a society means that there is only a weak common morality. Offenses are likely to be viewed as specific and limited, rather than as repudiations of the society itself. Second, because of the extensive interdependence fostered by the complex division of labor, each individual with their separate knowledge and skill set is potentially valuable to the whole. Thus, rather than exclude them, the authorities require the offender to make restitution to those who have been harmed, so that the individual can be restored to a productive role in society.

What does this mean for mediation? First of all, understand that small groups and organizations—families, clubs, churches, etc.—can be characterized by mechanical solidarity. In this situation, conflict can be created when someone is perceived as violating the overarching rules. The solution may be understood as zero/sum: either capitulation to the rules or expulsion from the group. It may be possible, however, to move the parties toward a restitutive solution if they can come to understand the complexities of their interdependence. In situations clearly characterized by organic solidarity, the emphasis of the mediators ought to be on restitution—i.e., exploring what would make it right for an offended party.

THE FLOW OF CONFLICT

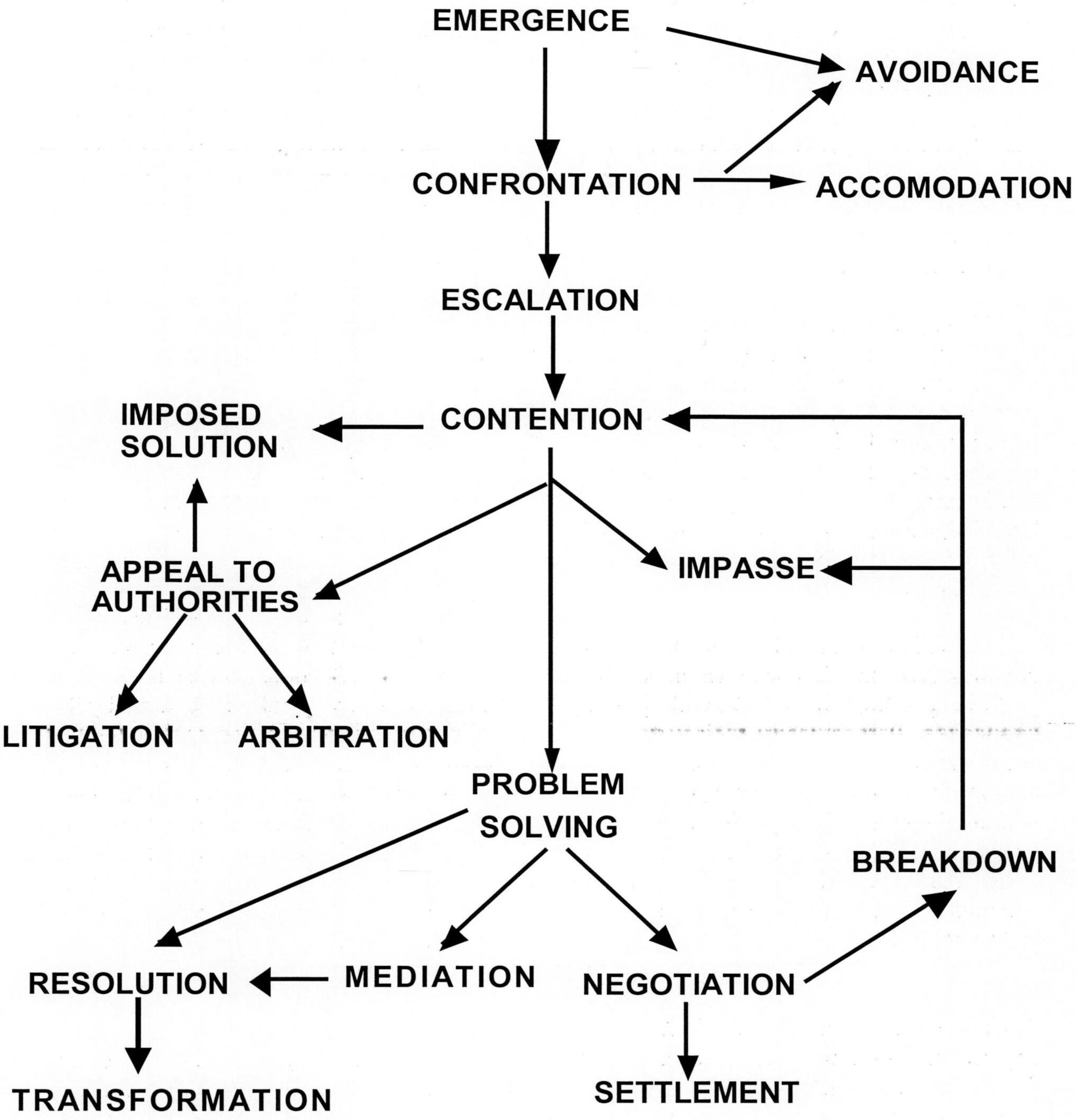

This diagram represents, not the inevitable progression of a given conflict, but rather various possibilities along the way. One important distinction is that resolution is based upon collaboration, whereas a settlement is frequently based upon compromise or accommodation. One embodies the possibility of transformation; the other does not. The difference in nuance and implications may be seen by examining conflict resolution processes in more detail.

Models of Third-Party Intervention

	Litigation	Arbitration	Directive Mediation	Common Ground Mediation	Transformative Mediation
Process	Judge decides based on legal principles	After hearing the parties, the arbitrator imposes the best decision	Mediator actively facilitates a settlement between the parties	Mediator facilitates conversation in which interests and needs are discussed and common ground identified	Mediator facilitates conversation that empowers the parties and builds the relationship between them
Orientation	Win/Lose Lose/Lose	Win/Lose	Win/Lose Win/Win	Win/Win	Win/Win
Outcome	Imposed	Imposed	Facilitated through 3-way negotiation	Controlled by parties	Controlled by parties
Method	Application of legal principles	Fairness enforced by an unbiased third party	Problem solution through informal negotiation	Problem solution based on joint discussion of underlying needs and interests	Empowerment and Recognition
Focus	Problem solving	Problem solving	Problem solving	Problem solving	Relationship building

What is Community Mediation?

Mediation is an informal, structured discussion between two or more disputants, aided by a neutral third party (one or more mediators), aimed at resolving conflict by producing a mutually satisfying, lasting agreement between the disputants. Additionally, common ground mediation or conciliation seeks to build and nurture the relationship between the disputants and to educate and empower them to solve their own problems.

Community mediation is designed to increase community capacity, which may be defined as the set of skills and knowledge, leadership, sense of efficacy, extent of trusting relationships, and existence of a culture of learning that exists within a given community. This ability to solve community problems as well as to resolve community conflicts is a major influence on the quality of life in a community. (Colorado Trust, 1998).

Community mediation traces its roots in the United States to the 1960s. The first programs were alternative dispute resolution programs (ADR), designed to reduce the logjam in the courts by diverting cases that could be settled out of court. Over time, courts in many states began to offer mediation of civil cases on a mandatory or voluntary basis. The U.S. Department of Justice began to fund the creation of Neighborhood Justice Centers during the 1970s. These centers generally mediated court-referred disputes, though they were often available for walk-in business as well.

The first authentically grassroots community mediation program was the Community Boards Program in San Francisco. This group helped create a model based on having panels of volunteer mediators who reflected, to the extent possible, key demographic characteristics of the disputants. In the 1980s, there was a veritable explosion in the number and type of mediation organizations. Today, mediation organizations tend to fall into one of three types: (1) justice-system-based, which are usually court-sponsored and often involve an element of coercion, as well as paid mediators; (2) community-based, which are usually run by nonprofit organizations and utilize volunteer mediators; and (3) hybrid organizations which take court-referred cases as well as cases from other sources (Duffy 1991).

Research Note

Mediation Outcomes

Research on the outcome of mediation indicates that it is a highly successful dispute resolution technique. Duffy (1991) notes that 80 to 90 percent of disputes that go to mediation are resolved to the satisfaction of the disputants. Not all disputes, of course, go to mediation. Nationally, about half of all disputes referred to mediation centers actually wind up in a mediation session.

The most frequent reasons disputes are ultimately not mediated include the fact that one party would not agree to mediate, or that the disputants felt that the dispute had already been resolved to their satisfaction. This is really a positive outcome in many cases because it is the very fact of intervention by a third party—the mediation center—that provokes or inspires the disputants to resolve the dispute themselves.

Notes on Transformative Mediation

Goals of Transformative Mediation

Education — During mediation, disputants should have the opportunity to learn and practice positive responses to conflict. Mediation organizations should be actively engaged in promoting and teaching the principles of nonviolent conflict resolution.

Empowerment — Mediation should empower disputants to solve, not only their immediate conflict, but future conflicts as well. By acting as facilitators and educators, mediators assist disputants to discover their capacity to solve their own problems.

Recognition — Mediation should evoke in the participants acknowledgment and empathy for the problems and life situation of others.

Note that the goal is not primarily reaching an agreement, but rather transforming the relationship between the parties. Success in transformative mediation is defined not by a settlement agreement, but by empowerment and recognition of the parties. Agreements may indeed flow from empowerment and recognition, but achieving an agreement is not the primary focus of the process.

Primary Vehicle of Transformative Mediation: Compassionate Strength

Two important dimensions of moral growth are autonomy, or strength of self, and concern for others, or compassion. Healthy, mature individuals exhibit both of these qualities. Transformative mediation is a vehicle for developing and exercising both of these capacities in a healthy mix. Compassionate strength emphasizes the individual overcoming adversity but with concern for others' welfare.

Primary Patterns of Transformative Mediation

- Microfocusing on the parties' moves
- Encouraging deliberation and choice making
- Fostering perspective taking

Pitfalls of Transformative Mediation

- Thinking empowerment means mediator passivity
- Carrying "positive pushing" too far – i.e., into directive action
- Protecting too much or too little
- Focusing on either empowerment or recognition alone
- Losing sight of the transformative orientation and becoming a problem-solver

Drawn from Bush and Folger 1994.

Theory *Models of Mediation*

	THE PROBLEM-SOLVING MODEL	THE TRANSFORMATIVE MODEL	THE SOCIAL JUSTICE MODEL
GOAL	To find optimal solutions to disputants' problems, thereby maximizing the satisfaction of individual needs.	To transform individual human character toward greater strength and com--passion, thereby facilitating individuals to solve their own problems.	To promote equality among individuals by organizing people and communities to obtain fairer treatment.
PREMISE	Conflicts arise due to the perceived incompatibility of parties' needs and interests.	Conflicts arise due to individual weakness and selfishness; conflicts provide opportunities for moral growth.	Conflicts arise from the unequal distribution of power and resources in society.
ADVAN-TAGES	•Focus on win/win outcomes, collaborative rather than adversarial model produces better agreements •Not bound by legal cate-gories or rules, the dispute can be reframed to facilitate solution •Result: a high settlement rate	•Empowers people to solve their own problems •Fosters moral growth by helping individuals to: •clarify their own needs and values •develop empathy for & humanize the other party •By building relationships, it creates more stable, long-lasting agreements	•Not bound by legal cate-gories/rules, dispute can be reframed to empower the disenfranchised •Helps individuals and communities define their values, needs and interests •Provides a vehicle for balancing power, thereby limiting exploitation
PRACTICE ORIENTA-TION	Mediator assists the parties in defining the issues and crafting the solution.	Mediator creates a process & an environment in which all parties are empowered to discover themselves and humanize each other.	Mediator structures the process to empower the disenfranchised and thereby obtain more just agreements.
CRITIQUE	Insertion of mediator's perspective/agenda potentially: •disempowers disputants •introduces mediator's biases •produces only the appearance of mutual satisfaction of parties' needs •undermines long-term satisfaction	•Absence of formal pro-cedure and substantive rules can magnify power imbalances •Focus on interpersonal relationships diverts attention from structural inequality and injustice •Focus on individuals privatizes issues which have community import	•Focus on achieving justice may prevent im-mediate, workable solu-tions to practical problems •Overlooks the oppor-tunity to humanize society by humanizing individual relationships •May exacerbate conflicts & move them to win/lose

adapted from Bush and Folger 1994

Some Thoughts on Mediation and Social Justice

True peace is not merely the absence of tension: it is the presence of justice.

Martin Luther King, Jr

There can be no real peace without justice. And without resistance there will be no justice.

Arundhati Roy

Recognition of the inherent dignity and of the equal and inalienable rights of all members of the human family is the foundation of freedom, justice and peace in the world.

Universal Declaration of Human Rights

No matter what someone else has done, it still matters how we treat people. It matters to our humanity that we treat offenders according to standards that we recognize as just. Justice is not revenge — it's deciding for a solution that is oriented towards peace, peace being the harder but more human way of reacting to injury. That is the very basis of the idea of rights.

Judith Butler

Washing one's hands of the conflict between the powerful and the powerless means to side with the powerful, not to be neutral.

Paulo Freire

If you are neutral in a situation of injustice, you have chosen the side of the oppressor. If an elephant has his foot on the tail of the mouse, and you say you are neutral, the mouse will not appreciate your neutrality.

Bishop Desmond Tutu

Key Features of Mediation

On the included DVD, go to the ***Client/Caseworker Mediation*** and view *Chapter 1: Introduction to Mediation.*

Characteristics of Mediation

Nonbureaucratic — Mediation is more informal, small-scale, spontaneous, and manageable than formal bureaucratic processes of conflict resolution.

Voluntary — Most community mediation is offered on a purely voluntary basis; even when a court has made mediation mandatory, the mediators stress that any agreement between the disputants is of their own voluntary making.

Nonadversarial — Mediation is an exercise in joint problem solving; disputants are encouraged to see each other as partners in finding a solution.

Principles of Mediation

Informed Consent — Parties to a dispute have the right to be informed in advance about the nature of the mediation process and their options within it before agreeing to mediation or to any mediated solution.

Impartiality — Parties in a dispute have a right to a process that serves everyone fairly. Mediators may not take sides in the disputes they mediate. They must refrain from actual or perceived bias or favoritism.

Confidentiality — All information related to the mediation process — the names of the parties, the issues they discuss, and the agreement they reach — is private. Information and may not be revealed unless the parties to the dispute agree to let it be known.

Self-Determination — The parties to a dispute have the right and the ability to define their needs and the issues they want to address and to determine the solutions they want to adopt. The conflict, like the agreement, belongs to the disputants.

Situations Where Mediation Can be Useful

Transformative mediation is most effective when the disputants have an ongoing relationship or they cannot avoid dealing with one another. It is also a way to avoid formal proceedings.

The principles and process of mediation laid out here can apply to a wide variety of situations. Here are some examples:

- Neighbor-to-neighbor disputes
- Landlord/tenant disputes
- Business/customer disputes over products and services
- Agency/client disputes
- Peer mediation at school
- Teacher/administrator/parent/student disputes at school
- Family disputes
- Employee conflicts in the workplace
- Employee/supervisor disputes
- *Organizational disputes
- *Divorce and child custody disputes
- *Victim/offender mediation
- *Policy disputes
- *Diplomatic or international disputes

*These situations require additional training and sometimes formal certification.

Situations Where Mediation is Not Appropriate or Effective

On the other hand, mediation is not effective or appropriate when

- the parties are too emotional to discuss the problem together
- one or more parties refuses to mediate or to demonstrate good faith
- power between the parties cannot be adequately balanced
- the issue is one of social justice that is better handled by courts or other formal processes.

Characteristics of Mediators

Role of the Mediator

A mediator is basically the ***guardian of the process*** of mediation. The *substance* of the mediation belongs to the disputants; the mediator is there to facilitate a discussion between the parties to a dispute in such a way that the parties achieve empowerment and recognition and acquire or enhance their ability to resolve the conflict themselves. In doing so the mediator will:

- ✓ choose and arrange a physical setting that is conducive to mediation.
- ✓ establish confidence and trust in the process by reinforcing the shared agreement of mutual respect (no name-calling; no or minimal interrupting) and maintaining control of the process.
- ✓ establish rapport by validating each of the parties without endorsing or opposing the expressed views of those parties.
- ✓ empower each of the parties to be heard, understood and recognized.
- ✓ use prompts and probes to intervene and maintain communication and move the discussion along when necessary.
- ✓ reality test the provisions of a tentative agreement with each of the parties to make sure it is workable.

Who Can be a Mediator?

Anyone who successfully completes a 40-plus hour training program can be a community mediator. Most states have additional guidelines and requirements for those who want to be professional mediators, especially in the area of family mediation. New mediators can gain experience by co-mediating with experienced mediators. All mediators should engage in continuing education to keep their skills sharp and to keep abreast of new developments.

Qualities of Good Mediators

A good mediator is one who is:

- ✓ a good listener.
- ✓ able to establish rapport with a wide variety of people.
- ✓ not uncomfortable with displays of strong emotion.
- ✓ able to empathize with people.
- ✓ not uncomfortable with disagreement and dissension.
- ✓ patient.
- ✓ tolerant of mistakes and differences.
- ✓ able to be impartial and withhold judgment.
- ✓ confident in their knowledge and understanding of the mediation process.
- ✓ thoughtful and reflective; able to listen to their intuition.
- ✓ emotionally fluent.
- ✓ able to "think on their feet" and respond quickly and creatively to challenges.
- ✓ able to let other people take the credit.

How Mediation Works: Common Ground's ***Process***

When neighbors, co-workers, fellow members of a church, or family and friends have a dispute that they cannot resolve by themselves, *Common Ground, Inc.* is available to help. Those who are in need of help in resolving a dispute begin by calling *Common Ground* directly or by being referred by the Citizen's Advocate office of the City of Fort Wayne or other local agency. The callers may have been referred to *Common Ground* from their neighborhood association, the police, the prosecutor's office, a telephone crisis hotline, or a wide variety of community agencies. The *Common Ground* volunteer who answers the phone gathers specific information from the caller about the nature of the dispute and the names and, if possible, addresses and phone numbers of the disputing parties. This case developer initiates contact with the parties who are in dispute. While talking separately with each of the disputing parties, the case developer explains the process of mediation, the rules of participation, and seeks permission from each disputant to participate in mediation to resolve their dispute.

If the parties agree to mediation, they each sign an agreement to mediate (copies of forms are in Appendix VI). The case developer then selects and solicits the participation of other members of *Common Ground* to serve on the mediation panel. *Common Ground* tries to establish panels of at least three mediators. Given their knowledge of the characteristics of the parties and the nature of the dispute, case developers select mediators who they think would work best in helping the parties to resolve their dispute. One priority in forming the panel is to try to ensure that the social, economic, and cultural characteristics of the disputants that are relevant to the nature of the dispute are represented on the panel of mediators. Once the mediation panel has been selected, the case developer works with the panel and the disputants to determine a mutually acceptable time and place for the mediation to take place. Case materials describing the nature of the dispute and the parties in the dispute are shared with all members of the mediation panel.

At the agreed-upon time and place, the members of the mediation panel and the disputants gather together to resolve the dispute. Mediation sessions should not last more than three hours. If the dispute cannot be resolved during this time, a second session is arranged to continue the mediation of the dispute. During the mediation session, mediators neither offer advice nor propose solutions. Rather, the mediators construct an environment and facilitate a process which allows the disputants to fully and freely communicate with one another, to find common ground, and to work toward a solution in which all parties have ownership. At the end of a successful mediation, the disputants will have worked out an agreement that resolves the dispute to their mutual satisfaction. Each party signs and receives a copy of the agreement as a sign of good faith in following through on the resolution. Several months later, *Common Ground* attempts to contact the parties to discover if the agreement is working and to determine their overall satisfaction with the process. If there are continuing problems, further mediation is suggested.

Based on the process of *Common Ground Community Dispute Resolution Service, Inc.*

Practitioner's Notes — *Conflict Analysis*

In seeking to understand and mediate a conflict, it is vital to consider the following issues:

Parties

- ✓ Who are the **primary** parties to the dispute?
  Primary parties are central to the conflict and its resolution.
- ✓ Who are the **secondary** parties?
  Secondary parties are constituencies *of the primary parties or are affected in some important way by the conflict. Secondary parties must be kept in mind because they also will be affected by the resolution.*
- ✓ What are the **relationships** among the parties to the dispute?
  Understanding these relationships may be key to resolving the conflict.

Positions

- ✓ Positions are stances that are specific, concrete, and appear non-negotiable.
- ✓ What is the position of each party with regard to the dispute?
- ✓ While you want to acknowledge the positions the parties take, *this is the least important aspect of the conflict.*
  Very little time should be taken with this. It is not important for mediators to understand the details of parties' positions. The point is to empower the disputants to move beyond positions to needs and interests.

Perceptions/Assumptions/Expectations

- ✓ How does each party perceive the dispute?
- ✓ How do the parties perceive each other?
- ✓ What assumptions are the parties making about each other?
- ✓ What expectations do the parties have for each other? for mediation?

Feelings

- ✓ What emotions does each party have about... the issues in conflict? the other parties to the dispute? being involved in this conflict? the involvement of third parties in the conflict? (e.g., mediators)

Interests/Needs/Values

- ✓ In relation to the issues in conflict here, what are each party's underlying needs, concerns, and fears?
  Underlying interests define the problem.
  Each party has multiple interests; only some of these interests are in conflict.
  Other interests are shared or compatible.
  The most powerful interests are basic human needs (i.e., Maslow's Hierarchy).
- ✓ What does each party value?
- ✓ What would "make it right" for each party?

Power

- ✓ What kinds of power does each party possess?
- ✓ What kinds of power imbalances need to be addressed in order to pursue a collaborative resolution?
- ✓ What power currencies can be created for each party?

Common Ground

- ✓ On what basis might common ground be recognized and established among the parties? e.g., commitment to similar goals or values; similar underlying needs; important relationships with the same people; shared focus of concern; similar vocational or avocational orientation; a wish to communicate better

Based on material developed by Fisher and Ury (1983) and
Education for Conflict Resolution (1995); modified by Patrick J. Ashton

Exercise *Doing Conflict Analysis: A Dispute in the Dorm*

Read the following scenario and then do a conflict analysis using the categories above.

Roger vs. Jim

Roger's perspective: Your neighbor in the dorm, Jim, has been a real pain lately. He's always hassling you about stuff. Nothing is good enough for him. For example, he is all the time complaining about the noise when you have some of your friends over to your dorm room in the evening, even though no one else on the floor seems to mind. You aren't trying to give him a hard time, but you get tired of being bugged, especially the way Jim handles it; he acts as though you are really inferior.

Last week you needed a library book. The friend working the desk at the library told you that the book was checked out to Jim. He wasn't in the room, but Phil his roommate found it for you on Jim's desk. After you reminded Phil that Jim has often let you borrow his things, Phil said he guessed you could borrow the book for a few hours. You put the book on your bookshelf and went to dinner. When you returned, an hour and a half later, the book was gone and a clay sculpture you purchased in Mexico several years ago lay broken on your desk. You knew right away who had done it.

Upset, you went over and knocked on Jim's door. But when he saw who it was, he just told you to "chill" and slammed the door in your face. Since then you and Jim haven't spoken. Your resident assistant has suggested mediation.

Jim's perspective: You are really tired of all the hassles caused by your neighbor in the dorm (and former friend), Roger. You have an early morning job to pay your college bills and need to be asleep by 10 pm Sunday through Thursday nights.

Roger is a big partier, and several nights a week he and his friends play loud music and talk and laugh till late – to midnight or even 1 am. On several occasions you have gone over and knocked on his door, asking him to keep the noise down. Fifteen minutes later, the volume is blaring again.

Roger also borrows your things. You have no problem with borrowing, but he doesn't return things to your room (your tennis racket – still in his room – is one of dozens of examples). When you get items back, they are often dirty or not in good condition (your popcorn popper, for example).

Last week you were finishing a major paper. You needed a book which you checked out of the campus library. When you went to use it, you couldn't find it anywhere. After searching your whole room, you went over to Roger's room. There is stood on his bookshelf. Irritated, you yanked it down. Another book fell from the shelf and landed on a little pottery trinket below on the desk. You were in a hurry, so you left the broken pieces there.

An hour later Roger banged on your door. When you opened it, he began swearing at you. When he refused to let you explain, you slammed the door in his face after telling him to come back to talk after he cooled down. Your resident assistant has suggested mediation between Roger and you.

Roleplay authored by Ron Kraybill.

Parties

Perceptions/Assumptions/Expectations

Feelings

Interests/Needs/Values

Power

Common Ground

Theory *Impression Management in Social Interaction*

American sociologist Erving Goffman (1959, 1967) developed a pioneering and unique analysis of the complexities of face-to-face social interaction. Goffman called his approach *dramaturgical analysis* because he wanted to emphasize that interaction involves individuals staging performances in which they generally cooperate to save face for one another. He calls this the *interaction ritual*:

> During interaction the individual is expected to possess certain attributes, capacities, and information which, taken together, fit together into a self that is at once coherently unified and appropriate for the occasion. Through the expressive implications of his stream of conduct, through mere participation itself, the individual effectively projects this acceptable self into the interaction, although he may not be aware of it, and the others may not be aware of having so interpreted his conduct.
>
> At the same time he must accept and honor the selves projected by the other participants. The elements of a social encounter, then, consist of effectively projected claims to an acceptable self and the confirmation of like claims on the part of others (1967:105-6).

Poise, says Goffman, is the ability to project claims about the self with confidence. Because self-identity is not genetically determined, we must symbolically construct an identity and then convey its meaning to those with whom we interact. Goffman calls this process *impression management* or "face-work." How does an individual accomplish this? By using all the tools of drama, he says: scenery, costume, props, script, and body language. Goffman also distinguishes between the *front stage,* where the performance is stages, and the *back stage*, which the audience for the performance is not allowed to see.

What happens when someone is unable to successfully carry off a performance? As we all know from everyday experience, that individual "loses face." The result is not only embarrassment for the person losing face, but also for others present, because, at some level, everyone understands that social identity is symbolically constructed and claims to competence are always subject to challenge. So when others lose face it is a reminder of our own vulnerability.

Our first line of defense is to try to ignore the social *faux pas* entirely, if possible, even though everyone is aware that it occurred. Goffman calls this *studied nonobservance*—working really hard to pretend not to notice what was clearly noticed. This is the very definition of tact—staging an interaction in ways that avoid challenging the face of others.

What happens when, in spite of tactful precautions, someone loses face? Or—generally in situations of conflict—someone attempts to undermine another person's identity as an aggressive tactic? In this case, says Goffman, what is required to save the situation is an *interchange*—e.g., a denial of the deliberate intention to undermine another person's identity, an apology, or some form of offered recompense. A third party's intervention here can be important to the face-saving process.

What if an individual anticipates that they might lose face? One tactic, says Goffman, is to establish *role distance*—i.e., to suggest that one's investment in the performance is limited and therefore any failure of that performance is minimized. ("I didn't really care." "I wasn't really trying.") Or we can engage in *aligning actions* to "get our ducks in a row" in advance. ("Excuse me but...." "This may sound stupid but...." "I don't mean to change the subject but....")

Goffman's analysis generates a rich understanding of the mediation process and a wealth of constructive strategies for mediators to employ.

Seen through the lens of Goffman's analysis, a major task of the mediators is to make it possible for the parties to deal with conflict without losing face. The mediators do this by *facilitating the process* of interaction in ways that allow for the construction of aligning actions, blunt or redirect parties' efforts to undermine the face of others, and facilitate interchange when face-losing occurs. On the other hand, mediators should not allow the parties to express role distance as a means of escape from dealing with the interaction.

Contrary to everyday experience, however, mediators should not engage in studied nonobservance. They should surface all potential embarrassments and deal with them constructively. Similarly, mediators should ensure that there is no backstage in the mediation process—everything about the process is made transparent and there are no secrets. This inspires the parties to have confidence in the process.

First we will see how these techniques can be used in case development—when mediators try to get the parties to commit to mediation. Then we will see how Goffman's analysis and techniques inform the mediation process itself.

Case Development Notes

COMMON GROUND
COMMUNITY DISPUTE RESOLUTION SERVICE

"THANK YOU for volunteering to do Case Development!"

Please find the following FORMS:

- CASE DEVELOPMENT NOTES
- COORDINATOR/CASE DEVELOPER JOB DESCRIPTIONS
- CASE RECORD *from the Citizen's Advocate Intake Staff*
- CASE DEVELOPER REPORT *for you to complete & return.*
- 2 CONSENT FORMS

Some asked for reference information, so please use, but keep in mind that this was prepared to accompany a training program. This is for all case development, but particularly when attempting to convince a reluctant second party to consider conciliation.

You should speak with disputants personally, possibly in their homes, however the suggestions below may also assist in over the phone efforts as well. **"GOOD LUCK!"** Call 555-5555 and ask for Diana should you have any questions/updates/or require assistance for this case.

RELAX AND REHEARSE

Don't rush to case development from another job or task
Mentally rehearse (presentation/obstacles/arguments)
Review case form information (but don't take file with you)
Expect opposition, hesitancy
Check in with co-case developer regarding roles/work
Leave enough time for the visit
Take brochures, consent forms and any other materials that you'll need
Remember the primary purpose: to get parties to hearing, not to personally attempt to "referee" or solve the problem yourself!

GET IN THE DOOR

Use your name, "Volunteer", "With Common Ground", "Community dispute resolution service", "Live in community", "Help people solve problems".
Mention that there's a person who has a conflict that concerns them
Use "Conciliation/mediation/conflict resolution" etc., sparingly
Express desire to talk to them about the problem – inside
Mention the name of first party only if necessary at this point
Smile, be friendly…Do not explain conciliation process (unless you think you're not going to get any further)

LISTEN and LEARN

Explain first party concern (not necessarily in full detail) and their interest in neighborly resolution. Make sure they know you are not a representative of first party.
Get their story first
Ask open ended questions, but don't go after "all the facts"
Active listen; empathize
Don't take too many notes, concentrate on the person
May need to reimmerse person in conflict if they seem to feel it doesn't exist or isn't serious
Think: What do they feel, need, want?

PRESENT and PERSIST

Don't go for hearing "pitch" right away
Use what you've heard to identify/validate their issues/concerns
Get person to start saying "yes" to you, to what they feel, what their issues are, and what they want
Focus on need for changed (improved) situation, not on going to panel hearing
Thank party for their desire to change situation for the better
Reinforce potential benefits for the party should they work on improving the problem
May be useful to ask "How is the problem for you now? How might it develop if unaided? How would it be if situation corrected?

MAKING THE PITCH

Give brief description of hearing in general terms
Specifically refer to/endorse party's needs and wants, and the potential for improved outcome.
Mention practical benefits (free, informal, convenient, quick, etc.)
Use success stories
Ask "Can I set up a hearing?"
Act as if you expect a yes answer (but expect that it won't be that easy!)

PERSIST, PERSIST

Give no indication of taking "no" for an answer (use courtesy & common sense however)
Isolate and respond to party's concerns, fears, etc.
Don't emphasize hearing itself (unless the hearing is the "problem")
Return to their issues/needs/wants – to help them see an improved situation, imagine what it would be like
Take their concerns about panel participation seriously (treat fear of retaliation as a legitimate concern, validate, then discuss how it might be overcome)
Check in – will they come just for you (personal pitch)
Reinforce: previous successes with such problems, convenience, etc.
Ask, "Can I set up a hearing?"

WRAP-UP

Do people have all the information they need?
Do you have all the information you need (suggested times for hearing, other involved parties, their phone number, etc.)?
Do they know what the next steps are?
Leave appropriate materials & **Thank them again!**

Revised 12/22/95 dmg

An Overview of the Mediation Process

The Briefing (before the disputants arrive)

- Develop teamwork among the mediators; discuss how you want to work together.
- Review the basic rules and principles of mediation that will be followed by everyone in this particular mediation.
- Review the background details of the case with fellow mediators; do a brief conflict analysis.
- Discuss individual strengths and weaknesses, personal styles and how they might affect the process.
- Assign roles for the mediation process.
- Appropriately arrange the room for mediation (seating, lighting, noise, etc.).
- Prepare yourself mentally and emotionally for mediation; do a centering exercise.

The Opening

- Greet the parties, put them at ease, and show them to their seats.
- Introduce yourselves to the parties; agree on names to be used in mediation.
- Describe the mediation procedure and the role of the mediators.
- Develop shared expectations for the process and get agreement.

The Storytelling Phase

- Have each party explain the situation from their viewpoint to the mediators.
- Balance the interaction with each of the parties; move back and forth between them to keep anger and tension from building up.
- Paraphrase frequently so that the parties will know that you are listening to them.
- Reduce tension and hostility by reflecting feelings and validating the parties.
- Microfocus on each party's moves by "following them around" as they tell their story.
- Probe for underlying needs and interests.
- Encourage perspective-taking by each party; strive for mutual recognition.
- Summarize each viewpoint, checking with the respective parties to make sure that the summary of their view is accurate.
- Evaluate the process to date.

. . . Separate Meetings

- Use this strategy only as a way to support face-to-face mediation — i.e., to help any of the people involved to participate more effectively and/or respectfully in the mediation, or to move the mediation forward. Do NOT engage in shuttle diplomacy.
- Call for separate meetings if and only if they will advance the process.

- Possible uses for separate meetings include: allowing hostile parties to cool down, confronting parties in private about their behavior or an issue, encouraging parties to take the perspective of the other party, receiving private information, and allowing the mediators to work through serious disagreements among themselves.

The Understanding Phase (also called the Exchange Phase)

- Guide the parties in talking directly to one another.
- Allow each party to understand the other's concerns and feelings by modeling and encouraging them to use active listening techniques.
- Especially early on, request that each party paraphrase what they heard the other say. Ask the first party to verify the accuracy of the understanding and correct any misperceptions.
- Begin with an easy issue or an area of common ground between the parties.
- Allow new information or concerns to surface.
- Encourage perspective-taking by each party; strive for mutual recognition.
- Help the parties establish common ground between themselves.

The Resolution Phase

- Help the parties, if they wish, to develop a wise, efficient, and fair agreement.
- Do not suggest solutions yourself; make sure that the parties own the agreement.
- Elicit options from the parties; don't be judgmental at this point.
- Evaluate and refine the alternatives.
- Write the agreement in terms of behaviors, and be as specific as possible.
- Make sure that the agreement seems workable to both parties (reality test it).
- Discuss what to do if there are future problems.
- Write out the agreement and have the parties sign it.

The Closing

- Evaluate the process.
- Validate and affirm the parties; acknowledge what they have accomplished.
- Thank the parties for participating.
- Inform the parties about follow-up procedures.

The Debriefing (after the disputants leave)

- Validate the other mediators; evaluate your teamwork and what you learned about the process.
- Discuss problems or difficulties, but only in a constructive way.
- Prepare a report for the dispute resolution center.

Research Note: Conversation Analysis of Mediation

Angela Garcia (1991) analyzed the process of dispute resolution in a community mediation program in California. She used conversation analysis as the lens to examine this process. In particular, she was interested in how conflict-laden conversations during the mediation process might differ from the conflict resolution procedures used in everyday conversation.

Garcia noted several features of the mediation process that reduce the frequency and volume of interpersonal conflict. First is the fact that, unlike in everyday conversation, in mediation the mediator is in charge of the process. This allows the mediator to serve as a buffer between the disputants.

And what about the process itself limits confrontation? Garcia notes that in mediation the disputants initially address their remarks to the mediator rather than to each other, reducing opportunities for direct personal confrontation.

Second, the prohibition on interruptions while each party tells their story during the mediation process significantly mitigates hostile interactions, whereas in everyday life [as well as in political debates], interruptions are key factors in escalating the conflict.

Thirdly, the specific conversational techniques employed in the mediation process not only reduce overt conflict, but allow disputants to save face Garcia observed the following:

1. Accusations and denials are not adjacent to one another in the turn-taking system of a mediated dispute, thereby reducing the likelihood of escalation to a confrontation.

2. Denials are not made directly to accusations by the other disputant, but to queries from the mediator.

3. The structure of the mediation process creates a delay between accusation and response, allowing a disputant to bypass or ignore some accusations while still saving face.

4. The mediator is able to soften potentially harsh accusations through the use of specific conversational techniques.

As a result, Garcia concludes that "in mediation, the adjacent and directly addressed oppositional utterances that constitute argument do not occur" (1991:827).

DEAR LANDLORD: A Scripted Mediation Roleplay

by Barbara Daté

Participants: Phyllis/Paul; Linda/Larry, Mediator

AUTHOR'S NOTE: In teaching the "classical" mediation process, I've found it helpful to demonstrate the process and its stages in a time-efficient way. I developed this transcript to be read by three volunteers from the audience to illustrate an easy, typical conflict "successfully mediated." It was written to show a few typical problems, but basically to depict the steps as an introduction to "What is mediation?" or the "classical" mediation process. This demonstration roleplay is self-contained and can merely be read out loud. Please note there is a "Before" scene (the usual way we handle conflict) and an "After" scene (one way to mediate) to be read in series simply noting the two scenes. Good Luck!

Scene One: Before Mediation

Phyllis/Paul: Aha!! I finally caught up to you after your Hawaii vacation! You've been late with all your rent checks each month. I want my money right now.

Linda/Larry: I don't have it. I can't pay you right now. And I didn't go to Hawaii for vacation!!!

P: When I came looking for you when your rent was late, your neighbors told me you were in Hawaii! You even sent me a postcard from Hawaii! What do you think I am, dumb?

L: I don't have the money. I just can't pay you now.

P: You think I'm a bank – that I'm loaded?

L: Yes. I don't think you need the money as bad as I do. You can wait.

P: I've been waiting – for two months, and I'm tired of waiting. In fact, I've waited for your check late each month! If you don't pay today, I'll evict you or take you to small claims court. Your choice.

L: You're threatening me! You can't get any money out of me, because I don't have any today. I can pay you with my next paycheck.

P: You have money. You went on vacation. You owe me over $600! I want it today.

L: I don't, I didn't, and I won't.

P: You'll be hearing from me or my lawyer.

Scene Two: The Mediation

[I. INTRODUCTION PHASE]

Mediator: Mediation traditionally has four or five major steps. Today we are going to use five. A typical mediation process includes:

Step 1 Introduction: The mediator facilitates introductions, describes the purpose and process of mediation, gains agreement about certain items (e.g. time constraints, listening) and establishes rapport.

Step 2 Story Telling: Each participant is given the chance to explain his or her problem, giving historical information and identifying the problems – who did or didn't do what when and what the consequences were.

Step 3 Shared feelings: Each participant is given the opportunity to (a) share some more about his or her feelings, the source or evolution of the problems, etc., and (b) reassure understanding of the other person's feelings.

Step 4 Problem solving: Everyone is invited to brainstorm solutions, sift through the alternatives and develop the most promising options.

Step 5 Agreement: The participants are encouraged to fashion workable agreements – to make it clear, concrete and do-able (who, what, when), identify concerns and ways to make the agreement more secure. Finally, they work to agree to mediate any future problems which they are unable to resolve on their own.

If you have any questions, I'd be glad to answer them now or any time along the way.

It would help me out if we could agree in advance about two things. First, how much time we have to work on this today, and second, that we will take turns listening to each other. I understand that we each agreed to take up to two hours today if that becomes necessary. Is that still the case for each of you?

P and L: (nodding) Yes/sure.

Med: Also, I'd like some agreement about taking turns listening to each other. I'd like to know if that is agreeable to each of you…

P and L: OK/yes.

Med: Thanks for your help in this way. It really will help keep the process moving along smoothly.

[II. STORYTELLING STAGE]

Med: The next step in the mediation process is called the Storytelling Stage. It is the opportunity for each of you, in turn, to share your memory of the experience – that is, what you remember happening and what kind of impact that had on you and the problems that have occurred because of it. Since you look quite upset, Phyllis/Paul, I'd like to begin with you. I'd like you to fill me in on the details of the situation from your point of view.

P: I have been renting an apartment to Linda/Larry for six months now. I have our signatures on the rental agreement. S/he refuses to pay me the rent s/he owes me.

L: *(interrupts)* That's not true!

Med: Linda/Larry, please jot down your concern on a piece of paper, you can share that in a few minutes. Now it is Phyllis's/Paul's turn to talk.

P: I can't run a business if the renters won't pay their rent. I can't keep on putting up with this nonsense.

Med: You're frustrated with the nonpayment and disrespect for the contract.

P: You can say that again! When s/he signed the agreement, s/he paid the first month's rent and also the deposits, and I thought, very good, here is someone who will be responsible and I won't have any hassles. But then the second and third month's rent came ten days late. That made me worry. Then the last three months s/he hasn't paid me a cent yet! S/he says s/he can't pay it. I just can't run my rentals this way.

Med: You've consistently experienced her/his failure to pay the rent on time.

P: You've got it. I have to pay the bills and earn money.

Med: Phyllis/Paul, thanks for explaining this clearly to me so I have a picture of what has been happening for you. I may come back to you to get more information later. In the meantime, I want to hear from Linda/Larry. If, while Linda/Larry is sharing you have some comments or information to add, please jot your ideas down on a piece of paper, and I'll make sure you get a chance to talk again later. Linda/Larry, now I'd like to hear what you've experienced.

L: (to P) You act like I'm never going to pay you!

P: That's right. That's what I'm worried about. You went to Hawaii for vacation – you have money.

Med: Phyllis/Paul, this is Linda's Larry's time to speak.

L: The reason I couldn't pay the rent was that I had a family emergency. My mother suddenly had a heart attack. I used my rent money to buy an airplane ticket to Hawaii to see her during surgery. She moved there to live near my sister and her children. Then when I came back I didn't have the money right away. I plan to pay my rent, even though it is late.

P: I didn't know your mother had surgery.

L: You never bothered to ask! My mother almost died!

Med: Linda/Larry, your family emergency prevented you from paying your rent, but you fully intend to pay it.

L: I even sent a postcard from Hawaii explaining this.

P: I didn't get it in time, and I couldn't read the handwriting very well. All I could read was "Dear Landlord."

[III. SHARING FEELINGS]

Med: It would help if each of you would share just a bit of how you are feeling right now.

L: I have been so distressed about my mother. We have always been a close family. Then to get the phone call that my mother had the heart attack. I could only think about getting to her. I didn't stop to think about anything else, bills to pay or anything. Then, Phyllis/Paul got so upset after I got back, s/he seemed totally unreasonable, shouting at me and not listening to anything I was trying to say. I feel like s/he was worse than old Mr. Scrooge!! Just a money grabber. I felt helpless, like there wasn't anything I could do to pay it all and make her/him get off my case.

Med: Phyllis/Paul, it would help here If you would paraphrase what you heard Linda/Larry say – say in your own words a brief summary.

P: Linda/Larry felt…

Med: Say it to Linda/Larry: "You…"

P: You felt frantic about your mother and did what you had to do to pack and get to her. You felt like I was over-reacting and I was deaf to you.

L: Yes.

Med: Ok, Phyllis/Paul, how do you feel about this situation?

P: Well, I feel differently now, since I understand more. But I did feel like Linda/Larry was irresponsible about paying her/his bills on time. That s/he might never pay it, and I'd be out two, maybe three, months rent, and s/he would be living in the apartment so I couldn't rent it to someone else. I have all sorts of bills to pay – electric, garbage, repair bills, saving for a new refrigerator for Linda's/Larry's apartment. I get real worried when I don't get income so I can pay my bills on time! I feel helpless and angry. I knew small claims court wouldn't really solve the problem quickly, so I got madder and madder.

Med: Linda/Larry, I'd like you to paraphrase Phyllis/Paul.

L: You thought I wouldn't pay at all. You felt frustrated – no, worse, victimized.

P: Yes, I did, and I don't like that feeling.

Med: It sounds like there are a number of concerns here.

1. Phyllis/Paul needs to have the rent paid on time or have some agreement about emergency payments.

2. Linda/Larry wants to be assured that if there is a personal emergency, Phyllis/Paul will be flexible.

3. Phyllis/Paul needs to receive back rent payments.

[IV. PROBLEM-SOLVING BRAINSTORMING]

Med: OK. What are some possible options here. Let's brainstorm. Any idea is a good idea in brainstorming. *(**Mediator** should write responses on newsprint or blackboard.)*

L: Phyllis/Paul can be more understanding in an emergency and give me a break!

P: Linda/Larry can pay the rent before the rent is due! S/he can move to a different apartment and then we won't have this problem anymore.

L: You can apply my deposit toward rent.

Med: Linda/Larry, can you offer some creative specific proposals about payment?

L: OK. What if I paid one month's rent today and another month's rent in two weeks?

P: How about paying all three months today?

L: I could do some yard work for rent due.

Med: You've generated a number of options, let's eliminate the ones less acceptable first.

L: I don't want to move.

P: I need the rent paid. The yard work was just done by a landscape architect.

Med: Of the options, I'd like to hear what sounds especially good.

L: Maybe I could pay half of my back rent today. And in two weeks I could pay the other half. Then by the 1st of next month I would pay everything I need to be all caught up.

Med: Phyllis/Paul, I'd like to hear whether you think you could live with that.

P: I'm not thrilled, but I'm willing to be reasonable – as long as I get the money. Will you put it in writing?

Med: All our agreements are written down.

L: This was a bad experience. I'm not planning on any more emergencies, but what if one happens? How can I be sure that Phyllis/Paul won't drag me into small claims court if I have another problem.

P: I could give you 10 days' grace. It would help me if you would let me know as soon as possible what the problem is so I can plan.

L: OK, I will do that.

P: I really want you to pay on time each month, not like the first few months.

L: I will make a real effort. I forget that you have lots of rental-related bills to pay, too. I keep thinking it's just extra income to you.

Med: Phyllis/Paul, if you could say something to Linda/Larry about being open to hearing about a personal emergency, that would help.

P: I thought I did. Well, I see myself as a reasonable and understanding person. So if you can call me right away, I will at least listen to your story. You have 10 days' grace.

Med: Phyllis/Paul, how would you feel about coming back to the mediation table, if there is some difficult problem in the future?

P: Certainly. I think this is a very helpful process to solve this kind of problem.

Med: Linda/Larry?
L: I agree. I thought Phyllis/Paul was a mean, uncaring money monger. I can see now that s/he just needs good information and a bit more responsible payment schedule from me.

[V. Agreement]

Med: So the written agreement states these things:

1. Linda/Larry will make every effort to pay on time.

2. Phyllis/Paul will give Linda/Larry 10 days' grace when necessary due to an emergency.

3. Linda/Larry will inform Phyllis/Paul ASAP if s/he has a problem paying on time.

4. Phyllis/Paul will listen to any problem Linda/Larry brings up.

5. Linda/Larry will pay half the back rent now. The rest of the back rent will be paid in two weeks. By the first of the month Linda/Larry will pay everything necessary to be caught up on the rent.

6. Both of you will call me to mediate any further problems you can't work out alone first.

Does this do it?

L and P: Yes.

Med: Linda/Larry, are you ready to write a check now and both of you sign this?

L and P: Yes.

L: Here is the check, and thank you for working this out. I felt like it was hopeless. I just don't know how to solve this.

P: I appreciate your help,too. This was a lot quicker than going through the litigation system and it was a much better outcome. In fact, I know you much better now – and I sure hope your mother is feeling better soon.

L: She is up and moving about again, thank you for your concern.

Mediation Roleplay: Client/Caseworker Dispute

Below is an example of a case report that would be provided to a mediation team.

DISPUTANTS: Sheryl Johnson, client. 26 year old single parent receiving public assistance
Billie Wilson, caseworker for 11 years

CASE REPORT

Jon, the Director of Family and Social Services, has asked the center to mediate a conflict between a client and caseworker. He received a complaint from the client saying her caseworker was "unprofessional," "on a power trip," and "not really interested in doing her job and helping people." When she was denied benefits, Sheryl Johnson, the client, requested that the Director "do something about this."

Billie Wilson, the caseworker, has said that she was only doing her job. When Ms. Johnson came in for her three-month redetermination of eligibility for benefits, Ms. Wilson attempted to obtain the required information, but Ms Johnson became hostile. She said some bad things about the caseworker, stormed out of the office, and later filed a complaint with the Director. Ms Wilson feels that the complaint is unfair and unjustified. With the new welfare-to-work program, there have been a lot of changes in rules and procedures, and Ms. Wilson feels that the client is confused and/or misinformed. Because the client refused to supply the needed information, the caseworker closed the case and the client was denied benefits.

Both parties have agreed to mediation.

Insert the included DVD and go to the roleplay entitled ***Client/Caseworker Mediation***.

View the following chapters:

Chapter 2: The Opening

Chapter 3: Storytelling

Chapter 4: Exchange

Chapter 5: Agreement

In preparation for your own mediation roleplaying, you may want to read the private background information given to each disputant to help them play their role. Read this material only **AFTER** you have viewed the mediation roleplay. You will find the additional background information in Appendix II in the back of this manual.

Mediation Roleplay: A Landlord/Tenant Dispute

Here is the case report that would be provided to a mediation team.

DISPUTANTS: Marlon Williams, college student
Joan Wells, landlord

CASE REPORT

Marlon Williams, originally from Jamaica, is a student at IPFW who rents an apartment in the Lakeside neighborhood. Marlon has contacted the mediation service about a dispute with his landlord. He says that his landlord, Joan Wells, has recently raised his rent by $75 per month, but has never kept the building up, and it is getting worse. Marlon feels that the roof is in such bad shape that this will be a difficult winter for him. He wants the repairs made and does not want to pay the rent increase until he sees some results. Joan Wells states that she is justified in raising the rent as she has not raised it in three years. She believes that the tenant has caused damage to the property.

Insert the included DVD and go to the roleplay entitled ***Landlord/Tenant Mediation***.

View the following chapters:

Chapter 1: Introduction

Chapter 2: Opening/Storytelling

Chapter 3: Exchange

Chapter 4: Agreement/Closing

After viewing this simulated mediation, you may want to read the private background information given to each disputant to help them play their role. Read this material only **AFTER** you have viewed the mediation roleplay. You will find the additional background information in Appendix II in the back of this manual.

Practitioner's Notes

Roles of Co-Mediators in the Mediation Process

Advantages of Co-Mediation

- Co-mediators provide emotional support and enhance each other's confidence.
- Co-mediators can help keep each other on track in the process.
- Multiple mediators provide a greater number and variety of creative solutions when an impasse is reached.
- Because each mediator has a different personality conflict resolution style and approach, co-mediation provides greater flexibility in responding to the parties.
- Co-mediation allows for the selection of mediators who share some of the salient characteristics of the parties to the dispute.
- When multiple mediators work together they can learn from each other.
- A group of mediators working together models collaboration for the parties to the dispute.
- When multiple mediators work together they can divide up the tasks involved in facilitating the mediation session. One possible way to do this follows.

Guidelines for Working Together

- ✓ Respect, trust, and support your co-mediators.
- ✓ Keep the process transparent.
- ✓ Check in with your co-mediators.
- ✓ Don't interrupt your co-mediators.
- ✓ Promote participation by all the mediators.

Theory

The Social Geometry of Group Size

Georg Simmel [GAY org ZIM el] was a pioneer in the development of sociology in the early 20th century. One of his many interests was in developing a geometry of social relations. In this the number of people in the group was a key factor.

Simmel (1950) began with a group of two people, or a dyad (from the Greek for two). In a dyad there is only one relationship, and therefore the active participation of both members is necessary for the functioning and survival of the group.

1 possible interaction

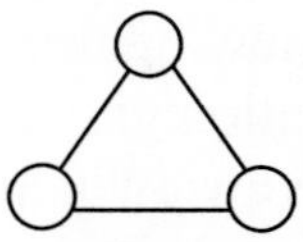

3 possible interactions

In a triad, or group of three people, there are a total of three possible interactions. The group can still function if one of the members chooses not to participate. However, there is also the possibility of coalition formation, in which two members unite against the third. Or the third party can act as a mediator or go-between.

When group size moves beyond three people, the quality of interactions changes rather dramatically, since there are now more interactions than there are members. For instance, in a group of four people there are six possible interactions. In a group of five people the number of interactions is ten.

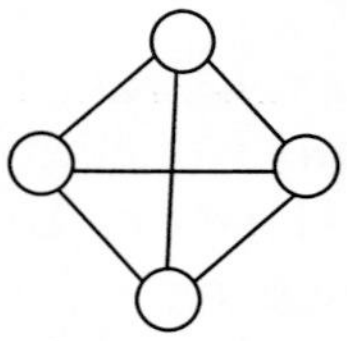

6 possible interactions

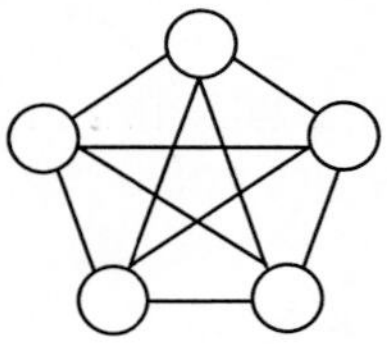

10 possible interactions

From this point on, the number of possible interactions increases exponentially as the size of the group increases. The formula for calculating the number of possible interactions for any size group is

$$\frac{n(n-1)}{2}$$ where **n** = the number of people in the group.

What does this mean for mediation? Generally the conflict relation is a dyad—i.e., the primary parties to the conflict. On the one hand, the pressures of a single relationship may exacerbate the intensity of the conflict. On the other hand, the necessity of both members participating to maintain the relationship may actually facilitate a constructive resolution.

In a conflict situation, a triad introduces the Third Side, with all the benefits that we have seen. A third party can play the roles of bridge-builder, arbiter, mediator, facilitator, equalizer, witness, referee, or peacekeeper.

In this course, you will learn to mediate with a team of two or three mediators. If there are two mediators and two disputants, that is a group of four, with six possible interactions. If there are three mediators and two disputants, that is a group of five, with ten possible interactions. If there are four disputants (see the Get Away From My Bench mediation roleplay later in this manual) and three mediators, that is a group of seven, with twenty-one possible interactions. Managing all of the possible interactions gets complex. To cope, the mediators need to tune into the process and take good notes. Suggestions follow below.

Practitioner's Notes — *Taking Notes in Mediation*

- ✓ Good note-taking is a vital part of the mediation process. It is important to record the concerns of the parties accurately and completely. Good note-taking can help mediators identify common concerns and common ground between the disputants. Further, many disputants are complimented by the fact that you are taking the time to get their concerns recorded accurately.

- ✓ On the other hand, taking notes during mediation can make the disputants nervous or uneasy. When someone is writing down something while we are speaking, we naturally wonder what it is. And when people are nervous or distraught they may expect the worst. First of all, explain to the parties at the outset *why* you will be taking notes. During the session, try to be subtle. If one party notices that you write down more of what the other party said as opposed to what they said, that party is likely to get defensive or hostile. Be aware of the nonverbal messages your writing may convey and avoid the negative ones. Finally, keep your notes concise – don't let note-taking get in the way of actively listening to the parties.

- ✓ One mediator should be the designated note-taker, and should be identified as such to the disputants. This note-taker is responsible for recording all of the important issues raised during the Storytelling and Exchange phases, and for getting the exact wording of what the parties agree to in the Agreement phase. However, keep in mind that the note-taker is not trying to generate a complete record of what everyone said – just the main issues.

- ✓ Assure the disputants of the confidentiality of all notes taken during the meeting. After the mediation is complete, keep the notes with the case file or destroy them.

- ✓ If disputants are interrupting each other because they don't want to forget to respond to what the other person said, consider offering each of them paper and pencil to record their concerns. Just don't allow them to write, doodle, etc. instead of listening to one another.

Suggested format for the note-taker to use:

Disputant #1 [write down the name they wish to be called]	Common Ground	Disputant #2 [write down the name they wish to be called]
[issue]	[Identify areas of common ground. Use arrows or lines, if desired, to connect their issues]	[issue]
[issue]		[issue]
[issue]		[issue]
[issue]		[issue]

Practitioner's Notes

Some General Reflections on the Process of Mediation

Trust the process.

- The process is everything. As mediators you are guardians of the process. Make sure that it is explained and followed. Validate the disputants for following the process.
- Practice the zen of mediation. Study the process and master it. Then, in the mediation itself, let go of all prior expectations, fears, and anxieties. Relax and open yourself up to the process.
- **MAKE THE PROCESS TRANSPARENT.** Don't worry about making mistakes or having false starts; they are inevitable. But remember: you can increase disputants' comfort level by dealing openly and honestly with your own concerns and actions. Communicate openly with your teammates on the mediation panel—there shouldn't be any secrets!
- The disputants are generally ignorant of the process and are looking to you for guidance. Don't be afraid to provide that guidance. While the process is everything, it is not magic or mystical. Educate the disputants on the process as you go.

Use the process.

- **"R-E-S-P-E-C-T. FIND OUT WHAT IT MEANS TO WE."** Convey it to the disputants through frequent validations; model it by demonstrating it toward fellow mediators; help the disputants discover it for each other.
- Be aware of and consciously look for "signpost" moments that can be used to further transformation. Don't let a signpost pass by without dealing with it.
- Don't allow the disputants to get hung up in *positions*—it is the mediators' job to help them see their underlying *interests*, and what interests they might have in common.
- Paraphrasing is less than half restating—most of it is *reflecting* the emotional content.
- Validate the disputants early and often. While it is especially important at the beginning, don't forget to validate throughout.
- Metaphors for mediation:
    - a river – "go with the flow" "it will follow it's own course"
    - a spoked wheel (zen: focus on the spaces)—or, use silence productively
    - "peeling the onion"—peel back the layers of positions to find the interests
    - "learning to drive a stick shift" or "learning to ride a bike"—it seems impossible at first, but once you get it, it's easy

Practitioner's Notes

A "Take" on Emotions in the Mediation Process

Take up the topic of emotions

"Emotions are present in any dispute that touches people's ways of making meaning and their identities or concepts of self." (LeBaron 2002:54) "…personal experiences open up space, inviting listeners to consider context, feelings, and dynamics relating to issues….Asking participants or parties to remember or imagine experiences evokes smells, tastes, sensations, sounds, and images. These sensory memories are recorded in our bodies in ways that connect to the feelings associated with experiences. When we bring the sensory memories into out awareness, the feelings come back, too." (58-9)

"Do my questions and statements to participants include positive references to emotional ways of knowing? Do I share my feelings about the process as it unfolds? Am I modeling attunement with my own and others' emotions, recognizing when breaks are needed, noticing feelings that are expressed but not named?" (58) When talking about the mediation process, use words associated with both positive and negative emotions (e.g., hopeful, optimistic, confident, concerned, apprehensive, worried) Ask parties to talk about situations that worked, that they were pleased with, proud of. Ask about their where they want to be in the future with each other or in their lives.

Do not let emotions **take over** the process

"Although we recognize that emotions are resources, it is also important not to let them 'take over' a process. Because we feel them viscerally, emotions are powerful and have a powerful impact. Emotionally fluent processes are most effective when emotions inform but do not control—when emotions are part of the atmosphere but not the whole weather system." (63) Physiologically, when strong emotions are triggered, our brains are washed in chemicals. Daniel Goleman calls this a neural hijacking. Makes us want to act before the rational part of the brain can figure things out. So: develop strategies for surfacing emotions and validating them.

Do not **take on** the emotions of the parties

As mediators we can unconsciously take on the emotions of the parties. Some of us are more like emotional sponges than others. But we are all tempted.

Take care of yourself as a mediator and a person

The way to deal with this is through specific preparation and closure activities. Before: meditation and visualization. After: meditate and visualize. Imagine the parties as they were. Surround them with goodwill and give them back their realities and their feelings. "Parties don't need you to take over their problems; they need you to help them manage, resolve, or transform them. Make sure you don't offer to carry them along the way. After a few mediations, your bag will be so heavy that you have to put it down if you do." (63-4)

Adapted from Michelle LeBaron (2002)

Practitioner's Notes | *Tips for Role Play Practice*

Role playing is a crucial part of learning mediation. No amount of "book learning" can replace the experience of actually mediating a dispute. The roleplays create a safe environment where trainees can experience the process, try out their developing skills, and experiment with different approaches. Most mediators-in-training will point to roleplays as the best part of the learning process.

The key is to make the roleplay as realistic as possible. Once you are in role, try to stay in that role. Resist the urge to "come out of character." You will learn more about how to handle real-life situations if you treat the roleplays as those situations. Roleplays, as you will no doubt experience, are potentially transformative. Yes, it's "just pretend," but you will find that people generally become absorbed into their roles, and the interactions and feelings generated are both real and pretty much identical to those experienced in a real mediation.

Key to the success of the roleplays is a mutual agreement among everyone involved that, when it comes to those playing the disputants, the group will not confuse the role with the person. This frees the disputant roleplayers to go ahead and play the role authentically, being somewhat hardheaded, obnoxious, or even offensive if the role calls for it (racist, sexist, homophobic, etc.).

Before the roleplay begins, take a moment to center yourself and get into character. You have a responsibility to yourself and your fellow learners to contribute to the best of your ability to an important learning experience.

Tips for Disputants

- Read through the description of your character. Try to imagine yourself as them. What would they be feeling about this conflict? What would their underlying interests be? How would this person behave toward the other disputant(s) and toward the mediators?

- You will probably need to make up some additional details about your character. Just be sure to stay in the spirit of the character as written, and don't make up something that adds a whole new issue of conflict or barrier to a resolution.

- Play the role as realistically and naturally as possible. Present your emotions authentically. Reveal your concerns gradually rather than just state them all at once at the beginning of the mediation.

- Resist the temptation to take the role to extremes: don't be too easy, but don't be too hard on your fellow mediators. After all, they are just learning! You want the mediators to have to work to recognize and empower the disputants and to help them resolve the conflict, but you don't want to make it impossible, either!

- Use your experience as a disputant to see what the mediation process looks and feels like from the perspective as a disputant. Use this knowledge productively when you are a mediator.

Tips for Mediators

- Don't overlook any aspects of the Briefing. In your nervousness and haste to get started, it is too easy to just assign roles for the Opening discussion and then invite the disputants in. Make sure that you leave time to discuss styles and teamwork with your fellow mediators. Also, be sure to do a conflict analysis. This will give you clues to help you decide where to go with the Storytelling phase. Finally, before you start, take time to just breathe and center yourself.

- When you are first learning to mediate, the process seems complex and even overwhelming. But if you get too wrapped up in details, you will miss the big picture of transformation and conflict resolution. Prepare as thoroughly as you can with your fellow mediators, but when the mediation process begins, try to relax into the process and tune in to the disputants. (Practice "the zen of mediation.")

- As you learn to mediate (and even after you are experienced!), it is inevitable that you will make mistakes, become confused, or find yourself at a loss for what to do next. As Buddhist teacher Pema Chödrön (1994) observes, these difficult moments can be the "perfect teacher," if only you will let them. The truth is, we probably learn more from situations that seem to go wrong than from those that seem to go well. You just have to stay present and tune into the moment—which is, of course, exactly what you *don't* feel like doing at that time. You want to escape, to disappear, to melt into the floor. "Most of us do not take these moments as teachings....[Moments like this can] teach us to perk up and lean in when we feel we'd rather collapse and back away." So when you feel frustrated, lost, overwhelmed and not sure what to do next, take a moment and *breathe.* Then tune into what's really going on, not your embarrassment or fear.

- **Make the process transparent**. If you forget a step, explain that you did so and what you're going to do about it. If you forget a disputant's name or misstate something or commit some other social faux pas, don't gloss over it. Acknowledge it, apologize if appropriate, and move forward. Remember: you don't have to be the all-knowing expert. You're basically just a sympathetic fellow human being, albeit with some valuable training, trying to do your best. Your sincere effort will be appreciated.

- Trust and rely on your fellow mediators. If you've prepared properly, you all should be on the same wavelength with regard to this mediation. And if you find you're not, use an I-message to deal with the situation. Remember: you are modeling constructive conflict resolution for the disputants. Consult with your fellow mediators out loud and directly – no whispered side conversations or passing notes!

- Remember that in a mediation roleplay, the mediators are playing roles, too. Go ahead and play the role of an experienced and competent mediator, no matter how confused or uncertain you are ("Fake it till you make it."). Resist the temptation to stop and ask your coach for help. You will learn much more by trying to "muddle through" a difficult situation than you will by getting outside intervention. And it's more realistic!

Tips for Observers

- Observe carefully the impact of the behavior of the mediators on the disputants. Not having to speak or act in the mediation gives you the luxury of observing closely. From what you can see, how does what the mediators say and do affect the disputants? What moves by the mediators are effective and what ones seem less effective or counterproductive?

- Imagine yourself on the mediation panel. In difficult situations, rehearse in your head (or on paper) what you would say or do next if it was up to you. Compare that to what the mediators actually do?

- Try to expand your repertoire of mediation moves by building on the strengths of what you observe the mediators do.

- Imagine yourself as one of the disputants. How would you feel at various points in the mediation? What would you most like the mediators to know and do? Use these insights to build your own skills as a mediator.

- Prepare to give constructive feedback to the mediators when the roleplay is over. Emphasize the positive, pointing out what the mediators said and did that was effective.

Debriefing Roleplays

- When the time comes to stop the roleplay, everyone should take a moment to relax and take a few deep breaths. You've all been working hard!

- The first order of business is for the disputants to take turns telling the panel what they felt and how their feelings changed (or didn't change) during the course of the process. It is helpful if the disputants basically stay in character and speak in the first person about their experience.

- After the disputants have conveyed their experience, they should come completely out of their roles. They should begin to talk about their characters in the third person, and the former members of the mediation panel should address them by their real names and treat them as fellow mediation learners. It is important to make this separation between the person and the role.

- Allow the members of mediation panel to discuss their feelings about the process.

- As a general rule, emphasize the positive. What strategies worked to move the process along? What elements of teamwork were present on the panel? What did the mediators tell the disputants that made them feel safe, engaged, empowered? In retrospect, what might you change about the way things were done? What do you still want to work on?

A Shorthand Guide to Mediation

Here is a 2-page "cheat sheet" that embodies both the main principles of transformative conflict resolution and the steps of the mediation process.

危 danger

機 crucial turning point

CRISIS

Conflict: the expressed struggle of interdependent people who perceive incompatible goals, scarce resources, and interference from each other in achieving their goals.

[adapted from Wilmot & Hocker 1998]

Perception:
"A situation defined as real is real in its consequences."

STYLES	**Accommodating/ Harmonizing**	**Analyzing/ Preserving**	**Achieving/ Directing**	**Affiliating/ Perfecting**
Metaphor	*Human radar*	*Turtle with a computer*	*Semi in the fast lane*	*Bicycle built for 2*
Tactics	Validate; make it safe	Allow reflection; stay calm	Respect autonomy; validate movement	Appeal to principles; hear them out

LISTENING

PARAPHRASING: Restate and **Reflect**

✓ 3-12 words every 3-5 sentences

"You feel ___________ when _____________."
"You're _________ because _______________."

Centered Communication

- **Agreement Stating**
- **Preference Stating**
- **Purpose Stating**
- **Posture of Puzzlement**

Conflict Analysis

- **Perceptions/Assumptions/ Expectations**
- **Feelings**
- **Interests/Needs/Values**
- **Power**
- **Common Ground**

Mediator's Toolbox

- **Paraphrasing**
- **Validating the parties**
- **Expressing confidence in the process**
- **Developing and using shared expectations**

"To change the game, change the frame."

The Power Paradox: The harder you make it for them to say no, the harder you make it for them to say yes.

The Mediation Process

The Briefing (before the disputants arrive)

- Develop teamwork; review basic rules and principles; do a brief conflict analysis.
- Discuss individual strengths and weaknesses, personal styles
- Assign roles for the mediation process; Appropriately arrange the room
- Prepare yourself mentally and emotionally for mediation; do a centering exercise.

The Opening

- Greet the parties, put them at ease; introduce yourselves; agree on names to be used.
- Describe the mediation procedure and the role of the mediators.
- Develop shared expectations for the process and get agreement.

The Storytelling Phase

- Have each party explain the situation from their viewpoint; balance the interaction.
- Paraphrase frequently; reduce tension and hostility by reflecting feelings and validating.
- Probe for needs and interests; encourage perspective-taking; strive for mutual recognition.
- Use externalizing language that makes the problem the problem, not the person.
- Identify and validate, through dialogue, the effect of the conflict on each party.
- Uncover the dominant, taken-for-granted assumptions behind each party's conflict story.
- Help the parties to define and operationalize what they mean by important concepts.
- Draw attention to unstoried experience—i.e., unnoticed, overlooked events.
- Watch for signpost events that can foster empowerment and recognition.
- Highlight agreement, common ground, etc., and ask about its impact on the parties.
- Facilitate the parties in the construction of an alternative story.
- Summarize each viewpoint, check with the respective parties; evaluate the process to date.
- The purpose of this phase is to get to the Understanding Phase. Go slow to go fast.

. . . Separate Meetings

- Use this strategy only as a way to support face-to-face mediation—no shuttle diplomacy.

The Understanding Phase (also called the Exchange Phase)

- Guide the parties in talking directly to one another; encourage them to use active listening.
- Begin with an easy issue or an area of common ground between the parties; allow new information or concerns to surface.
- Encourage perspective-taking by each party; strive for mutual recognition.

The Resolution Phase

- Help the parties, if they wish, to develop a wise, efficient, and fair agreement.
- Do not suggest solutions yourself; elicit options from the parties; don't be judgmental.
- Evaluate and refine the alternatives; reality test them.
- Write the agreement in terms of behaviors, and be as specific as possible.
- Discuss what to do if there are future problems; write out the agreement; everyone signs it.

The Closing

- Evaluate the process; validate and affirm the parties; inform them about follow-up.

Mediation Roleplays: Case Reports and Notes

Below is a list of possible mediation roleplays. You will probably find it useful to record your observations and reflections on each one.

Noise in the (Neighbor) Hood: Gambino vs. Baughman

Case report: Mrs. Alice Gambino, 72, called the mediation center because for the past six months her next door neighbor, Joe (or Jo) Baughman, has been disturbing her with loud music and wild parties. One of her main problems is that she can't get to sleep at night. Mrs. Gambino says that lots of Joe's friends frequently hang out in front of his house, and she says she doesn't feel safe anymore. She has called the police on Joe twice, but the noise is still a problem. Joe Baughman, 25 and single, is Mrs. Gambino's neighbor. He is embarrassed and upset that the police were called – in his judgment, unnecessarily. He has agreed to come to mediation as a way to work on the problem.

Your role:

Other participants in the roleplay:

Observations:

What you did well:

What you'd like to work on:

Fuel for Conflict: Fowler vs. Henson

Case report: Jenna Henson lives in a house next door to a gas station managed by Brook(e) Fowler. Mrs. Henson has a long list of complaints about the gas station, including a drain on the street in front of the gas station that gets plugged up and floods her property, noise and inappropriate activity by teens who frequent the gas station (especially during car washes), and an alarm that goes off frequently, both day and night. Mr. Fowler is tired of being hassled by Mrs. Henson. She is always calling him up and making demands. He doesn't feel that he can do anything to please her. Both parties have agreed to try mediation.

Your role:

Other participants in the roleplay:

Observations:

What you did well:

What you'd like to work on:

Feuding Farmers: Kramer vs. Olson

Case report: Kramer and Olson are feuding over upkeep of their common lane and other issues. Both farms originally belonged to Kramer's father. Kramer bought his farm from his father 15 years ago. Kramer's brother farmed the other land until recently. Two years ago Olson bought Kramer's brother's farm. When Kramer's brother owned Olson's farm, the two would order truckloads of gravel dumped along the entire lane every few years and would split the cost. Legally, the lane belongs to Olson, but the deeds of both farms contain an easement giving Kramer permanent right of access to use the lane. The deeds say nothing about who should pay upkeep expenses on the lane. Recently Olson installed speed bumps on the lane, which are a huge source of irritation to Kramer. At their wits end about how to solve the conflict, both farmers have somewhat reluctantly agreed to mediation.

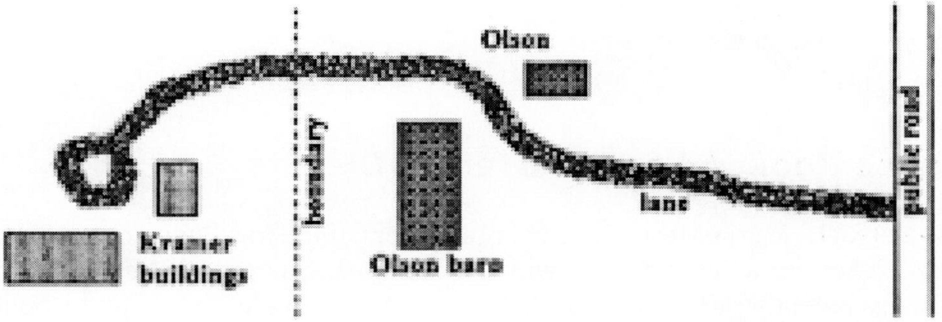

Your role:

Other participants in the roleplay:

Observations:

What you did well:

What you'd like to work on:

The Problem Next Door: McKee vs. Malone

Case report: Misty Malone, her 3 children, and a live-in boyfriend moved in 1 year or so ago next door to Mary McKee. Mrs. McKee, 58, owns her home and has lived there for 22 years. Malone rents her house from a landlord who lives out of town. Mrs. McKee's complaint is that, ever since Ms. Malone moved in next door the place has gone downhill. The grass doesn't get mowed very often and there's trash in the yard that doesn't get picked up. The kids seem to "run wild" around the neighborhood and don't show Mrs. McKee proper respect when she speaks to them. People seem to come and go from the Malone house at all hours, and they drive cars and motorcycles with loud engines and they play loud music on their radios. Misty and her boyfriend both seem to be unemployed. In the eyes of

Mrs. McKee, who works full-time, Ms. Malone seems satisfied to live on welfare and not even try to better herself and her children. In the past, Ms. Malone has not responded to Mrs. McKee's complaints. Mrs. McKee went to the neighborhood association, and the president suggested that she contact the local mediation service. Misty Malone has agreed to mediation as a way to "get Mrs. McKee off my back."

Your role:

Other participants in the roleplay:

Observations:

What you did well:

What you'd like to work on:

Raising the Roof: A Landlord/Tenant Dispute

Case report: Maria/Mario Sanchez is a student at the local university who contacted the mediation service about a dispute with her landlord. She says that her landlord, Joan (John) Wells, has recently raised her rent by $35 per month, but has not kept the building up, and it is getting worse. Maria feels that the roof is in such bad shape that it will be a difficult winter for her. She wants the repairs made and does not want to pay the increased rent until she sees some results. Joan Wells states that she is justified in raising the rent, as she has not raised it in three years. She believes that the tenant has caused damage to the property.

Your role:

Other participants in the roleplay:

Observations:

What you did well:

What you'd like to work on:

Smashing Mailboxes: Victim/Offender Mediation

Case report: The offender, 16, admits to smashing 8 mailboxes with a baseball bat while out joyriding in a friend's car one Friday night. The victims were all on the same street in a neighborhood near the offender's home. The victims complain that this sort of thing happens all too frequently in their neighborhood, which is very close to the local high school. They perceive vandalism and general disrespect from the high school kids to be on the rise lately. The offender admits what he has done, and seems remorseful. The local prosecutor has recommended that this case go to victim/offender mediation. The victims, who are anxious for a resolution of the vandalism problem, have agreed to nominate two representatives to speak for them in the mediation.

Your role:

Other participants in the roleplay:

Observations:

What you did well:

What you'd like to work on:

Workplace Worries: Kelly vs. Pat

Case report: Kelly is head of the claims department of a branch office of a major insurance company. Pat is one of four area coordinators in the office, which includes a total of fifteen employees. This morning there was an angry confrontation between the two over a report which Kelly had assigned to Pat to prepare. Kelly talked to the branch office's Conflict Resolution Coordinator, who has assembled a team of mediators (none of whom are from the claims department). The mediation takes place the next afternoon.

Your role:

Other participants in the roleplay:

Observations:

What you did well:

What you'd like to work on:

Get on the Bus? An Intra-Agency Dispute

Case report: Community Services, Inc. is a five-county social services agency serving the needs of families and children, primarily through administering programs funded with state and federal monies. Two of its programs are Heart Start and a teen program called What's Up? Staff of these two programs generally get along pretty well, but recently a problem has come up. The teen program occasionally plans field trips to sports events, concerts, educational centers, or amusement parks, and has asked for the use of the Head Start buses for transportation to these events. Head Start has resisted the idea, saying the buses were purchased specifically for their program and they don't want to risk damage from the teens. The coordinator of each program has agreed to mediate the conflict.

Your role:

Other participants in the roleplay:

Observations:

What you did well:

What you'd like to work on:

Benched: A College Roommate Dispute

Case report: This is a roommate dispute, between Bob and Ali (or Bobbie and Alia). Bob and Ali, both first year students, decided to room together last fall (it is now March) because they thought that they had a lot in common. Both are immigrants and their families now live in NYC. Ali was born in Egypt, came to the US two years ago, and speaks Arabic at home. He speaks English passably but with some trouble. Bob was born in St. Moritz, Switzerland, and speaks Italian at home. His English is fluent including American slang, and he also speaks French and German. He has lived in the US for five years. Ali was raised as a Muslim and Bob was raised as a Roman Catholic.

At the university, Bob immediately made lots of friends, and at first invited Ali to join in to their activities. Ali always refused and Bob has quit inviting him. At first they did a lot together but now Bob mostly does things with his other friends. Now Bob rarely even comes in their room alone except to sleep. Bob and Ali rarely speak. Ali does not like most of Bob's other friends. Bob's friends come over to the room a couple of times a month. Very often they drink and their voices get loud. Ali complains and says he can't study. Ali also objects to alcohol on religious grounds.

Last week Bob and his friends were chugalugging in the room, and tried very hard to get Ali to join in. The more he resisted, the nastier the comments became, until finally one of the friends made some really insulting comments. Ali was so upset that he left the room and has since slept on a bench in the lobby. Ali and Bob have reached a hurtful stalemate. Ali's TA called Bob to discuss mediation. Bob agreed to mediate but acts as though he does not take mediation seriously. Ali made the initial call to request mediation.

Your role:

Other participants in the roleplay:

Observations:

What you did well:

What you'd like to work on:

"Political" Studies: Books vs. Activism on Campus

Case report: Chris Billups, DeShaun Johnson, and Terry Michaels are students in the same residence hall. DeShaun and Terry (both African-American students) are roommates while Chris (a Euro-American student) has a single room next to them. There have been some problems between Chris and DeShaun and Terry over what is an acceptable level of activity and noise. DeShaun and Terry hold frequent meetings in their room. Last week, Chris and some of his/her friends called the campus police because Chris found it difficult to concentrate because of a meeting being held in DeShaun and Terry's room. After the campus police confronted them and asked them to "keep it down," DeShaun, Terry, and their guests were furious and went to Chris' room and angry, accusatory words were exchanged. The head of the residence was alerted and after an hour, she was able to quiet things down. Since these problems seemed to have gone on for some time, the residence manager referred Chris, DeShaun, and Terry to the mediation program.

Your role:

Other participants in the roleplay:

Observations:

What you did well:

What you'd like to work on:

Trouble in the House: The Stuckyville Home Dispute

Case report: Anne Nicholson is 43 years old and has a daughter, aged 16, named Julia. Anne's brother, Robert Stewart, recently died in an automobile accident at age 47. Robert had a will in which he left all of his property, belongings, assets and accounts to his wife, Susan. Robert and Susan have two children, ages 8 and 12. Since her divorce seven years ago, Anne and Julia have lived in Anne and Robert's parents' home in Stuckyville.

Both Anne and Robert grew up living in the Stuckyville home, which the parents owned for over forty years. Both parents had moved into a nearby assisted-living facility two years before Anne moved back to Stuckyville. During that time, Robert arranged for renters to live in the home for a year. The tenants paid their monthly rent to Robert, and Robert took care of minor maintenance repairs. Robert terminated the tenants' lease so that Anne and Julia could move into the home. Anne has not paid rent while living in the home but has taken care of the home as her own, as well as paid for major renovations and new appliances.

Because of his education and expertise as an accountant, Robert handled the parents' financial affairs. The parents had ownership title to the Stuckyville home placed in Robert's name because they feared their mounting medical bills would cause creditors to take the home. The parents also listed Robert as a joint account holder to their bank accounts, cars, and as sole beneficiary to their life insurance policies. Both parents have passed away in the past 2 years.

Robert has owned a home three blocks from the Stuckyville property since he got married 20 years ago. Robert was very successful in business and worked as a partner with a national accounting firm. Susan is also an accountant and has a part-time tax service business, which she runs out of her home.

Unlike her more studious and ambitious older brother, Anne was somewhat of a "free spirit" growing up. Despite her parent's protests, Anne dropped out of high school. She moved to various places around the country and worked mainly temporary clerical jobs. After her divorce, Anne reconciled with her parents and was a committed mother and daughter. Anne's parents were pleased that she had come home and invited her to live in the Stuckyville home with Julia. Anne has not had a steady job but is actively involved in her child's schooling and other community volunteer projects. Anne also made daily visits and brought special meals to her parents during the last five years of their life.

After Robert's death, Susan instructed her attorney to evict Anne and Julia from the Stuckyville home. The home has appreciated substantially in value over the years. Stuckyville has become a popular resort town, and real estate is extremely valuable. Although the parents paid only $35,000 for the home years ago, the home is currently valued at $1.5 million. Anne has filed a legal action against Susan, seeking to enjoin the eviction and to establish that the home belongs to her and Julia. Prior to the hearing, the two have agreed to meet in a mediation.

Problem drafted by Maureen Weston to be used for the 2001 ABA Representation in Mediation Competition. Modified by Patrick J. Ashton. Permission to reproduce for individual classroom use granted.

Your role:

Other participants in the roleplay:

Observations:

What you did well:

What you'd like to work on:

Once in a Blue Moon: A Smashing Success?

Case Report: Katrin is the owner of a popular restaurant called the Blue Moon Café which is located in the center of Tomsk. The restaurant has been open for the past three years and has established a reputation for excellent quality food at reasonable prices. Recently Katrin converted the back room of the restaurant into a martini bar. She bought nice tables and chairs for the bar and installed a beautiful custom designed granite counter for the bar. She picked moon shaped lights to hang over the bar and set up a small stage area so that she could have a space for jazz musicians to play.

Katrin decided to have a grand opening where she would serve only top quality vodka. She spent a lot of money promoting and advertising the grand opening and hired a band to play at the martini bar for the first night. The Blue Moon Martini Bar was all ready and the only things Katrin had to do were stock the bar with top quality vodka and buy the glassware for the bar. Leo, the guy who supplies the meat for the restaurant, offered to supply both the vodka and the glassware. He sent Katrin a proposal for 10 cases of vodka and 300 glasses and she approved it.

On opening night, the delivery was late, and included vodkas in a range of qualities, instead of top quality only. Furthermore, the glasses were wine glasses, not vodka glasses. Because Katrin was embarrassed by the mistakes, she felt she had to offer free drinks to her patrons. Because Leo's errors caused her to be humiliated and lose money, Katrin sent a note to Leo saying she has no intention of paying for the vodka and that he should pick up the remaining glasses before she smashes them. Leo filed a claim with the Arbitrazh Court for $2,100 – $2,000 for the vodka and the glasses plus $100.00 for a delivery fee. He has requested filing fees as well.

Russian/American Rule of Law Consortium. Modified by Patrick J. Ashton

Your role:

Other participants in the roleplay:

Observations:

What you did well:

What you'd like to work on:

Get Away From My Bench: Multiparty Dispute at the Community Center

Case report: Chas' Place is a community center funded by the United Way. It has a full-time director (Richard/Renee McMurtry) and several part-time activity directors, as well as a number of volunteers. The mission of Chas' Place is to serve the primarily low-income neighborhood in which it is located. To do this, the center provides programming directed at residents of all ages. Many of the programs during the day are for senior citizens; there is an after-school program for teens, and evening activities for adults. In front of the center there is a grassy park area which includes benches and all-weather chess boards molded onto tables. The senior citizens enjoy congregating in this area, sitting on the benches, playing chess, and chatting with one another before and after their programs. When the teenagers come after school for their programs, they too meet and hang out in the park area. Lately the teens and seniors have not been getting along. There have been loud shouting, some name calling, and complaints registered on both sides. The main complaints center around the music the teens play on boomboxes they bring. The seniors say the music is too loud. The teens say that they have a right to use the center, too – and the seniors have had it to themselves all day. Each group claims to be disrespected by the other. As complaints and confrontations escalated, the director decided to contact the local mediation service. Each group has chosen 2 representatives to mediate the dispute. The director will attend as well.

Your role:

Other participants in the roleplay:

Observations:

What you did well:

What you'd like to work on:

Practitioner's Notes *Detailed Description of Each Phase of the Mediation Process*

The Briefing (before the parties arrive)

Purpose
- To develop teamwork among the mediators.
- To ensure that the mediators are in basic agreement about principles and process.
- To generate ideas about the process.
- To prepare the mediation space and the mediators.

✓ **Arrive at least a half hour before the mediation is scheduled to begin.**
It is important to have time for some friendly small talk with your fellow mediators to build solidarity and a sense of teamwork. This is especially important if you don't know each other well or haven't mediated together before.

✓ **Review the basic rules and principles of transformative mediation.**
Don't assume that everyone is on the same page. Go over the principles of empowerment and recognition and the priorities of each phase of the mediation process.

✓ **Review the background details of the case before you.**
Do a brief conflict analysis of the dispute, focusing on underlying needs and interests and potential common ground. The idea is not to decide the outcome of the dispute in advance (that is for the parties to decide), but rather to share ideas about how to help the parties tell their individual stories and to shape a new common story.

✓ **Discuss how you will each contribute to the mediation team.**
Discuss each mediator's personal style and how it contributes to the team. Share personal strengths and weaknesses with regard to mediation, potential blind spots, personal flash points, and how the other mediators can help you to become a better mediator. Give each other permission to intervene, guide, and support one another during the session.

✓ **Establish the roles each of the mediators will take during the process.**
Different teams will decide differently how to handle this, based on the members of the mediation team, the nature of the dispute and the parties involved. It is generally useful to have one person serve as the primary notetaker for the mediation, and to identify them as such to the parties. Some mediation teams may assign one member to pay particular attention to the socioemotional state of the parties—or a member of the team may be assigned to each party. Regardless of how the roles are distributed, it is important for the mediation team to present itself as a team of peers, with no one individual "in charge."

✓ **Plan carefully how you will open the mediation session.**
First impressions are important. Discuss how the parties will be greeted and brought into the room. (Will all the mediators greet the parties? One mediator? One mediator for each party?) Plan who will cover what during the Opening phase. It is important that each

mediator have a role in explaining the process so that it is apparent to the parties that the mediators are a team of peers. Here are issues covered in the Opening to which you may want to assign individual mediators:

- Welcome the parties and validate their decision to mediate their dispute.
- Give an overview of how the session will work.
- Lead the discussion on shared expectations of how to work together (ground rules).
- Explain the role of the notetaker.

Discuss how you will decide which party will start the Storytelling Phase. Will the mediators make a suggestion? Will you offer to let the parties decide? Which strategy will best advance the process? You may want to assign one mediator to each of the parties to be the first to address and paraphrase that party. After that, of course, the whole team of mediators should be involved. But sometimes assigning a mediator to begin with each party ensures that the conversation gets off to a smooth start.

✓ **Arrange the mediation space appropriately.**
Examine the mediation space carefully and prepare it so that it best facilitates transformative mediation.

- Know the smoking and parking regulations for the location where you are meeting. Where are the nearest restrooms? Are they open? Where will the parties wait? Think carefully about the security and comfort of the parties and the mediators.
- Examine the mediation space. Is the room temperature comfortable? Is the lighting appropriate? Can it be adjusted? Is there privacy? What can be done to minimize interruptions? Do what you can to screen out any extraneous noise.
- Think carefully about the type and placement of seating. Are the chairs moveable? Will tables be used? How might they be benefits or barriers? Create a seating arrangement that will
  - allow everyone to see and hear one another
  - neither create nor allow distractions
  - create a feeling of safety and comfort
  - allow the mediators to facilitate the process
  - suggest mediator impartiality

✓ **Prepare yourself for the mediation.**
Sometimes in the effort to work out all the practical details of the mediation—assigning roles, arranging space, etc.—mediators can temporarily forget or overlook the primary reason they are there: to facilitate the process of transformative mediation. Take a moment before you transition to the actual mediation to center yourself and focus on the process, both as an individual and as a team. A short breathing exercise is recommended. The team may also engage in a brief, informal ritual of affirmation and commitment to the process.

The Opening

Purpose

- To put the parties at ease with the mediators and the process.
- To set a confident, positive, and respectful tone.
- To make clear the roles of each person present.
- To establish clear ground rules or guidelines for the mediation, including those that the parties agree to establish themselves.
- To establish empowerment and recognition as goals of the process.

✓ **Greet the parties when they arrive.**
Greet each party in an equally friendly fashion. Engage in small talk if you wish, but not too much, as you don't want to seem overly friendly toward one party over the other. Do not get drawn in to discussing the case. Find out how each party wishes to be addressed. Escort them into the room, show the parties to their seats, and perform introductions.

✓ **Make the Opening a conversation, not a statement or speech.**
Speak in a conversational tone; look at and address the parties directly. Attempt to draw them in in a polite and friendly way. Empower the parties right from the beginning by telling them that the purpose of the mediation is for them to have a conversation about what is important to them.

✓ **Acknowledge and validate the parties.**
Let the parties know that you appreciate and respect their decision to mediate their dispute. Acknowledge that conflict can be uncomfortable, but assure them that, as a mediator, you will help them to make the process as respectful and productive as possible.

✓ **Establish the roles of the mediators and the parties.**
Explain that the mediators are completely neutral and will not take anyone's side against anyone else; that the mediators are not judges or jurors and are not there to determine who is right or wrong. Rather, the mediators are there the help the process of mediation work by helping the parties to talk with one another. The parties themselves are in charge of the issues and any resolution. Stress to the parties that there is no agreement unless they both (or all) agree to it. The mediators facilitate the process; the parties control the direction of the process and any outcomes.

✓ **Develop the shared expectations and ground rules and get agreement to them.**
Explain that the mediation process is fundamentally about empowering each party to be able to tell their story and be heard and to establish or build on mutual respect between the parties. Suggest that, in order for the process to work well, there ought to be some shared understandings or ground rules. Elicit ideas from the parties by asking, "How would you like to work together on this?" Don't just focus on creating a lot of rules. Instead focus the discussion on principles and social dynamics. Include positive statements if at all possible. The mediators may want to ask the parties how they want to deal with interruptions. For instance: Let the other person finish speaking before you reply. Another topic mediators may want to bring up if the parties do not is mutual respect. For instance, what does it mean

in relation to name-calling or sarcasm? When you've got a set of basic guidelines, ask each party in turn if they agree to follow them. The mediators should explicitly agree to abide by any guidelines as well. Let the parties know that by mutual consent they can modify existing ground rules or establish new ones as the process unfolds.

✓ **Assure them of mediator confidentiality and check the parties' expectations of each other.**
Explain that the mediators will not disclose outside of the mediation session the names of the parties, the nature of their concerns, or anything that is discussed during the session. Ask the parties about their expectations of confidentiality of each other. If one party is concerned about the other party keeping information confidential, that can be made part of the written shared understandings. The parties can, of course, agree to disclose to others anything they discuss, but the agreement must be mutual and should be put in writing during the Resolution Phase.

✓ **Explain how the mediation process will work.**
Briefly explain each phase of the mediation process and what you will ask the parties to do in each phase. Don't go into too much detail at this point, as the parties are likely to be nervous and not processing a lot. Don't portray the mediation process as a search for truth or an effort to "get to the bottom of things." Emphasize that it's about empowering the parties to make their own resolution. Note that a resolution statement can include a variety of things, including statements about new information discovered in the process, new understandings reached, as well as actions that will be taken in good faith afterwards. Explain why one or more mediators will be taking notes during the session. Clarify the time frame for the session, and mention the possibility of a subsequent session if you don't finish.

✓ **Express confidence in the process and set a positive tone.**
Acknowledge and validate the parties again for choosing to mediate their dispute. Express your confidence in the process of mediation. Reinforce that the mediation belongs to the parties. Any agreement that is reached will be their agreement—i.e., one to which they both (or all) agree. There is no agreement unless they agree. The parties will be nervous as you move closer to actually discussing the conflict, so it is important here to set a confident, positive tone. According to Dukes et al. (2000:108), "People tend to attribute their success or failure to four things: ability, effort, luck, or difficulty of the task. If people can be encouraged to attribute their success or failure to effort, then they will believe that the matter is within their control. If they attribute the outcome to ability, luck, or difficulty of the task, then they believe it is beyond their control. Recognizing effort and accomplishment derived from effort motivates and inspires people."

✓ **Ask for questions and get agreement to continue.**
Ask each party if they have any questions. Answer any questions briefly and specifically, especially if they are about rules, process, or policy. Don't get dragged into assuming the outcome or discussing what might happen. Tell the parties that you want the process to unfold and that your job as a mediator is to make sure the process and the ground rules are followed. Ask each party if they are willing to go ahead with the mediation session.

NOTES:

- The Opening does not consist of mere "preliminaries" to get out of the way so that you can get to the "real" business of mediation. Rather, the Opening is an integral part of the process itself. It sets the tone and provides the first opportunities for empowerment and recognition. Taking the time here to focus on process will almost always pay off later. It is a prime example of "going slow to go fast."

- If there is more than one mediator, make sure that you take turns talking during the Opening Phase. If only one mediator talks, it may seem to the parties that the talkative mediator is "in charge." You want to present the mediators as a team.

- Use simple, everyday language in your opening statement. Don't talk down to the parties, but don't use specialized jargon from the field of mediation, law, psychology, or any other professional area. By communicating clearly with the parties, you empower them to be part of the process.

- Model teamwork among the mediators. Be supportive and helpful of one another.

- Make the process transparent. If you or another mediator skip a step or a part of the opening, go back and cover it. No apologies are necessary. It is important to convey to the parties that the mediators are only human and can make mistakes, but the process is powerful.

The Storytelling Phase

Purpose

- To give each party an uninterrupted chance to tell their story and be heard.
- To reduce tension and hostility by giving each party a chance to vent their feelings toward the mediators rather than each other.
- To foster empowerment of each party and recognition between the parties.

✓ **Explain this phase to the parties.**
Explain that you will give each party an uninterrupted opportunity to describe the situation from their point of view to the mediators. Emphasize that each party should talk to the mediators and not to the other party at this point. Acknowledge that it may be difficult for the party not speaking to sit quietly and listen, but assure them that they will have their turn to speak as well. Suggest that the party who is listening try to listen for something new — something that they didn't know before. In addition, suggest that if the listening party thinks of something they want to say, they make a short note to themselves. Be sure to provide paper and a pen or pencil, if desired, so that they can do this.

✓ **Select one of the parties to begin.**
You may want to begin with the party that initiated the complaint, or the party who seems to be the most agitated, or you may want to ask one of the parties to volunteer. Or you may

want to just arbitrarily choose one of the parties. Whatever you do, briefly explain the rationale for your choice so that the process is transparent.

✓ **Use active listening and centered communication techniques.**
Attend carefully while each party is speaking. Take cues from the speaker about what is comfortable and culturally appropriate in terms of eye contact, distance, language, etc. After a party has presented 2–3 paragraphs of information, paraphrase what you heard them say so that they know that they were heard. Reflect the feelings that you hear each party express. *Don't worry that you might be interrupting the flow of their story by paraphrasing. It is vitally important that you let the person know that you hear what they are saying, and that you establish the pattern of paraphrasing early in the process.* In general, try not to ask questions. As you paraphrase, be conscious of framing the story in a way that legitimates, not undermines, the speaker. Remember: it is their story and they should not lose face by telling it. Model centered communication by using I-messages. ("I'd like for you to tell me more about the problem.")

✓ **Paraphrase each party's story in a way that avoids stereotypes, unsupported generalizations about people and groups, and holds them accountable for their own views.**
While you want to paraphrase the parties accurately, at the same time you want to avoid repeating or in any way lending support to stereotypes and unsupported generalizations about categories of people. Use of stereotypes undermines the process because they are contrary to the goals of empowerment and recognition. Among other things, stereotypes potentially deny the individuality and humanity of the other party. Whether stereotypes are expressed out of sheer ignorance or used as a conscious tactic, they should be constructively challenged by the mediators through reframing. (See information and exercises later in the Manual.) Inflammatory or hateful language should always be challenged by the mediators (through reframing or the use of an I-message), since silence is most often interpreted as agreement. Finally, paraphrasing should be done in a way that encourages each party to take responsibility for their own views and be accountable for their own actions. Encourage the parties to talk about specific behaviors, not just generalized wrongdoing or failure: e.g., when someone says "He's just a lousy neighbor," you say, "I'd like you to tell me some of the things that ________ does that you find problematic." Similarly, don't let the parties speak for others. "No one in the neighborhood likes him." You say: "I'd like for you to tell me about your specific experience with ________."

✓ **Validate each party, early and as often as is helpful.**
Validate them for the hard work that they are doing in discussing the conflict and observing the shared expectations or guidelines. Positive reinforcement is a powerful motivator. The components of effective praise are that it (1) follows the behavior immediately; (2) is specific, i.e., tied to behavior; and (3) is credible and appropriate.

✓ **Remind the parties as necessary about their shared expectations of how to work together.**
Do this in a supportive, empowering fashion. Don't act as a judge, police officer, or parent. Too much emphasis on "the rules" can impede the process. You want to encourage the parties to be respectful, not scold them for not following the rules. NEVER "shush" a

party. If interruptions are a problem, assure the party who interrupts that they will have an uninterrupted time to speak as well. Continued violations of the guidelines or shared expectations may indicate a need to revisit them. Don't hesitate to bring this up if you feel the process is being impaired. Remember: you want to empower the parties to own the process as well as the resolution.

✓ **Move the uninterrupted speaking time back and forth between the parties to keep anger and hostility from building up.**
Try to give each party as much uninterrupted speaking time as they seem to need at one time. However, if the other party is becoming agitated (i.e., if their "emotional balloon" is growing and in danger of exploding), look for an opening and gently but firmly stop the first party, assuring them that you will come back to them and that they will have an opportunity to say everything they want to before you're finished. When you get multiple interruptions by the same party, it can mean that you're not paying enough attention to them. Consider exploring with them why they are having difficulty listening to the other party. The goal is to be respectful and draw them into the process.

✓ **Don't interrogate the parties about the facts of the dispute.**
Don't portray the process as a search for truth. Remember: as a mediator, you are neither judge nor jury. You are there to facilitate the process; the parties will decide about the dispute. *Only rarely* do questions need to be asked to obtain clarification of an important detail. For the most part, the mediators should "follow the parties around" as they tell their stories. Microfocus on each move a party makes: paraphrase, summarize, and reframe what each party tells you in order to probe for underlying needs and interests and foster empowerment and recognition. Never badger, confront, or try to trap a disputant. Remember: the *mediators'* need for specific information about the dispute is *largely irrelevant.* The issue is: what do the disputants need to hear *from each other* in order to allow them to move on? The whole point of this phase is to make it possible for the disputants to get to the next phase—the Understanding Phase. Don't waste time doing anything else here.

✓ **Don't get bogged down in the history or the details of the dispute.**
Often parties come in with a detailed mental list of accumulated grievances. They believe that they can "win" by having a longer list or more details. You can avoid getting overwhelmed in detail by looking for underlying needs and interests and paraphrasing those. Once a party is confident that you really understand their underlying concerns, they will have less need to provide endless details. Remember: the history of the dispute is not what's important—improving the relationship is.

✓ **Try to avoid discussion of an agreement at this point.**
Until the parties have vented their feelings and begun to listen to one another, any discussion of an agreement is premature. Tell the parties that you will make note of any suggested points of agreement and come back to them later. Then be sure that you write these points in your notes.

✓ **Probe for underlying needs and interests; look for common ground.**
Don't encourage confrontation and don't emphasize differences; look for commonalities. Use paraphrasing and reframing to assist the parties in recognizing underlying needs and interests. Help the parties discover and identify areas of common ground, as this will be the

basis of a wise resolution. Launder and reframe negative or confrontational comments into neutral or positive statements. Remember that the most important kind of common ground is *emotional* common ground. It is the key to the transformative model.

✓ **Use silence appropriately and creatively.**
Don't be afraid of silence. Don't feel that you need to rush in and fill all the empty spaces with conversation. Sometimes parties need time to process the new information that they are getting or to review and revise their personal agenda. Respectful silence allows them to do this. Also, silence can heighten the impact of a powerful emotional statement, or reinforce a moment of recognition. Silence can also allow the mediators to mentally regroup.

✓ **Summarize the issues, needs, and interests of the parties as you have heard them.**
Periodically summarize what you have heard each party tell you. *Never ask "Is there anything else?" unless you summarize first.* Make sure that you summarize feelings as well as facts. Keep the list relatively short—3-5 issues is generally about right. Much more than that and you risk having the parties feel overwhelmed. Restate, reflect, and probe until each party agrees that you understand all their main points—especially their underlying interests. Help the parties with mutual recognition by identifying areas of potential common ground.

✓ **When everyone is ready, prepare to move on.**
When both parties are satisfied with the summaries of their concerns, and the mediators are satisfied that the parties are sufficiently empowered, it is time to move on. The mediators should be able to answer the following questions in the affirmative: 1) Have the main issues, needs, and interests of each party been heard? 2) Have these issues been clearly and succinctly identified and summarized by the mediators? 3) Are the parties ready to talk with each other now? (Consider asking them this question directly.) If not, then additional restating and reflecting are needed. If you're ready to move on, validate the hard work the parties have done so far and express confidence about their ability to find a resolution.

✓ **Check in on the process.**
Ask the parties how they are doing with regard to their shared expectations. Is there anything that they would modify or add at this point? By discussing this now before moving on, you are contributing to empowerment and recognition.

✓ **Take a brief break and regroup.**
Tell the parties that you need a brief break to prepare for the next phase. Have at least one mediator show the parties the restrooms and where to get a drink of water, if necessary. The remaining mediators decide how they will begin the Understanding Phase. The usual custom is to choose something upon which the parties already seem to be moving toward agreement, or some area of common ground.

NOTES:

- Model the process. If we expect the parties to listen to one another in the next phase, then we should "walk the talk" by modeling the techniques of active listening from the beginning. Paraphrase the parties and validate them for doing good paraphrasing.

- ***Make the mediation process transparent.*** Mediators should avoid whispering among themselves or writing notes to one another during the mediation. In order to build confidence and trust, there should be no secrets. Talk about the process, if necessary, out loud in front of the parties. This will give them confidence that the process is not mysterious and there really are no secrets.

. . . Separate Meetings

Purposes:

- To empower parties to more effectively participate in mediation.
- To facilitate the mediation process by dealing constructively and privately with unhelpful behaviors.
- To give the mediators an opportunity to confer privately.

✓ **Call for separate meetings whenever you think that they are the most productive way to advance the goals of transformative mediation. Among other things, use separate meetings to:**

- calm down and cool off people who are in a rage.
- interrupt unhelpful behaviors and seek compliance with the rules or shared guidelines while saving face for the party involved.
- confront people privately about destructive or hostile behaviors that undermine the mediation.
- empower a shy or fearful person a chance to speak their mind.
- empower people to think about their needs and interests.
- get at private information that one party isn't comfortable sharing with the other party.
- encourage parties to take the perspective of the other party.
- help the discussion get unstuck.
- consult with your co-mediators about strategy, disagreements over process and style, and concerns about impartiality or confidentiality.

✓ **Once you decide separate meetings are necessary, make them a seamless part of the process.**

Call for separate meetings in a straightforward, matter-of-fact way. Emphasize the potentially helpful role of separate meetings; avoid portraying the decision to use them as a crisis, a failure, or a lack of nerve on the part of the mediators. Again, be transparent about the process. Empower the parties, if possible, to be part of the decision to go in this direction.

✓ **Make sure the separate meetings are balanced and evenhanded.**

Always meet with each of the parties so that impartiality is maintained. If all the mediators meet with one party at a time, give the other party something to do, and tell them when you will get back to them. Check in with them if you run longer than anticipated.

✓ **Assure the parties in each separate meeting of confidentiality.**
State that you will not repeat anything a party says during a separate meeting without their permission. If you think it would be beneficial to share some of what they said with the other party, ask their permission to share it.

✓ **Be clear about the purpose of a separate meeting.**
The mediators should be clear themselves on why they called a separate meeting and what they hope to accomplish. They should convey this, in the most appropriate way, to the parties in the meetings. Once again, it is inappropriate to keep secrets from the parties.

✓ **Report the results of the separate meetings, as appropriate.**
When you reconvene, acknowledge the separate meetings and validate the parties. Report what you agreed to disclose and check with the parties to make sure you got it right. Ask if they have anything to add before moving on. Use the separate meetings as a springboard to move the mediation forward.

The Understanding Phase (or Exchange Phase)

Purposes:

- To foster mutual understanding between the parties by encouraging and facilitating direct communication between them.
- To allow the parties to develop empathy for one another.
- To allow the parties to discover areas of common concern.
- To allow new information, concerns, and feelings to be shared by the parties.

✓ **Establish the context for the parties to talk directly with one another.**
Seat the parties so that they are facing one another at a comfortable distance. Explain that, in this phase, they will primarily be talking to one another. Check to see if the parties are willing to go with the same ground rules or shared guidelines established at the beginning of the mediation, or if they would add or modify anything at this point. Get agreement from everyone to any changes.

✓ **Guide the parties in talking with one another.**
Begin with the issue you have chosen during the break. Ask one party to speak to the other party about it. Ask the other party to listen without interrupting, then to paraphrase what they heard, and verify their perception with the first party. *Don't be afraid to intervene to make each chunk of information manageable to paraphrase.* ("Janelle, I'd like you to stop there so that Betsy can paraphrase what you just said.") Especially at the start, coach the parties in using "I" messages and in restating before responding. Also, gently remind the parties not to refer to each other in the third person. They should be talking to each other and using second-person pronouns: *you, your, yours.*

✓ **Balance intervention with allowing the parties to talk to one another unimpeded.**
Gently remind the parties to use paraphrasing when you don't think they're hearing one another. If one of the parties has a hard time constructing an adequate paraphrase, model a good one for them, then the next time encourage them to try it themselves. Guide them

only when they get stuck or off the track. On the other hand, if the parties are talking with one another and building empathy, let them go. If they're communicating, that's good! Remember, it's their problem and it will be their resolution, so let them talk about it.

✓ **Model centered communication techniques to help the parties understand one another.**
Use these techniques—agreement, preference, and purpose stating, posture of puzzlement, and spirit of inquiry—to encourage each party to consider new information or the other party's point of view and as a model of how to communicate effectively.

✓ **Help the parties reframe issues.**
Reframing acknowledges an individual's experience while at the same time reconfiguring, reinterpreting, or reconstituting it in a more constructive way.

✓ **Listen for new information and common ground.**
When you hear a party surface new information, write it down and check to see if the other party heard it, too. Keep notes on possible areas of common ground. Reality-check these with the parties after they have talked for a while. When appropriate, summarize the discussion and check to see if they have anything to add.

✓ **Validate their efforts.**
This phase can be anxiety-provoking, emotional, and uncomfortable. Acknowledge and validate the efforts and successes of the parties. Remember that framing success as attributable to effort will encourage the parties.

✓ **Don't let them move to the Resolution Phase too soon.**
Make sure that the parties have really heard one another and have acknowledged new information. In the rush of good feeling when a transformative breakthrough has been achieved, the parties will sometimes want to immediately move to discussing an agreement. Encourage them not to do so until you make sure that they've dealt with all the underlying concerns and interests that surfaced during the Storytelling Phase. Check your notes and then check with the parties.

NOTE: You know the parties are ready to move on when they have developed some level of empathy and trust in addition to an understanding of the issues at hand and the underlying interests.

The Resolution Phase

Purposes:

- To allow the parties to recognize and acknowledge what they have accomplished.
- To develop, if the parties wish, an agreement that is wise, efficient, and fair.
- To ensure that any agreement is workable for the parties.

✓ **Help the parties set an agenda for discussing resolution.**
Summarize the issues discussed. Ensure that the list includes each party's concerns, but present problems as shared concerns wherever possible. Help the parties clarify the

principles that will guide their decisionmaking in this phase. Elicit from the parties principles that will be used to evaluate any solutions. Help the parties brainstorm ways to reframe their concerns as issues that can be resolved. Be clear about what is off limits for any agreement. Use positive, impartial language. Prioritize the agenda.

✓ **Begin with shared understandings.**
Begin by writing down areas of consensus or common ground as well as new understandings or ways of communicating established by the parties. This not only sets a positive tone for any resolution, but it empowers the parties to note how they have improved their ability to resolve this and future problems. It also provides for mutual recognition.

✓ **Elicit options for resolution.**
Don't let the parties get locked into specific options too early. Brainstorm nonjudgmentally to get a number of options. Solicit suggestions by asking what they might be doing already that works, or what they would offer if they were the other party. Empower each party to discover their options and resources.

✓ **Evaluate and refine the alternatives.**
Discuss the advantages and disadvantages of the various options. Encourage the parties to explore possible consequences. Reality test each option: Can the parties really do it?

✓ **Avoid imposing solutions or guiding the parties to the mediator's favored outcome.**
Any agreement that is made must belong to the parties. Though the mediators may be able to come up with a resolution that seems objectively better, if the parties don't have ownership of it, the agreement is not empowering and it isn't likely to last.

✓ **Check for agreement.**
Check to see if each party buys into a tentative agreement. Sometimes there is a tendency to rush into an agreement, or to minimize the need for it, particularly if a lot of empathy and good feeling has been generated earlier in the session. Avoid this trap. If one or more parties are unsure or uneasy about a tentative agreement, don't force them. Go back and explore alternatives.

✓ **Write action plans in specific behavioral terms.**
In any agreement, focus on what individuals will *do*, not how they should feel or what they should think. Be specific about who will do what when. Make sure you have a relative balance of actions for each party.

✓ **Build in alternatives for handling future disagreements.**
You don't want to expect the worst, but it is wise to think about what should happen if one party or the other perceives that the agreement has broken down.

✓ **Have the parties sign the resolution document and give copies to everyone involved.**
It is important that you emphasize to the parties that the resolution agreement is theirs, and they should sign it only if they agree with their ownership of it. You don't want to see them back out of a workable agreement, but they must own it. Make sure that everyone understands the resolution agreement. Provide for reading it out loud as well as silently, and give people as much time as they need. Sign and distribute the copies.

The Closing

Purposes:
- To affirm, acknowledge, and validate the parties.
- To evaluate the process.
- To make arrangements for followup activities.
- To bring closure to the session.

✓ **Validate the parties.**
Acknowledge the work that the parties have done and validate their efforts.

✓ **Evaluate the process.**
Ask the parties to evaluate their success in using their shared expectations. Compliment the parties on their willingness to participate in mediation and on their work in the session. Briefly and honestly point out what they were able to achieve (there's always something).

✓ **Remind the parties of any followup activities.**
Let them know if and when they will be contacted to evaluate the mediation session. Encourage their participation by emphasizing that the evaluation is of the mediation process, not the performance of the parties.

✓ **Wish the parties well and see them off if necessary.**
A clear, positive signal that the mediation session is over releases the parties and gives them permission to leave. It also maintains a business-like attitude on the part of the mediators.

The Debriefing (after the parties leave)

Purposes:
- To affirm, acknowledge, and validate the other mediators.
- To evaluate the process.
- To prepare a final report on the mediation.

✓ **Validate your mediation team.**
Acknowledge the hard work you all did and your commitment to the process. Note especially helpful actions of other mediators.

✓ **Evaluate the process.**
Discuss aspects of the process that went well and contributed to success. Discuss challenges that you faced, but only in a constructive way—e.g., what did you learn about how better to deal with this issue in the future? Share new understandings you gained from the process.

✓ **Prepare a final report.**
Prepare whatever paperwork you need to do for this mediation and make sure you know who has responsibility to file it or get it where it needs to go.

Theory *Mediation as a Narrative Frame or Account*

"Children love stories—in fact we all do, but children admit to it."

Marc Gopin

Humans are meaning-making creatures. We generally make these meanings in the form of stories, both on the individual and societal levels. These stories or narratives are inherently cultural, meaning that they are arbitrary, learned, shared, and adaptive. Erving Goffman (1974) called these culturally-generated stories *frames.* In the process of organizing their experience, he said, people choose among various available frames.

But any particular individual's knowledge of frames is likely to be limited, both in breadth and depth. Thus in conflict situations, the individual will fall back on frames provided by the media, popular culture, and personal experience. These frames might not be conducive to transformative conflict resolution.

Along the same line—as we have seen—ethnomethodologists suggest that individuals offer *accounts* to explain their behavior. The regularly reproduced patterns in these accounts constitute their *accounting practices.* As with frames, these learned symbolic practices are often not productive of transformative conflict resolution.

In mediation, each party brings their own story or frame or account of the dispute. Moreover, "a sense of injustice and unfairness is part and parcel of most conflict scripts" (Gopin 2005: 67). Indeed, most of us have learned that, when there is a problem, someone must be at fault. Thus parties usually come to mediation as aggrieved victims and look to the mediator to rescue them and/or grant justice.

Michelle LeBaron (2002:269) pictures the most common account this way:

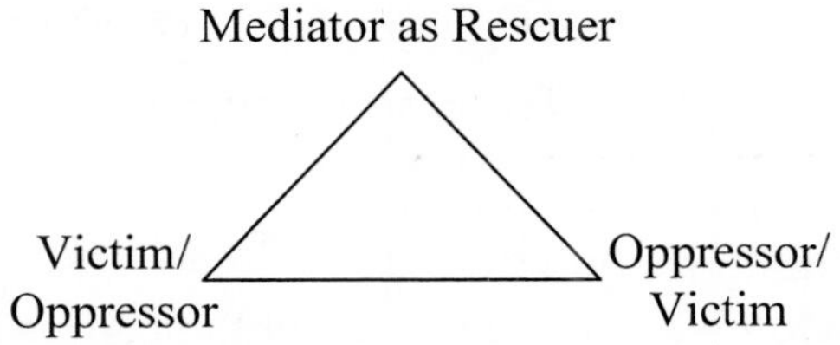

In this model, each party provides an account of themselves as a victim, oppressed by the other party. They expect the mediator to rescue them by scolding or punishing the other party and compelling the oppressive behavior to stop. Transformative mediation, however actually looks like this:

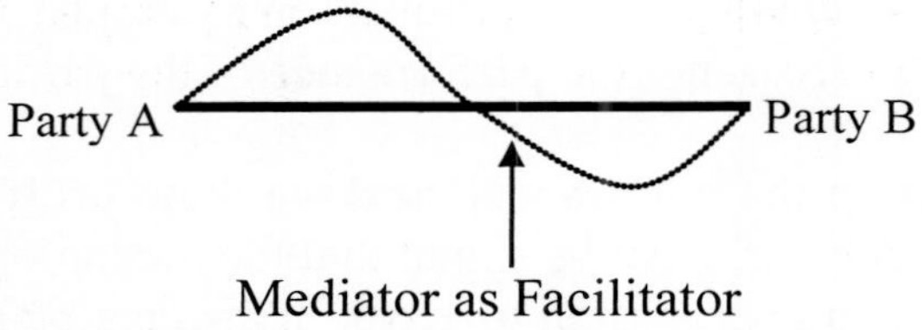

Functioning as a witness and guide, the mediator facilitates communication and humanization of each party to the other. This is accomplished through storytelling and helping the parties to rewrite their conflict-saturated story.

Christensen and Jacobson (2000: 1-13) suggest that there are at least three stories in a conflict script: one for each of the aggrieved parties, and a third that could be written by a neutral observer. One way to look at mediation is to see it as an attempt to get the parties to see this third story as a basis for rewriting their own personal conflict narrative. John Winslade and Gerald Monk (2000:38) put it this way:

> The task of mediation can be considered to be a teasing out of these stories in order to open up possibilities for alternative stories to gain an audience.... It follows, then, that the

success of a mediation might depend not so much on the extent to which a mediator can separate the story of the dispute from the realities or facts, but on the extent to which the mediator can work with the parties to create an alternative story. Such a story needs to be plausible and to include the significant events of the conflict story in a way that makes sense to the participants.

The narrative approach to mediation has three phases: engagement, deconstruction of the conflict-saturated story, and construction of an alternative story. In order to promote engagement, the mediators have to build trust. One important way to do this is to make the process transparent. In order to deconstruct the conflict-saturated story, the mediators will need to surface feelings, expectations, hopes, and desires. Christensen and Jacobson (2000) note that the construction of an effective common "problem story" narrative will focus on:

- ✓ differences rather than defects
- ✓ vulnerability rather than violation
- ✓ description rather than evaluation
- ✓ valid rather than invalid aspects of each person's experience
- ✓ complex dilemmas rather than simple solutions
- ✓ conscious consequences of actions rather than unconscious intent
- ✓ emotional reactions rather than motives
- ✓ the big picture rather than the little behaviors

Attention to the relationship of the parties through empowerment and recognition helps them to find common ground and to construct an alternative narrative. "Perhaps much of our conflict practice is about helping parties compose redemptive stories they can live into." (LeBaron 2002: 168)

How do we help the parties rewrite their conflict narrative? Following are some practical suggestions.

Practitioner's Notes **Techniques for deconstruction and reconstruction**

- Use externalizing language that makes the problem the problem, not the person.

  Perhaps solicit agreement on what to call the problem.
  Ask: "How has the problem caused you to feel about __________?"

- Identify and validate, through dialogue, the effect of the conflict on each party.

  In addition, ask them to project the continuing effect of the conflict forward into the future.

- Uncover the dominant, taken-for-granted assumptions behind each party's conflict story.

  Help the parties to define and operationalize what they mean by important concepts.

  These assumptions are often based on a sense of entitlement drawn from the larger cultural context. It may require separate meetings to tease these assumptions out.

- Draw attention to unstoried experience – i.e., unnoticed, overlooked events.

  Identify the ways in which the conflict is *not* totalizing, in terms of time or space.

  Highlight agreement, common ground, etc., and ask about the impact on the parties of hearing about it.

- Facilitate the parties in the construction of an alternative story by validating their expressed desire and experience of being different.

  Help the parties to articulate their hopes and positive expectations.
  Find common language and build common expectations.
  Perhaps ask the parties to roleplay each other in order to help develop an alternative story.

Practitioner's Notes *Reframing*

A specific technique for deconstructing and reconstructing a conflict narrative is reframing. Reframing is a process by which the mediators restate the parties' concerns in a way that removes the hateful/hurtful, potentially offensive aspects of a speaker's statements while at the same time acknowledging the validity of their experience. Reframing thus contributes to the goals of transformative mediation by recognizing the inherent dignity of all the parties while educating and empowering them. Reframing can also be used to hold a speaker accountable for their own opinions and views by moving them away from unsupported generalizations.

Reframing is used to:

- ✓ Launder hateful or hurtful language.
- ✓ Challenge and move beyond the use of stereotypes and generalizations about categories of people.
- ✓ Encourage the speaker to be specific about the nature of their concern.
- ✓ Encourage the parties to take responsibility for their own views and opinions and not presume to speak for others.

Party's statement	Mediator's reframe	Comment
"She's just a ___________ (fill in racial, ethnic, sexist, etc. slur)."	"I prefer not to use that language. I'd like you to tell me about the specific things she does that you find problematic."	Launders offensive language and focuses on specific behaviors
"You know how *they* are."	"As a matter of fact, I don't know about all people who fit in this category. I'd like for you to tell me about the specific behaviors of Mr. X."	Denies stereotype/ generalization, but still encourages party to talk about their concerns – only in specific terms.
"He never does anything to help."	"I'd like you to tell me about some specific times when you don't feel you got the help you needed."	Does not acknowledge the absolute generalization, but still focuses on the party's concern.

"It's like she enjoys bossing people around and being a bitch."	"You are concerned about how she uses her authority."	Omits the slanderous characterization but validates the underlying concern.
"I don't like anything about them."	"I'd prefer that you tell me the specific things they do that irritate you."	Focuses on behaviors, not generalizations.
"Any idiot could see that …."	"I don't know how everyone else sees the problem, but I'd like you to tell me more about how you see it."	Denies the generalization, but invites them to say more about their own perception.

Exercise *Practice Reframing*

Reframe each of the following statements in a way that acknowledges the concern of the speaker but launders the language or holds the speaker accountable.

1. He's a complete asshole.

   frustrated please explain

2. Isn't that just like a _____________? (fill in ethnic group, sex, or other category)

   Call one another by name rather than stereotypes

3. He must be some kind of moron not to see what the problem is here.

   You must be frustrated please be more clear

4. No one can deny that ….

   Very

5. Nobody in this neighborhood gives a shit.

   Explain your feeling rather then every one else

6. Everyone on the block has trouble with him.

Explain how you feel rather than everyone else

7. You know, that's just the way men are.

No Stereotypes, not all past experiences are the same

8. If he'd just start acting responsibly, we could fix this problem.

You can't always rely on certain people actions for an out come

9. I've dealt with his kind before and I know that you just can't trust them.

7

10. What are you going to do? You know how those people are!

7

11. Everything she says is a lie.

12. I hate this kind of bickering. If you'd just act reasonably we could solve this mess.

13. If you had done what I asked you to six months ago, this never would have happened!

14. Clearly [the other disputant] is an idiot! Any intelligent person can see what must be done!

15. They're just jealous, that's their problem.

Practitioner's Notes — *Keeping the Focus on the Parties*

Most mediators are initially attracted to mediation primarily because they perceive that it can help people solve problems constructively. Would-be mediators are often good problem-solvers themselves, and they are eager to see the benefits extended to others. As we have seen, however, a focus on problem-solving is antithetical to the transformative model of mediation. In transformative mediation, the focus must be on the empowerment and mutual recognition of the parties in the process. And yet, mediators often find themselves wanting to offer helpful suggestions to the parties about how they might constructively solve their problems. This is a natural tendency, especially for people who are generally known for giving good advice and in the past have been positively reinforced for dispensing it. AS A MEDIATOR, YOU MUST RESIST THIS TENDENCY!!! It will neither empower the parties nor provide them opportunities for mutual recognition if the mediator solves their problems for them. Remember: the mediator's role is to facilitate the process. The conflict belongs to the parties, and the solution, if any, must belong to them as well.

When you experience a desire to help solve the parties' problems, focus instead on the process. Examine what is going on at that point, and think about what needs to happen next to promote empowerment and recognition between the parties. Then ask yourself what you can do to promote movement toward that goal.

A potentially more difficult problem arises when parties express values, opinions, or ideas that contradict or conflict in some way with your own values. Be aware of the conflict, but keep the focus on the parties. Do one party's expressed values conflict with those of the other party? Then figure out what one party needs to hear from the other to clarify or accept the difference or promote further dialogue. But if the conflict is between the party's expressed viewpoint and your own ideas, then you must work to neutralize your bias. Try to mentally adopt the party's viewpoint and try to understand what they want or need. If you find that your views agree with one party more than the other, make sure that you work to acknowledge each party's view as valid for them.

Theory — *Labeling and Secondary Deviance*

One of the basic insights of sociology, going all the way back to one of its founders, Emile Durkheim, is that deviance is socially defined. No act is inherently deviant; it becomes deviant when it is socially defined as such.

Contemporary symbolic interactionists take this further and argue that powerful social groups as well as agencies of social control have the power to label certain acts and certain people as deviant. This explanation for deviance is called *labeling theory* (Lemert 1951; Becker 1963).

An important insight of labeling theory is that once an individual has been labeled as a deviant, they may come to accept this new identity and to engage in further deviance precisely because they now see themselves as "deviants."

This new round of deviance is called secondary deviance.

In mediation, the mediators must take care to manage the discussion process and the inevitable violations of ground rules and procedures in ways that do not label parties as deviant. The risk is that, once a party believes that they have been labeled, they may begin acting in accordance with that label.

Practitioner's Notes

Handling Difficult Situations

What do I do when one or both parties display one of these behaviors?

EXTREME ANGER

First, determine why a party is displaying anger at this point.

✓ **Does the person just need to express a strong emotion?** Not all displays of anger—even intense anger—are counterproductive. Sometimes a person just needs to vent. They need to release the energy of their pent-up emotions, and they don't know how else to do it. If the other party is not intimidated or provoked, then let the angry party go a bit. Restate their concerns and reflect their strong emotions frequently. Letting them know they are heard is the surest path to calming an angry person down. But if you are concerned that things might get out of control, then take a break and let the angry party cool down. Be sure to have one of the mediators stay with the angry party during the break. And check in with the other party to make sure that they are okay.

✓ **Does the person just need to be heard?** Sometimes people get angry because they feel they are not being listened to. Make sure you step up your paraphrasing when one of the parties gets angry. Another thing you can do is to ask the other party to summarize (or paraphrase, if they can) what they think the angry person is trying to tell them.

✓ **Is the person using anger as a weapon?** If one party angrily attacks another, interrupt immediately. Acknowledge that the person feels strongly about the issue, and assure them that they will be heard. Reassure everyone of your commitment to a fair and respectful process, and remind everyone that they agreed to mutual respect at the beginning of the mediation. Help the angry party to reframe the issue. If they cannot or will not, then call for a break and possibly a separate meeting. In that meeting be sure to paraphrase extensively, both to let them know their concerns are heard and to help them get a deeper understanding of their interests and needs.

CRYING

The strong emotions attached to many conflicts can result in tears and anguish.

✓ **Offer tissues, some generalized sympathy, and support.** Reassure the parties that expressing strong emotions under the circumstances is healthy and normal.

✓ **Maintain a respectful silence.** Sometimes your silence can create the space for the other party to recognize the emotional party's pain. Not intervening immediately can create a breakthrough—but don't appear heartless.

- ✓ **Take a break.** After a display of strong emotion all the parties may need a moment to regain control.

- ✓ **Call a separate meeting.** The party expressing the strong emotion may be too fragile, embarrassed, or vulnerable to continue facing the other party. A separate meeting gives them a chance to recover.

SILENCE

Silence is not always a negative.

- ✓ **Be respectful of silence.** Some people need time to reflect and process information. Allow them that time by remaining respectfully silent. Sometimes silence can be an effective tool to allow a point to sink in or to emphasize the gravity of a statement. Don't feel that you need to fill up all of the silences.

- ✓ **Empower the quiet person to speak.** If a person is quiet because they are shy or intimidated, think about how to empower them to speak. How can you create a safe space for them? Call for a separate meeting if you think that is necessary to empower them.

- ✓ **Don't allow silence to be used as a weapon.** If you think that one party is using "the silent treatment" to provoke the other party or to gain a perceived edge, don't hesitate to respectfully call them on the strategy by using an "I" message. Don't accuse them of anything or impute any motives to them. Just report the behavior that you have observed and allow the parties to develop a plan for dealing with it.

LYING

- ✓ **Ignore suspected lying that doesn't really impact the process.** Sometimes people will lie or distort the truth because they are afraid. Figure out how you can make the parties more comfortable. Create a safe space for them to open up. Moreover, since transformative mediation is not about a search for facts, you as a mediator don't have to very concerned with "getting to the truth." The process should be your focus. Empower the parties to signal their discomfort with aspects of the other's story.

- ✓ **If a party seems to be using lying as a tactic, respectfully call them on it.** If apparent lying is disruptive of the process, use an I message to convey your observation of the behavior and its effect on you and/or the process. Don't make accusations.

REFUSAL TO COOPERATE

There are a number of ways in which one or more parties may demonstrate refusal to cooperate.

- ✓ **Consistently breaking the rules.** Calmly but firmly emphasize to the offending party the importance of following the agreed-upon rules. If they won't agree to any, or won't abide by the agreement they made, inform them that the mediation cannot continue. Make it a factual statement; do not threaten them. Probe for natural consequences of halting the mediation.

- ✓ **Threatening to leave.** Do not beg someone to stay who clearly doesn't want to be there. If a party is threatening to leave as a tactic, indicate your desire that they stay and engage in dialogue, but emphasize their free choice to leave at any time. At the same time, probe the consequences of their leaving with them. Make sure that you leave the decision about leaving with them.
- ✓ **Going out of control.** If someone is out of control, your first duty is to protect everyone involved. Act firmly and decisively, but calmly. Do what is necessary to get the person's attention. Take a break and/or go to separate meetings. If the person becomes calm enough, probe for what set them off and enlist their help in developing strategies to keep things under control.

Practitioner's Notes

Afterward: Personal Reflections on Common Ground Mediation

General Principles

- Conflict, disagreement, and emotion are not inherently bad. In fact, the expression of them is necessary to a successful process.

- Try to get at the interests that underlie the positions disputants take.
  - — "Peel the onion" by making successive preference statements.

Case Development

- Emphasize to the parties that no solution will be forced on them.
  "There is no solution unless YOU agree that there is one."

The Mediation Process

- Don't try to analyze the "real" reason for people's problems.
  - — Remember that the goal is to empower people to solve their own problems.
  - — So don't offer possible solutions. Rather, ask questions in such a way that the parties may come up with ideas.

- RESTATE AND REFLECT! RESTATE AND REFLECT! RESTATE AND REFLECT!
  - — especially at the beginning of each phase

- Watch the "emotional balloons" over participants, and don't let those balloons explode!
  - — Make sure to move back and forth between the participants.
  - — Make sure that each party feels heard and respected.

- Focus on getting feelings expressed, rather than information recorded.
  - — Don't let your own curiosity get the better of you and dictate that you ask a lot of informational questions.
  - — It's important that the disputants understand the situation; less so the panel.

- Make sure that each party is fully heard, but don't get bogged down in repeating or fishing out minor details.
  - — e.g., "What would you most like X to know about you or this situation?"

- Move people forward, pulling them along with hope and affirmation.
  - e.g., "You're really making progress here." "It sounds like you can really solve this."
  - e.g., "Can you visualize what this would look like if/when it was solved?"
    - — use journey metaphors: e.g., "I think you're really on the road to a solution."

- Communicate as openly and honestly as possible; it inspires trust in the process and models appropriate behavior
  - — Communicate openly on the panel and with the disputants as well.
  - — There is no "magic" in the process, so make the disputants partners in directing it.

Large Group and Organizational Mediation

Conflicts occur in all kinds of social settings, of course. And the basic principles and techniques of transformative conflict resolution that you have learned apply whether the conflict involves two or three individuals in a small group, large informal groups of relatives, friends, or neighbors, or members of a formal organization. However, the sociological dynamics of a large group or organization are different enough from those of a small group that special versions of the techniques are required.

Historically, indigenous cultures developed a variety of techniques for community conflict resolution. Most, if not all of them are based on the talking circle. Here community members meet in a ritualized process that promotes sharing and respect. There is often some sacred or highly symbolic object which must be held in order to have the right to speak (e.g., a talking stick, eagle feather, stone, etc.) The object may be passed around sequentially or it may be obtained in turn from a central location. Regardless, there is a process of turn-taking and listening, often interspersed with respectful silence and reflection. This traditional process is highly adaptable to modern groups and organizations. Below is one updated version.

THE DATÉ DISCERNMENT CIRCLE

The Daté Discernment Circle is a combination of the traditional indigenous talking circle and a Western counseling procedure called "Neutralizing History." While the process is based on the basic principles of mediation and transformative conflict resolution, it requires a trained facilitator. NOTE: Because this technique deals with conflict resolution in large groups and organizations, there is always the possibility of setting in motion or enhancing existing dysfunctional, out-of-control social dynamics in which potentially irreparable harm is done to individuals and/or the group or organization. Therefore *this process should not be attempted without a facilitator specifically trained in this technique.*

Purpose: To promote understanding and discernment through careful, caring, and skillful listening in a group context.

Goals:

Educational

- Share information, history, memories
- Collect data
- Teach listening and paraphrasing skills
- Teach the model for future use
- Establish rapport between participants and the facilitator/consultant

Healing

- Instill respect for others' feelings and ideas
- Offer support
- Provide a safe atmosphere for sharing; protect individuals' vulnerability
- Improve and/or enhance relationships
- Express hopes and visions for the future

Problem-solving

- Initiate discussion
- Define and clarify issues, concerns, problems, conflicts
- Brainstorm options
- Seek and explore solutions

Structure and Process

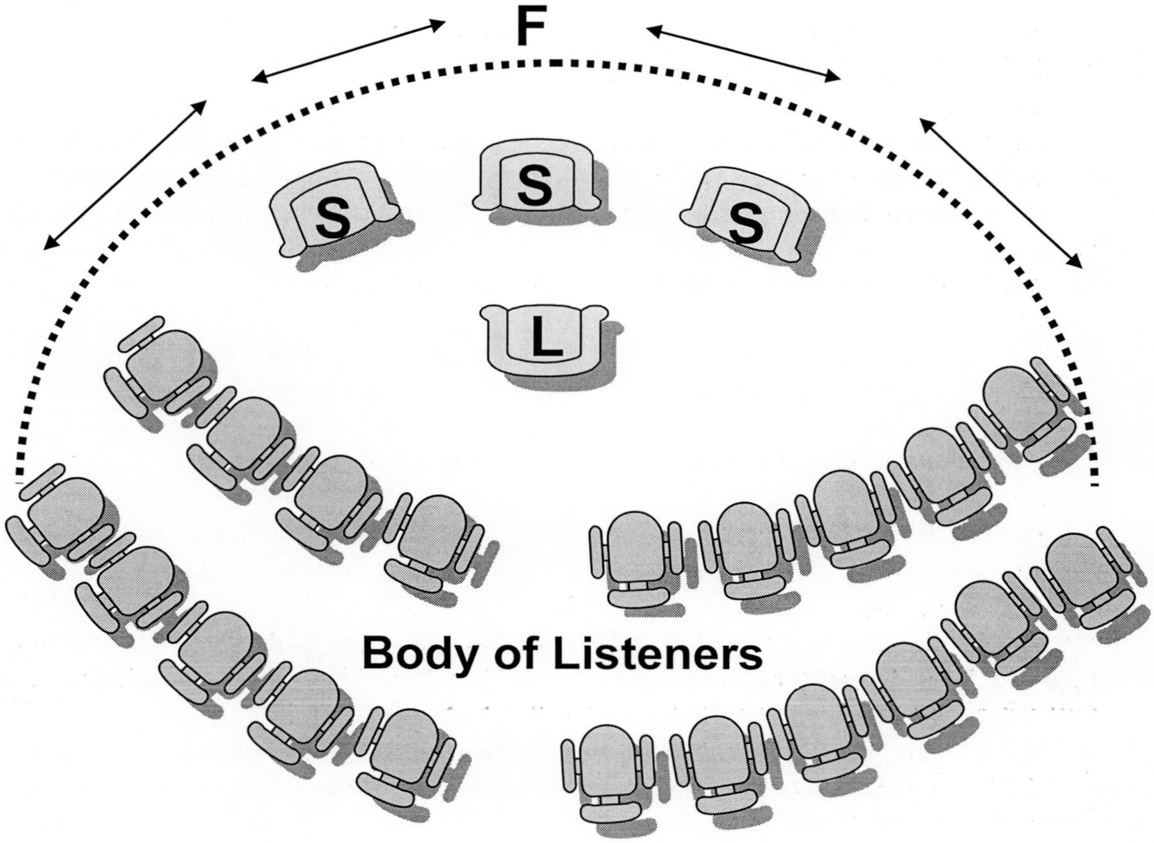

S = Speakers

- The three Speaker chairs are arranged at the front of the room.
- Other than the Facilitator, the only person who may speak is a person seated in a Speaker's Chair, and then only when it is their turn.
- Each person speaks in the order in which they occupied the Speaker's Chairs. The first person to come forth and occupy a chair speaks first, the second person second, and so on. After the first person has finished speaking, they vacate their chair and return to the Body of Listeners. Another person may come forward and occupy that seat and wait for their turn to speak.

- Each Speaker speaks only to a Listener of their own choosing. The Speaker can choose the Listener on any relevant criteria, for instance:
    - By name
    - By group membership (age, gender, race, experience, etc.)
    - Or they can ask for a volunteer.

- Each Speaker speaks until they are through. Then they and their Listener return to their seats in the Body of Listeners.

L = Listener

- The Listener is selected by each person who takes a turn as a Speaker. The Speaker makes the determination of the specific individual or category of the person they want to listen to them and announces it to the Body of Listeners when it is their turn to speak.

- A requested Listener may respectfully decline the request.

- The task of the person in the Listener's chair is ONLY to listen carefully to the Speaker and to paraphrase the Speaker's message. The Listener may not ask questions, agree, disagree, criticize, offer support, apologize, or add information in any way. The Listener is there exclusively to engage in active listening for the Speaker.

- The Facilitator will help the Listener to paraphrase if they are unsure of how to do it or they get stuck.

Body of Listeners

- The relevant group of people who wish to engage in discernment are seated in a half-circle or a series of half-circles where everyone can see each other if at all possible.

- The task of people seated here is to listen attentively. They may not make comments or engage the Speakers or the Listener in conversation. If someone wants to speak, they must go forward and sit in a Speaker chair.

F = Facilitator

- The Facilitator is responsible for the healthy movement of the process and the safe atmosphere of the space, while protecting the vulnerability of everyone in the room. The Facilitator generally stands behind or adjacent to the Speaker's chair of the person who is currently speaking.

- The Facilitator will
    - Initiate and conclude the process
    - Confirm agreement with the process guidelines among all present before going forward

- Be visible and present in the process
- Offer verbal and nonverbal support to the Speaker and the Listener
- Facilitate the pace of the discussion
- Deal constructively with any disruptions from the Body of Listeners
- At appropriate points, make observations of an educational nature (teaching moments)

There are many advantages to this process for dealing with group conflict.

✓ It provides a safe way for vulnerable people to express their thoughts and feelings.

✓ It forces speakers to take responsibility for what they are saying.

✓ It helps individuals clarify their message and thereby clarify the pattern and dynamics of the conflict for the group.

✓ It compels people to really listen to one another and thereby promotes mutual respect.

✓ It can educate the participants about how to deal with conflict constructively.

Developed by B. Daté and M.A. Smith
Used with permission.
Additional material by Patrick J. Ashton

Exercise *Finale: Personal Self-Assessment*

Purpose: The purpose of the self-assessment is to encourage you, at the end of this course, to assess your learning and to develop a plan to integrate the knowledge and skills learned into your life.

Assignment: Write an assessment of your learning in this course, *in the form of a letter or notes to yourself.* (You can write it in the first or second person, according to your own personal preference.) Note that the audience for this paper is *yourself,* not the instructor. I will be "reading over your shoulder" of course, but you should write the paper to and for yourself. Among the points you should cover are the following:

- After reviewing your initial goals for this course, discuss the extent to which those goals were met (or how and why those goals changed during the course). What features of the course contributed to meeting your goals? What features were detrimental? Could you have done anything different to better meet your goals?

- Assess your own effort at meeting your goals for the course. Did your effort match your expectations? What if anything could you have done differently? Evaluate your level and quality of participation and explain your rationale.

- Discuss the most important knowledge and skills you obtained from this course. Why are these particular things important to you? What has been their real impact upon you?

[continued on next page ⟶]

- Use the metaphor of the bridge to develop a vision for how you want the conflict resolution and mediation skills you have learned in this course to impact your life. Where are you now (**Here**)? Where do you want to be in the future (**There**)?

There

Here

- Imagine the knowledge, skills, and insights you gained from this course as the bridge that will help you move toward your vision. How will you use them? Challenge yourself to develop a specific plan.

Appendixes

MODEL STANDARDS OF CONDUCT FOR MEDIATORS

AMERICAN ARBITRATION ASSOCIATION
(ADOPTED SEPTEMBER 8, 2005)

AMERICAN BAR ASSOCIATION
(APPROVED BY THE ABA HOUSE OF DELEGATES AUGUST 9, 2005)

ASSOCIATION FOR CONFLICT RESOLUTION
(ADOPTED AUGUST 22, 2005)

SEPTEMBER 2005

available at

http://www.americanbar.org/content/dam/aba/migrated/2011_build/dispute_resolution/model_standards_conduct_april2007.authcheckdam.pdf

The Model Standards of Conduct for Mediators
2005

The Model Standards of Conduct for Mediators was prepared in 1994 by the American Arbitration Association, the American Bar Association's Section of Dispute Resolution, and the Association for Conflict Resolution[1]. A joint committee consisting of representatives from the same successor organizations revised the Model Standards in 2005.[2] Both the original 1994 version and the 2005 revision have been approved by each participating organization.[3]

---

[1] The Association for Conflict Resolution is a merged organization of the Academy of Family Mediators, the Conflict Resolution Education Network and the Society of Professionals in Dispute Resolution (SPIDR). SPIDR was the third participating organization in the development of the 1994 Standards.

[2] Reporter's Notes, which are not part of these Standards and therefore have not been specifically approved by any of the organizations, provide commentary regarding these revisions.

[3] The 2005 version to the Model Standards were approved by the American Bar Association's House of Delegates on August 9, 2005, the Board of the Association of Conflict Resolution on August 22, 2005 and the Executive Committee of the American Arbitration Association on September 8, 2005.

Preamble

Mediation is used to resolve a broad range of conflicts within a variety of settings. These Standards are designed to serve as fundamental ethical guidelines for persons mediating in all practice contexts. They serve three primary goals: to guide the conduct of mediators; to inform the mediating parties; and to promote public confidence in mediation as a process for resolving disputes.

Mediation is a process in which an impartial third party facilitates communication and negotiation and promotes voluntary decision making by the parties to the dispute.

Mediation serves various purposes, including providing the opportunity for parties to define and clarify issues, understand different perspectives, identify interests, explore and assess possible solutions, and reach mutually satisfactory agreements, when desired.

Note on Construction

These Standards are to be read and construed in their entirety. There is no priority significance attached to the sequence in which the Standards appear.

The use of the term "shall" in a Standard indicates that the mediator must follow the practice described. The use of the term "should" indicates that the practice described in the standard is highly desirable, but not required, and is to be departed from only for very strong reasons and requires careful use of judgment and discretion.

The use of the term "mediator" is understood to be inclusive so that it applies to co-mediator models.

These Standards do not include specific temporal parameters when referencing a mediation, and therefore, do not define the exact beginning or ending of a mediation.

Various aspects of a mediation, including some matters covered by these Standards, may also be affected by applicable law, court rules, regulations, other applicable professional rules, mediation rules to which the parties have agreed and other agreements of the parties. These sources may create conflicts with, and may take precedence over, these Standards. However, a mediator should make every effort to comply with the spirit and intent of these Standards in resolving such conflicts. This effort should include honoring all remaining Standards not in conflict with these other sources.

These Standards, unless and until adopted by a court or other regulatory authority do not have the force of law. Nonetheless, the fact that these Standards have been adopted by the respective sponsoring entities, should alert mediators to the fact that the Standards might be viewed as establishing a standard of care for mediators.

STANDARD I. SELF-DETERMINATION

A. A mediator shall conduct a mediation based on the principle of party self-determination. Self-determination is the act of coming to a voluntary, uncoerced decision in which each party makes free and informed choices as to process and outcome. Parties may exercise self-determination at any stage of a mediation, including mediator selection, process design, participation in or withdrawal from the process, and outcomes.

1. Although party self-determination for process design is a fundamental principle of mediation practice, a mediator may need to balance such party self-

determination with a mediator's duty to conduct a quality process in accordance with these Standards.

2. A mediator cannot personally ensure that each party has made free and informed choices to reach particular decisions, but, where appropriate, a mediator should make the parties aware of the importance of consulting other professionals to help them make informed choices.

B. A mediator shall not undermine party self-determination by any party for reasons such as higher settlement rates, egos, increased fees, or outside pressures from court personnel, program administrators, provider organizations, the media or others.

STANDARD II. IMPARTIALITY

A. A mediator shall decline a mediation if the mediator cannot conduct it in an impartial manner. Impartiality means freedom from favoritism, bias or prejudice.

B. A mediator shall conduct a mediation in an impartial manner and avoid conduct that gives the appearance of partiality.

1. A mediator should not act with partiality or prejudice based on any participant's personal characteristics, background, values and beliefs, or performance at a mediation, or any other reason.

2. A mediator should neither give nor accept a gift, favor, loan or other item of value that raises a question as to the mediator's actual or perceived impartiality.

3. A mediator may accept or give de minimis gifts or incidental items or services that are provided to facilitate a mediation or respect cultural norms so long as such practices do not raise questions as to a mediator's actual or perceived impartiality.

C. If at any time a mediator is unable to conduct a mediation in an impartial manner, the mediator shall withdraw.

STANDARD III. CONFLICTS OF INTEREST

A. A mediator shall avoid a conflict of interest or the appearance of a conflict of interest during and after a mediation. A conflict of interest can arise from involvement by a mediator with the subject matter of the dispute or from any relationship between a mediator and any mediation participant, whether past or present, personal or professional, that reasonably raises a question of a mediator's impartiality.

B. A mediator shall make a reasonable inquiry to determine whether there are any facts that a reasonable individual would consider likely to create a potential or actual conflict of interest for a mediator. A mediator's actions necessary to accomplish a reasonable inquiry into potential conflicts of interest may vary based on practice context.

C. A mediator shall disclose, as soon as practicable, all actual and potential conflicts of interest that are reasonably known to the mediator and could reasonably be seen as raising a question about the mediator's impartiality. After disclosure, if all parties agree, the mediator may proceed with the mediation.

D. If a mediator learns any fact after accepting a mediation that raises a question with respect to that mediator's service creating a potential or actual conflict of interest, the mediator shall disclose it as quickly as practicable. After disclosure, if all parties agree, the mediator may proceed with the mediation.

E. If a mediator's conflict of interest might reasonably be viewed as undermining the integrity of the mediation, a mediator shall withdraw from or decline to proceed with the mediation regardless of the expressed desire or agreement of the parties to the contrary.

F. Subsequent to a mediation, a mediator shall not establish another relationship with any of the participants in any matter that would raise questions about the integrity of the mediation. When a mediator develops personal or professional relationships with parties, other individuals or organizations following a mediation in which they were involved, the mediator should consider factors such as time elapsed following the mediation, the nature of the relationships established, and services offered when determining whether the relationships might create a perceived or actual conflict of interest.

STANDARD IV. COMPETENCE

A. A mediator shall mediate only when the mediator has the necessary competence to satisfy the reasonable expectations of the parties.

1. Any person may be selected as a mediator, provided that the parties are satisfied with the mediator's competence and qualifications. Training, experience in mediation, skills, cultural understandings and other qualities are often necessary for mediator competence. A person who offers to serve as a mediator creates the expectation that the person is competent to mediate effectively.

2. A mediator should attend educational programs and related activities to maintain and enhance the mediator's knowledge and skills related to mediation.
3. A mediator should have available for the parties' information relevant to the mediator's training, education, experience and approach to conducting a mediation.

B. If a mediator, during the course of a mediation determines that the mediator cannot conduct the mediation competently, the mediator shall discuss that determination with the parties as soon as is practicable and take appropriate steps to address the situation, including, but not limited to, withdrawing or requesting appropriate assistance.

C. If a mediator's ability to conduct a mediation is impaired by drugs, alcohol, medication or otherwise, the mediator shall not conduct the mediation.

STANDARD V. CONFIDENTIALITY

A. A mediator shall maintain the confidentiality of all information obtained by the mediator in mediation, unless otherwise agreed to by the parties or required by applicable law.

1. If the parties to a mediation agree that the mediator may disclose information obtained during the mediation, the mediator may do so.

1. A mediator should not communicate to any non-participant information about how the parties acted in the mediation. A mediator may report, if required, whether parties appeared at a scheduled mediation and whether or not the parties reached a resolution.

3. If a mediator participates in teaching, research or evaluation of mediation, the mediator should protect the anonymity of the parties and abide by their reasonable expectations regarding confidentiality.

B. A mediator who meets with any persons in private session during a mediation shall not convey directly or indirectly to any other person, any information that was obtained during that private session without the consent of the disclosing person.

C. A mediator shall promote understanding among the parties of the extent to which the parties will maintain confidentiality of information they obtain in a mediation.

D. Depending on the circumstance of a mediation, the parties may have varying expectations regarding confidentiality that a mediator should address. The parties may make their own rules with respect to confidentiality, or the accepted practice of an individual mediator or institution may dictate a particular set of expectations.

STANDARD VI. QUALITY OF THE PROCESS

A. A mediator shall conduct a mediation in accordance with these Standards and in a manner that promotes diligence, timeliness, safety, presence of the appropriate participants, party participation, procedural fairness, party competency and mutual respect among all participants.

1. A mediator should agree to mediate only when the mediator is prepared to commit the attention essential to an effective mediation.

2. A mediator should only accept cases when the mediator can satisfy the reasonable expectation of the parties concerning the timing of a mediation.

3. The presence or absence of persons at a mediation depends on the agreement of the parties and the mediator. The parties and mediator may agree that others may be excluded from particular sessions or from all sessions.
4. A mediator should promote honesty and candor between and among all participants, and a mediator shall not knowingly misrepresent any material fact or circumstance in the course of a mediation.

5. The role of a mediator differs substantially from other professional roles. Mixing the role of a mediator and the role of another profession is problematic and thus, a mediator should distinguish between the roles. A mediator may provide information that the mediator is qualified by training or experience to provide, only if the mediator can do so consistent with these Standards.

6. A mediator shall not conduct a dispute resolution procedure other than mediation but label it mediation in an effort to gain the protection of rules, statutes, or other governing authorities pertaining to mediation.

7. A mediator may recommend, when appropriate, that parties consider resolving their dispute through arbitration, counseling, neutral evaluation or other processes.

8. A mediator shall not undertake an additional dispute resolution role in the same matter without the consent of the parties. Before providing such service, a mediator shall inform the parties of the implications of the change in process and obtain their consent to the change. A mediator who undertakes such role assumes different duties and responsibilities that may be governed by other standards.

9. If a mediation is being used to further criminal conduct, a mediator should take appropriate steps including, if necessary, postponing, withdrawing from or terminating the mediation.

10. If a party appears to have difficulty comprehending the process, issues, or settlement options, or difficulty participating in a mediation, the mediator should explore the circumstances and potential accommodations, modifications or adjustments that would make possible the party's capacity to comprehend, participate and exercise self-determination.

B. If a mediator is made aware of domestic abuse or violence among the parties, the mediator shall take appropriate steps including, if necessary, postponing, withdrawing from or terminating the mediation.

C. If a mediator believes that participant conduct, including that of the mediator, jeopardizes conducting a mediation consistent with these Standards, a mediator shall take appropriate steps including, if necessary, postponing, withdrawing from or terminating the mediation.

STANDARD VII. ADVERTISING AND SOLICITATION

A. A mediator shall be truthful and not misleading when advertising, soliciting or otherwise communicating the mediator's qualifications, experience, services and fees.

1. A mediator should not include any promises as to outcome in communications, including business cards, stationery, or computer-based communications.

2. A mediator should only claim to meet the mediator qualifications of a governmental entity or private organization if that entity or organization has a recognized procedure for qualifying mediators and it grants such status to the mediator.

B. A mediator shall not solicit in a manner that gives an appearance of partiality for or against a party or otherwise undermines the integrity of the process.

C. A mediator shall not communicate to others, in promotional materials or through other forms of communication, the names of persons served without their permission.

STANDARD VIII. FEES AND OTHER CHARGES

A. A mediator shall provide each party or each party's representative true and complete information about mediation fees, expenses and any other actual or potential charges that may be incurred in connection with a mediation.

1. If a mediator charges fees, the mediator should develop them in light of all relevant factors, including the type and complexity of the matter, the qualifications of the mediator, the time required and the rates customary for such mediation services.

2. A mediator's fee arrangement should be in writing unless the parties request otherwise.

B. A mediator shall not charge fees in a manner that impairs a mediator's impartiality.

1. A mediator should not enter into a fee agreement which is contingent upon the result of the mediation or amount of the settlement.

2. While a mediator may accept unequal fee payments from the parties, a mediator should not allow such a fee arrangement to adversely impact the mediator's ability to conduct a mediation in an impartial manner.

STANDARD IX. ADVANCEMENT OF MEDIATION PRACTICE

A. A mediator should act in a manner that advances the practice of mediation. A mediator promotes this Standard by engaging in some or all of the following:

1. Fostering diversity within the field of mediation.

2. Striving to make mediation accessible to those who elect to use it, including providing services at a reduced rate or on a pro bono basis as appropriate.

3. Participating in research when given the opportunity, including obtaining participant feedback when appropriate.

4. Participating in outreach and education efforts to assist the public in developing an improved understanding of, and appreciation for, mediation.

5. Assisting newer mediators through training, mentoring and networking.

B. A mediator should demonstrate respect for differing points of view within the field, seek to learn from other mediators and work together with other mediators to improve the profession and better serve people in conflict.

Association for Conflict Resolution
www.ACRnet.org

FINAL REPORT OF ACR ETHICS COMMITTEE
MAY, 2010

Available at

http://www.acrnet.org/uploadedFiles/About_Us/ACR_News_Headlines/ACR%20Ethical%20Principles.pdf

INTRODUCTION

In October, 2008, the ACR Board of Directors set policy that initiated a committee to explore, for conflict resolution practitioners, the creation of ethical principles that would be supplemental to any and all such documents then in place.

After exhaustive research, it was found that the 2005 Model Standards of Conduct for Mediators, approved in its entirety by ACR and others, are the only behavioral standards approved by the ACR Board of Directors.

It is unclear what ACR ethical principles were used to make the 2005 decision. Although some suggest that the former SPIDR ethical principles were contemplated, no approval of record exists.

Nor are there ACR Section ethical principals, standards of behavior or grievance procedures formally approved of record. Thus the task of the Committee became to present universal Ethical Principles for ACR that will guide practice standards for all ACR neutrals and be in compliance with existent behavioral standards for dispute resolution processes contemplated by the various Sections of the organization.

An interim report was presented to the board in February, 2009, and again in June, 2009. In October, 2009, the report was approved by the Board of Directors for release for public comment, the deadline for such comment being December 10, 2009. Subsequently, input was again sought from the Board, as final comment. This final draft is submitted to the Board for approval and whatever subsequent action it chooses to take.

ETHICAL PRINCIPLES

□ **Principles of Professionalism:** An ACR Neutral must adhere to the highest standards of integrity, impartiality and professional competence in rendering her or his professional service.

1. A Neutral must not accept any engagement, perform any service, or undertake any act which would compromise the Neutral's integrity.

2. A Neutral must maintain professional competence in dispute resolution skills by staying informed of, and abiding by, all relevant practice statutes, rules, and administrative orders and by regularly engaging in educational activities that inform as to professional practices and promote professional growth.

3. A Neutral must decline appointment, withdraw, or request technical assistance when the Neutral feels that a case is beyond the Neutral's competence.

4. A Neutral must decline all cases where there is a conflict of interest or where there is the appearance of an impropriety.

5. A Neutral must not engage in conduct that is considered contrary to professional standards of justice, honesty and ethics, including but not limited to misrepresentation of credentials, crossing of professional boundaries and truth in advertising.

□ **Principles of Role:** An ACR Neutral must respect the principle of individual integrity by ensuring that in dispute resolution proceedings, other than arbitration or other leader-directed models of dispute resolution, decision-making authority rests with the participants. The role of the Neutral shall include assisting participants in identifying issues, reducing obstacles to communication, maximizing the exploration of alternatives and helping the participants reach voluntary agreements.

1. A Neutral must promote a balanced process and must promote mutual respect among the participants throughout the conflict resolution process.

2. A Neutral must not coerce or unfairly influence a participant into any settlement agreement.

3. A Neutral must not intentionally nor knowingly misrepresent material facts or circumstances in the course of conducting the conflict resolution proceeding.

4. A Neutral must be impartial and advise all participants of any circumstances bearing on possible bias, prejudice, or impartiality. Impartiality means freedom from favoritism or

bias in word, action, and appearance. Impartiality implies a commitment to aid all participants, as opposed to an individual participant in conducting the conflict resolution process.

5. A Neutral must promote informed decision making among the participants in the process, without offering legal, psychological or any other advice associated with the Neutral's background and training.

□ **<u>Principles of Process:</u>** An ACR conflict resolution process should emphasize the following principles:

1. Participants' Self-determination: The act of participants coming to informed, voluntary and uncoerced decisions.

2. Client Centered Negotiation: The needs and interests of the participants form the basis upon which resolution is sought.

3. Neutral's Impartiality: Freedom from favoritism or bias in word, action, attitude and appearance; ensuring a commitment to aid all participants, as opposed to an individual participant, in conducting the conflict resolution process.

4. Fairness of the Process: The balancing of the process to meet the needs and interests of the participants.

5. Procedural Flexibility: Designing the process to fit the circumstances of the situation, wishes and needs of the participants.

6. Confidentiality: Keeping all information shared in the process private unless such privilege is waived by all participants.

7. Full Disclosure: All information necessary for making informed decision by the participants.

8. Informed Decision Making: The capacity to make decisions with full understanding of all the information needed and shared.

Respectfully submitted:
Carol Berz, Crevon Tarrance, Co-Chairs
Jeffrey Cohen
Nancy Gardner
Marilyn McKnight

Appendix II: Detailed Mediation Roleplays

The following two conflicts are acted out and mediated on the included DVD. 

A CLIENT/CASEWORKER CONFLICT

DISPUTANTS: Sheryl Johnson, client. 26 year old single parent receiving public assistance
Billie Wilson, caseworker for 11 years

CASE REPORT

Jon, the Director of Family and Social Services, has asked the center to mediate a conflict between a client and caseworker. He received a complaint from the client saying her caseworker was "unprofessional," "on a power trip," and "not really interested in doing her job and helping people." When she was denied benefits, Sheryl Johnson, the client, requested that the Director "do something about this."

Billie Wilson, the caseworker, has said that she was only doing her job. When Ms. Johnson came in for her three-month redetermination of eligibility for benefits, Ms. Wilson attempted to obtain the required information, but Ms Johnson became hostile. She said some bad things about the caseworker, stormed out of the office, and later filed a complaint with the Director. Ms Wilson feels that the complaint is unfair and unjustified. With the new welfare-to-work program, there have been a lot of changes in rules and procedures, and Ms. Wilson feels that the client is confused and/or misinformed. Because the client refused to supply the needed information, the caseworker closed the case and the client was denied benefits.

Both parties have agreed to mediation.

SHERYL JOHNSON'S PERSPECTIVE

You are a single parent who has been receiving public assistance. You have had a hard life. Your daughter's father was violently abusive toward you. After yet another fight and your third visit to a hospital emergency room, you took your daughter and left. The two of you spent several weeks at the women's shelter while you got a restraining order on your daughter's father and figured out what to do next. You have a lot of pride and a strong desire to make a good life for yourself and your daughter. With the help of counselors at the shelter, you applied for and received a Pell grant and have started college. You are afraid that if your caseworker finds out about the Pell grant, it will reduce or eliminate your public assistance.

When you were called in for a "redetermination of eligibility," all your worst fears seemed confirmed. The caseworker started demanding to know the biological father of your daughter. Given the domestic violence you have experienced, this is a very painful subject for you. You don't think it's any of your caseworker's business anyway. When the caseworker was rude to you, you left the office. Later that week you received notice that your case had been closed and your benefits terminated. This has caused a real hardship for you and your daughter. You were even more upset when you noticed that your name had been misspelled on the notice (Cheryl instead of Sheryl). They have your paperwork, why can't they get it right? It seemed just another example of disrespect. Angry, you contacted the Director and asked him to fix things.

BILLIE WILSON'S PERSPECTIVE

You have been a caseworker for 11 years. You went into social work because you genuinely wanted to help people. But lately it seems to be getting tougher. There have been a lot of changes in laws and procedures regarding public assistance lately. Some of these changes, you feel, are punitive toward welfare moms, and are probably based on racist and sexist assumptions by state and national legislators. You keep your opinions to yourself at work, however, because you want to keep your job and continue to help people who need public assistance. You don't write the laws, but you have to follow them if you're going to be successful in getting people the benefits they deserve under the law.

When Sheryl Johnson came in for her three-month redetermination, you asked her the information you needed to maintain her eligibility, including who the bio father of her daughter is and whether she had any unearned income. With regard to identifying the father, Ms. Johnson became visibly upset and refused to do so. She accused you of being unprofessional, unfair, and unkind. This really hurt because you are required by law to ask this, although Ms. Johnson wouldn't see it that way. With regard to unearned income, it seemed to you that Ms. Johnson was being evasive. Since she couldn't answer the question, you couldn't certify her for benefits. Any chance of rectifying the situation was lost when Ms. Johnson stormed out of your office. But you were just doing your job, and actually trying to HELP her. The case continued to bother you, and you were really hurt when Ms. Johnson complained to the Director about you.

A LANDLORD/TENANT CONFLICT

DISPUTANTS: Marlon Williams, college student
Joan Wells, landlord

CASE REPORT

Marlon Williams, originally from Jamaica, is a student at IPFW who rents an apartment in the Lakeside neighborhood. Marlon has contacted the mediation service about a dispute with his landlord. He says that his landlord, Joan Wells, has recently raised his rent by $75 per month, but has never kept the building up, and it is getting worse. Marlon feels that the roof is in such bad shape that this will be a difficult winter for him. He wants the repairs made and does not want to pay the rent increase until he sees some results. Joan Wells states that she is justified in raising the rent as she has not raised it in three years. She believes that the tenant has caused damage to the property.

MARLON WILLIAMS' PERSPECTIVE

Marlon Williams is a junior at IPFW majoring in elementary education. He has been living in an upstairs apartment in a house owned by Joan Wells for four months. Marlon works hard, is quiet, but does enjoy having some friends over on the weekend sometimes to visit and relax. He takes good care of the apartment and enjoys living there. It is convenient to the university and his job. He likes having a family live downstairs from her.

The family that lives downstairs has a baby, and once in a while Marlon babysits for them. He and they get along fine, although there was one night, just two weeks after Marlon moved in, when he was having a party on Friday night and the music woke the baby. The couple was upset, and called the landlord the next morning. But that afternoon, Marlon stopped by to apologize for the noise, and they felt much better. There have been no problems since.

On the day he moved in, while everything was still packed in boxes, Marlon got an important phone call from his sister. He had a pencil, but nothing to write on, so he wrote the number lightly on the wall next to the phone. Just at that moment, the landlord walked in. She never said anything about the writing on the wall, but seemed upset. Later Marlon washed the writing off the wall.

Marlon is very upset with the landlord for not making repairs to the house that were promised at the time he was shown the apartment. The roof leaks, and the water that soaks the ceiling and wall in a heavy rain has not only damaged the plaster but also stained a blanket which is an important family heirloom. The building is old and not very well insulated, so Marlon's heating bills this winter are probably going to be huge. He feels that Wells is a typical absentee landlord who doesn't care and who takes care of other apartments better than she takes care of Marlon's. Marlon does not want to pay the rent increase until the roof leak and the ceiling plaster are fixed. He likes the apartment and doesn't want to move, but feels the rent increase is unfair if repairs are not being made.

Marlon came to the United States from Jamaica.. He has always had to work hard. His family is unable to help him with college costs, but Marlon has a partial scholarship and also works 15 hours per week.

JOAN WELLS' PERSPECTIVE

Joan Wells lives in Aboite Township southwest of Fort Wayne, but lived in the Lakeside neighborhood near the university for many years. She and her spouse built up a successful hobby shop business in the area, and she now owns three stores, as well as several housing rental properties in the city. Joan is successful now, but remembers when she had little and had to work very hard for a living; she still works hard, and is very busy. Ten years ago, Joan and her spouse bought 5 acres of wooded property in Aboite township and built their dream house. Joan's spouse died five years ago.

Joan feels that her rent increase is reasonable, and in line with what other similar properties charge. No one else has refused to pay the rent increase. Further, Joan feels that Marlon does not care for the property well, and that he has done damage to it - e.g., graffiti on the walls, plaster damage, etc. Three years ago she rented a small house to a Haitian family and it was a disaster. They stopped paying the rent after only a couple of months, and Joan had to go to court to get them evicted. Then when they left, the house was in really bad shape and cost over $1000. to repair. Joan feels that this family really took advantage of her and cheated her. She had some hesitation about renting to Marlon Williams because she feels that "those people" just do not have any respect for property. It seems to her that "people like that" are always trying to get something for nothing, and don't really want to work for it. But Joan knew that she couldn't legally deny Marlon the apartment, so she went ahead and rented it to him. Then, when Joan stopped by on the day Marlon moved in, she observed that Marlon had *already* started writing on the walls! Joan has not returned to the apartment since, because she is afraid of what she may find in terms of damage.

The couple who live downstairs called Joan on a Saturday morning shortly after Marlon moved in to complain about loud music and noise that woke them and their baby after midnight. Joan wrote a letter to Marlon about it but has received no response. Now Marlon is refusing to pay the rent increase, so it looks to Joan as if she is in the same kind of mess as before.

Marlon has complained about the roof leaking, and says he wants Joan to insulate the house before winter. Joan just can't afford major investments in such a low-rent, older property, especially if the renter is going to create damage that will have to be repaired as well. An additional problem is that Joan's regular maintenance person, who took care of repairs and alterations at both Joan's stores and rental properties, took another job two months ago, and she is still trying to find a capable, dependable replacement. Consequently, Joan is behind on repairs at present.

Appendix III: Handbooks, Training Manuals, and Curricula

Beer, Jennifer E. with Eileen Stief, *The Mediator's Handbook. Revised and expanded 3rd edition.* Gabriola Island, British Columbia: New Society Publishers, 1998.
A classic resource on community mediation. Developed through long experience by the Friends Conflict Resolution Programs in Philadelphia, this is a practical handbook filled with easy-to-digest handouts, graphics, and exercises.

Bellard, Jan and Hilda Gutiérrez Baldoquin. *Face to Face: Resolving Conflict Without Giving In or Giving Up.* Washington, D.C.: National Association for Community Mediation, 1996.
A modular curriculum developed to train AmeriCorps members. Addresses personal, interpersonal, and group conflict. Participant workbook also available.

Butler, C.T. Lawrence and Amy Rothstein. *On Conflict & Consensus: A Handbook on Formal Consensus Decisionmaking.* Portland, ME: Food Not Bombs Publishing, 1987.
A brief guide to the formal consensus decisionmaking process, a method to deal constructively with conflict in meetings.

Duryea, Michelle LeBaron. *Conflict Analysis and Resolution as Education: Culturally Sensitive Processes for Conflict Resolution.* Victoria, British Columbia: University of Victoria Institute for Dispute Resolution, 1994.
A rich source of information for mediators and trainers on dealing with cultural issues in mediation.

Folberg, Jay and Allison Taylor. *Mediation: A Comprehensive Guide to Resolving Conflicts Without Litigation.* San Francisco: Jossey-Bass, 1984.
A comprehensive guide aimed at independent mediation practitioners. Includes information on topics such as interviewing clients, keeping records, and setting fees.

Frager, Robert, ed. *Who Am I? Personality Types for Self-Discovery.* Tarcher-Putnam, 1994.
A useful collection of readings on personality types from a wide variety of cultural traditions, from both the East and West.

Gilmore, Susan K. and Patrick W. Fraleigh, *The Friendly Style Profile for People at Work.* Eugene, OR: Friendly Press, 2004.
Responses to a 20-question inventory provide personal style profiles under both calm and storm conditions. Useful for many settings in addition to work and organizations. Booklet has extensive information on each style, including strengths and excesses and self-management strategies for dealing with excesses.

Glaser, Rollin and Christine Glaser. *Negotiating Style Profile, revised ed. Negotiating Style Profile Facilitator Guide, revised ed.* King of Prussia, PA: HRDQ, 1996.
Self-scoring inventory based on responses to 30 statements about conflict and negotiating situations. Facilitator Guide includes instructions, more in-depth description of each of the styles, and national norms.

Hart, Lois Borland. *Learning From Conflict: A Handbook for Trainers and Group Leaders, 2nd ed.* Amherst MA: HRD Press, 1991.
A practical guide to conducting workshops on conflict analysis and resolution. Includes over 60 easy-to-use exercises.

Hogan, R. Craig and David W. Champagne. *Personal Style Inventory. Personal Style Inventory Trainer Guide.* King of Prussia, PA: HRDQ, 1990.
A Meyers-Briggs Type Inventory based on the personal style types first identified by psychologist Carl Jung. Self-scoring based on responses to 32 statements. Types include Extraversion/Introversion, Sensing/Intuition, Thinking/Feeling, and Perceiving/Judging. Trainer Guide includes suggestions on how the styles relate to individual conflict resolution strategies.

Katz, Neil H., John W. Lawyer and Marcia Sweedler. *Communication and Conflict Resolution Skills, 2nd ed.* Dubuque, IA: Kendall Hunt, 2011.
Manual for courses, workshops, and self-study. Includes theory, skill development, and self-testing, all from the point of view of communication theory.

Leviton, Sharon C. and James L. Greenstone. *Elements of Mediation.* Pacific Grove, CA: Brooks/Cole, 1997.
A brief practical guide on how to do problem-solving mediation. Short on theory and philosophy, but useful for practical tips and strategies.

Libove, Laurie Ribble. *Learning to Listen. Learning to Listen Facilitator Guide. 2nd ed.* King of Prussia, PA: HRDQ, 2004.
Self-scoring inventory based on responses to 30 statements. Provides feedback on individual skill in three listening areas: Staying Focused, Capturing the Message, and Helping the Speaker. Facilitator Guide provides tips for effective listening and its application to the workplace.

Luvmour, Sambhava and Josette. *Everyone Wins! Cooperative Games and Activities.* Gabriola Island, British Columbia: New Society Publishers, n.d.
Over 150 cooperative games that are easily adaptable to conflict resolution and mediation training. Most games are appropriate for children as well as adults; age levels are indicated.

MacBeth, Fiona and Nic Fine. *Playing with Fire: Creative Conflict Resolution for Young Adults.* Philadelphia: New Society Publishers, 1995.
A conflict resolution training program for young adults. Includes many practical exercises and makes creative use of the fire metaphor for conflict.

Mennonite Conciliation Service. *Mediation and Facilitation Training Manual: Foundations and Skills for Constructive Conflict Transformation, 4th ed.* Akron, PA: Mennonite Conciliation Service, 2000.
The most comprehensive and oft-cited manual in the field. Includes detailed information on the nature of conflict and conflict transformation, mediation, and group facilitation.

Mock, Ron, ed. *The Roleplay Book: 41 Hypothetical Situations, 2nd edition.* Akron, PA: Mennonite Conciliation Service, 1997.

An excellent source of training exercises. Includes various levels of interpersonal conflicts, complex multiparty disputes, and scripts, sociodramas, and case studies.

Moore, Christopher W. *The Mediation Process: Practical Strategies for Resolving Conflict, 3rd ed.* San Francisco: Jossey-Bass, 2003.

A very comprehensive handbook, written by a professional mediator. Contains more theory and research than most other manuals.

OJPCR: The Online Journal of Peace and Conflict Resolution

Intended as a resource for students, teachers and practitioners in fields relating to the reduction and elimination of conflict. It desires to be a free, yet valuable, source of information to aid anyone trying to work toward a less violent and more cooperative world.

Potter, Dr. Beverly. *From Conflict to Cooperation: How to Mediate a Dispute.* Berkeley, CA: Ronin Publishing, 1996.

A practical handbook, cleverly illustrated by nationally-syndicated cartoonist Phil Frank. Couched in both humanistic psychology and Eastern philosophy, the book offers many valuable tips and strategies. Because Potter is an organizational consultant, this manual offers more direct applications to the workplace than most.

Potter-Efron, Ronald T. and Pat Potter-Efron. *Letting Go of Anger: The 10 Most Common Anger Styles and What to Do About Them.* Oakland, CA: New Harbinger Publications, 1995.

A practical workbook by two therapists. Includes self-tests, examples, and techniques.

Reilly, Patrick M. and Michael S. Shropshire. *Anger Management for Substance Abuse and Mental Health Clients: A Cognitive Behavioral Therapy Manual.* DHHS Pub. No. (SMA) 03-3859. Rockville, MD: Center for Substance Abuse Treatment, Substance Abuse and Mental Health Services Administration, 2002.

Although developed for a substance abuse counseling program, the techniques suggested are valuable for conflict resolution as well. Available free (along with a Participant's Workbook) on the web at www.samhsa.gov/ or by calling the National Clearinghouse for Alcohol and Drug Information at 1-800-729-6686.

Russo, Eileen M. and Matthew P. Eckler. *Conflict Strategies Inventory. Conflict Strategies Inventory Facilitator Guide.* King of Prussia, PA: HRDQ, n.d.

Self-scoring inventory based on responses to descriptions of ten workplace-related conflict situations. Facilitator Guide provides instructions for administering the inventory as well as analysis of the conflict situations and interpretation of the results.

Sashkin, Marshall. *Conflict Style Inventory, revised ed. Conflict Style Inventory Trainer Guide, revised ed. Managing Conflict Constructively, revised ed.* Amherst, MA: HRD Press, 1995.

Self-scoring inventory based on responses to ten brief case studies, all of them employment-related. Trainer Guide provides analysis of the case studies and suggestions for workshops. Managing Conflict Constructively is a short pamphlet that describes the basic interpersonal strategies needed to discuss and resolve conflicts.

Schwarz, Roger M. *The Skilled Facilitator: Practical Wisdom for Developing Effective Groups.* San Francisco: Jossey-Bass, 1994.
A useful volume focused on group facilitation and dealing with conflict in groups.

Slaikeu, Karl A. *When Push Comes to Shove: A Practical Guide to Mediating Disputes.* San Francisco: Jossey-Bass, 1996.
A comprehensive manual of problem-solving mediation techniques and strategies, written by a professional mediator.

Timpson, William M. *Teaching and Learning Peace.* Madison, WI: Atwood Publishing, 2002.
A very personal narrative that shares stories from the author's over 30 years of working as a peace educator. Includes a comprehensive introduction to the literature on peacemaking as well as many practical tips.

Timpson, William M., Edward J. Brantmeier, Nathalie Kees, Tom Cavanaugh, Claire McGlynn, and Elavie Ndura-Ouédraogo. *147 Practical Tips for Teaching Peace and Reconciliation.* Madison, WI: Atwood Publishing, 2009.
Much more than a list of teaching tips, the authors situate their suggestions in the theories and literature of peace studies, and provide a rationale for their proposals.

Weinstein, Matt and Joel Goodman. *Playfair: Everybody's Guide to Noncompetitive Play.* San Luis Obispo, CA: Impact Publishers, 1980.
A wonderfully creative source of cooperative games that can easily be adapted for conflict resolution and mediation training.

Withers, Bill and Keami D. Lewis. *The Conflict and Communication Activity Book: 30 High-Impact Training Exercises for Adult Learners.* New York: AMACOM, 2003.
Almost any trainer could use each of these exercises successfully the first time out. The authors provide a valuable short introduction to transformative training. Each of the 30 activities is described in detail, with a suggested script for introducing and debriefing the exercise. Time and materials needed are clearly laid out, and handouts and flip chart material are provided where appropriate.

Appendix IV: Books for Conflict Resolution and Mediation

Boulding, Elise. *Cultures of Peace: The Hidden Side of History.* Syracuse, NY: Syracuse University Press, 2000.
Looks at the history of nonviolent and peaceful cultures for lessons about how to empower peacebuilding movements in the twenty-first century.

Burton, John. *Conflict: Resolution and Provention.* New York: St. Martin's Press, 1990.
Derives problem-solving and conflict-resolution processes from human needs theory. Coins the term "provention" to refer to the process of actively removing the bases for potential conflicts.

Bush, Robert A. Baruch and Joseph P. Folger. *The Promise of Mediation: Responding to Conflict Through Empowerment and Recognition.* San Francisco: Jossey-Bass, 1994.
Analyzes, critiques, and promotes the field of mediation today, focusing on its transformative potential. Criticizes mediation practices that focus primarily on solving problems as opposed to those that seek to empower participants and transform their personal relationship.

Bush, Robert A. Baruch and Joseph P. Folger. *The Promise of Mediation: The Transformative Approach to Conflict. Revised ed.* San Francisco: Jossey-Bass, 2005.
In an update of their earlier book, the authors reflect on changes in the field in the 10 years since the first book. Provides the transcript of a sample mediation that, in my opinion, is more anarchic than transformative.

The Colorado Trust. *Promoting Health by Building Community Capacity: Evidence and Implications for Grantmakers.* Denver, CO: The Colorado Trust, 1998.
Provides a succinct and perhaps definitive definition of community capacity, discussed in the context of community mental health and wellness.

Coser, Lewis. *The Functions of Social Conflict.* New York: The Free Press, 1956.
A classic work that draws on the roots of the sociological tradition to show the many ways that conflict can be functional for groups, organizations, and societies.

De Dreu, Carsten K.W. and Evert Van De Vliert, eds. *Using Conflict in Organizations.* London: Sage Publications, 1997.
A book of essays that takes the position that conflict in groups and organizations can be a productive force which can improve quality and group decision making.

Deutsch, Morton and Peter T. Coleman (eds.). *The Handbook of Conflict Resolution: Theory and Practice.* San Francisco: Jossey-Bass, 2000.
A comprehensive resource, it consists of original essays by leading authorities on processes of interpersonal and intergroup conflict generation and resolution.

Diamond, Louise. *The Peace Book: 108 simple Ways to Create a More Peaceful World. Third revised edition.* Bristol, VT: The Peace Company, 2001.
A handbook of practical strategies to create peace within ourselves, in our personal relationships, families, communities, and in the world. Includes good web resources.

Duffy, Karen Grover et al., eds. *Community Mediation: A Handbook for Practitioners and Researchers.* New York: Guilford Press, 1991.
An extensive collection of readings that provides research findings on conflict resolution processes as well as the success of community mediation centers and programs.

Dukes, E. Franklin, Marina A. Piscolish, and John B. Stephens. *Reaching for Higher Ground in Conflict Resolution: Tools for Powerful Groups and Communities.* San Francisco: Jossey-Bass. 2000.
An intriguing attempt to take mediation beyond common ground to *higher ground,* where the parties go beyond self-interest to envision creative joint solutions and to grow in a mutually supportive, principled way.

Fisher, Roger and William Ury. *Getting to Yes: Negotiating Agreement Without Giving In, 2nd ed.* New York: Penguin, 1991.
The fundamental resource on principled negotiation and collaborative problem-solving.

Fisher, Roger and Scott Brown. *Getting Together: Building Relationships as We Negotiate.* New York: Houghton Mifflin, 1988.
Another book emerging from the Harvard Negotiation Project. This one focuses on maintaining and enhancing relationships through principled negotiation.

Fisher, Roger, Elizabeth Kopelman and Andrea Kupfer Schneider. *Beyond Machiavelli: Tools for Coping with Conflict.* New York: Penguin Books, 1994.
A manual for dealing with conflict resolution on the international level.

Fisher, Ronald J. *Interactive Conflict Resolution.* Syracuse, NY: Syracuse University Press, 1997.
Theory, research, and practical strategies for resolving conflict on the international level.

Galtung, Johan. *Peace by Peaceful Means: Peace and Conflict, Development and Civilization.* London: Sage Publications, 1996.
A comprehensive overview of peace and conflict theory by the international father of peace studies.

Gilmore, Susan K. and Patrick W. Fraleigh, *Communication at Work, 3rd edition.* Eugene, OR: Friendly Press, 1993.
An accessible manual of knowledge and skills for improving communication at work. Covers, among other topics, coaching and conflict resolution.

Goffman, Erving. *Interaction Ritual: Essays on Face-to-Face Behavior.* New York: Anchor Books, 1967.
A unique sociological analysis of "facework," or the behaviors in which people engage in order to maintain the credibility of their self-image claims and avoid "losing face." Generates many insights applicable to the interactional process of conflict resolution and mediation.

Hanh, Thich Nhat. *Anger: Wisdom for Cooling the Flames.* New York: Riverhead Books, 2001.
Uses the wisdom of Zen Buddhism to show that mindfulness and compassion are the keys to transforming anger. Has many practical stragegies.

Iadicola, Peter and Anson Shupe. *Violence, Inequality, and Human Freedom, 2nd edition.* New York: Rowman & Littlefield, 2003.
A unique and insightful analysis that locates the roots of violence in the structure of inequality in society. After developing a general theory of violence, the authors analyze each level of violence, from interpersonal to structural. Useful in understanding the origin of conflict and determining which issues are amenable to mediation and which are not.

Katz, Neil H. and John W. Lawyer, *Resolving Conflict Successfully: Needed Knowledge and Skills.* New York: Corwin Press, 1994.
Presents core skills for conflict resolution and practical illustrations.

Kochman, Thomas. *Black and White Styles in Conflict.* Chicago: University of Chicago Press, 1981.
Useful for understanding how cultural differences impact the communication process.

Kolb, Deborah M. et al., *When Talk Works: Profiles of Mediators.* San Francisco: Jossey-Bass, 1994.
Interviews with mediators who talk about how they work to resolve conflicts.

Kriesberg, Louis. 2007. *Constructive Conflicts: From Escalation to Resolution.* Lanham, MD: Rowan and Littlefield.
A comprehensive, sociological examination of the origins of conflicts, both international and interpersonal, and their various resolution processes.

LeBaron, Michelle. *Bridging Troubled Waters: Conflict Resolution from the Heart.* San Francisco: Jossey-Bass, 2002.
A deeply personal discussion of mediation that focuses on the whole person, utilizing multiple ways of knowing.

Lederach, John Paul. *Preparing for Peace: Conflict Transformation Across Cultures.* Syracuse: Syracuse University Press, 1995.
An examination of culture and its relation to conflict resolution training by one of the giants of the field.

Merry, Sally Engle and Neal Miler, eds. *The Possibility of Popular Justice: A Case Study of Community Mediation in the United States.* Ann Arbor: University of Michigan Press, 1993.
An in-depth study of the pioneering community mediation program, Community Boards of San Francisco.

Mitchell, Christopher and Michael Banks. *Handbook of Conflict Resolution: The Analytical Problem-Solving Approach.* London: Pinter, 1996.
Develops the theoretical rationale and lays the strategies involved in collaborative, analytical, problem-solving conflict resolution between and among nations.

Mosten, Forrest S. *Mediation Career Guide: A Strategic Approach to Building a Successful Practice.* San Francisco: Jossey-Bass.
A comprehensive and practical guide to becoming a practicing mediator by one of the most successful individual practitioners.

Nicotera, Anne Maydan, ed. *Conflict and Organizations: Communicative Processes.* Albany: State University of New York Press, 1995.
Assumes that conflict is a naturally-occurring human phenomenon, and examines how it impacts and is impacted by communication processes at the organizational and interpersonal level.

Phillips, Barbara Ashley. *Finding Common Ground: A Field Guide to Mediation.* Austin, TX: Hells Canyon Publishing, 1994.
A description of the nuts and bolts of mediation, with emphasis on how to select a competent mediator, particularly with regard to family mediation.

Porter, Jack Nusan and Ruth Taplin. *Conflict and Conflict Resolution: A Sociological Introduction.* Lanham, MD: University Press of America, 1987. Reprinted in 1997 with a theoretical and bibliographic update by The Spencer Press, Newton Highlands, MA.
A good sociological overview of the field, from Simmel to contemporary theorists. Contains a useful bibliography.

Potter-Efron, Ronald T. *Working Anger: Preventing and Resolving Conflict on the Job.* Oakland, CA: New Harbinger Publications, 1998.
A useful, practical resource for both individuals in their own daily lives and for managers and supervisors in organizations.

Ramsbotham, Oliver, Tom Woodhouse, and Hugh Miall. *Contemporary Conflict Resolution: The Prevention, Management and Transformation of Deadly Conflicts, Second Edition.* Malden, MA: Polity Press, 2005.
A good overview of current conflict resolution theory and research. The bulk of the book focuses on war and international conflict.

Rosenberg, Marshall B. *Nonviolent Communication: A Language of Life, 2nd ed.* Encinitas, CA: Puddle Dancer Press, 1999.
Teaches how to communicate peacefully based on empathic listening and honest expressing, both of which include observations, feelings, needs, and requests. Promotes relationships based on mutual respect, compassion, and cooperation and the creation of social structures in which everyone gets their needs met.

Sandole, Dennis J. D. and Hugo van der Merwe, eds. *Conflict Resolution Theory and Practice: Integration and Application.* New York: Manchester University Press, 1993.
A wide-ranging book of readings on conflict theory and practice, from interpersonal resolution to international negotiations. Contains many insightful essays.

Schellenberg, James A. *Conflict Resolution: Theory, Research, and Practice.* Albany: State University of New York Press, 1996.
Combines an analysis of theories of conflict generation and resolution with case studies of conflict resolution from the interpersonal to the international.

Singer, Linda R. *Settling Disputes: Conflict Resolution in Business, Families, and the Legal System.* Boulder: Westview Press, 1990.
A survey of dispute resolution models, especially in relation to conventional legal models.

Tannen, Deborah. *You Just Don't Understand: Women and Men in Conversation.* New York: William Morrow, 1990.
An exploration of how gender impacts communication. Includes a chapter on gender styles in conflict.

Tavris, Carol. *Anger: The Misunderstood Emotion, revised edition.* New York: Simon & Schuster, 1989.
A landmark exploration of the subject from a social psychological point of view. Suggests that just as suppressing anger is not always healthy, neither is expressing it always a good idea. Revised edition looks more closely at gender differences and gender politics with regard to anger and more specific strategies for dealing constructively with anger.

Tjosvold, Dean. *Learning to Manage Conflict: Getting People to Work Together Productively.* New York: Lexington Books, 1993.
An accessible, practical manual that draws on organizational research. Provides useful examples of conflict resolution strategies in action.

Ury, William. *Getting Past No: Negotiating Your Way from Confrontation To Cooperation. Revised ed.* New York: Bantam, 1993.
Elaborates the model he developed with Roger Fisher, providing more handy techniques for resolving conflict constructively and maintaining and enhancing relationships.

Ury, William. *The Third Side: Why We Fight and How We Can Stop* (previously published as *Getting To Peace*). New York: Penguin, 2000.
Using his training as an anthropologist, Ury draws on extensive evidence to show that violent conflict is not an inherent part of human nature. Violence as a solution is relatively recent, and can be overcome by using the ancient human tradition of "the third side."

Wehr, Paul. *Conflict Regulation.* Boulder: Westview Press, 1979.
A pioneering work in the field. Explores conflict dynamics through the examination of case studies. Includes appendix of training exercises.

Weisinger, Hendrie. *Anger at Work: Learning the Art of Anger Management on the Job.* New York: William Morrow and Company, 1995.
An easily accessible handbook that describes the phenomenon of anger and gives practical strategies for using and managing it.

Weisinger, Hendrie. *Emotional Intelligence at Work.* San Francisco: Jossey-Bass, 1998.
Describes emotional intelligence and documents its importance in the work setting. Gives practical tips on how to master the core competencies of emotional intelligence, including such skills as mood management, assertiveness, listening and communication, giving and receiving criticism. Shows how to emotionally mentor others.

Wilmot, William W. and Joyce L. Hocker. *Interpersonal Conflict, 7th ed.* New York: McGraw-Hill, 2005.
An examination of conflict and conflict resolution through the lens of communication theory. Very thorough.

Winslade, John and Gerald Monk. *Narrative Mediation: A New Approach to Conflict Resolution.* San Francisco: Jossey-Bass, 2000.
A groundbreaking work that emphasizes the vital role of storytelling in both conflict generation and conflict resolution. Facilitating conflict resolution, according to the authors, is helping the parties to re-vision and retell the story of their relationship.

Zeigler, J.W. "Zig" Jr. *The Mediation Kit: Tools to Solve Disputes.* John Wiley & Sons, 1997.
Detailed information about conducting a mediation and the best way to prepare for it. Extensive resources including sample forms and case study examples.

Appendix V: Conflict Resolution and Mediation Organizations

Listed here are organizations providing mediation services and/or resources. New ones are created fairly frequently, and websites change, so be sure to search the Web.

Keywords to explore using your favorite computer search engine: conflict resolution, mediation, community mediation, peer mediation, family mediation, environmental mediation, conciliation, negotiation, nonviolent communication, peace, peacemaking, peace education, reconciliation, compassion, nonviolence, alternatives to violence

Alternatives to Violence Project
St. Paul, MN
877 926-8287
www.avpusa.org

Provides education in conflict resolution, alternatives to violence, and personal empowerment to people in prisons, schools, and communities. Begun in New York, it is now found in many states and foreign countries. Offers train-the-trainers training and consultation for groups around the country who want to do this work.

American Arbitration Association
Washington, DC
202 296-8510
www.adr.org

Promotes the use of voluntary dispute resolution. Its 35 regional offices have a pool of more than 50,000 trained arbitrators/mediators to assist in a wide variety of disputes. Publishes *Arbitration Journal.*

American Bar Association, Section of Dispute Resolution
Washington, D.C.
202 662-1680
www.abanet.org/dispute

Provides a clearinghouse for information on alternative dispute resolution; publishes *Dispute Resolution Magazine* quarterly, a free *Guide to Dispute Resolution Processes* and other resources. Check with your state Bar Association as well.

Association for Conflict Resolution
Washington, D.C.
202 464-9700
www.acrnet.org

The result of a merger between the Academy of Family Mediators (AFM), Conflict Resolution Education Network (CREnet), and the Society of Professionals in Dispute Resolution (SPIDR) in 2001, this organization serves a diverse international audience of more than 7,000 mediators and conflict resolution educators. Publishes the journal *Conflict Resolution Quarterly* and the magazine *ACResolution.* Provides access to affordable professional liability insurance for mediators.

CDR Associates
1-800-MEDIATE
www.mediate.org

A good example of a private organization providing conflict and dispute resolution services both domestically and internationally in the areas of cross-cultural, environmental, and organizational conflict resolution and collaborative decisionmaking.

Center for Nonviolent Communication
818 957-9393
www.cnvc.org

Describes and provides resources on the Nonviolent Communication model developed by Marshall Rosenberg. The model is based on empathic listening and honest expressing, both of which include observations, feelings, needs, and requests. The site has many good resources on education and parenting as well as personal transformation and interpersonal communication enhancement.

Community Boards Program
San Francisco, CA
415 920-3820
www.communityboards.org

Founded in 1976, this is one of the oldest and largest community-based dispute resolution programs. Provides training for mediators and mediation trainers. Has a variety of resource materials, including several curricula for conflict resolution in schools.

Community Relations Service
U.S. Department of Justice
Chevy Chase, MD
301 492-5929
http://www.justice.gov/crs/

Provides technical assistance to school systems and communities for conflict resolution and the prevention of violence.

Conflict Resolution Center International, Inc.
http://crinfo.org/crcii/

Maintains a resource database listing various types of conflict resolvers by fields of experience location. Publishes the quarterly newsletter *Conflict Resolution Notes.* Has extensive computer-catalogued library of conflict resolution materials.

Council of Better Business Bureaus, Inc., ADR Division
Dispute Resolution Division
www.dr.bbb.org

A public service agency designed to protect consumers, the BBB strives to solve disputes between companies and consumers through arbitration or mediation. The ADR Division provides training in arbitration and mediation and publishes a newsletter called *BBB Solutions.* Several BBBs also operate dispute resolution centers in local communities.

CRU Institute
Bellevue, WA
800 922-1988
www.cruinstitute.org/

Provides training for school-wide mediation programs, including parent training. Includes materials in Spanish as well as several award-winning training videos that can be previewed on the website.

Education for Conflict Resolution, Inc. (ECR)
P.O. Box 275
North Manchester, IN 46962
219 982-4621
www.workitout.org

Agency that began as an offshoot of the oldest Peace Studies program in the nation at Manchester College. Now provides mediation services as well as training for community mediators, school mediators, and mediation trainers. Publishes an extensive training manual.

Educators for Social Responsibility
Cambridge, MA
617 492-1764
www.esrnational.org

Offers curricula and professional development in the areas of conflict resolution, peace studies, and diversity education. Seeks to make social responsibility an integral part of education. Publishes a newsletter entitled *Forum.*

Indiana Network of Community Mediation Centers (INCOMM)
c/o Conflict Resolution Center
Indiana University East
PO Box 1564, Richmond IN 47375
765 973-8511
crcinc@indiana.edu

Electronic network of community mediators from all parts of the state of Indiana.

M.K. Gandhi Institute for Nonviolence
Memphis, TN
901 452-2824
www.gandhiinstitute.org

Founded by Mahatma Gandhi's grandson, the Mission of the Gandhi Institute is to promote and apply the principles of nonviolence locally, nationally, and globally, to prevent violence and resolve personal and public conflicts through research, education, and programming.

Mediate.com
www.mediate.com

Claims to be the most visited conflict resolution site in the world. Offers training, resources for mediators, and a mediator locator service. Has a free email newsletter.

Mennonite Conciliation Service (MCS)
Akron, PA
717 859-3889
www.mcc.org/us/peaceandjustice/mcs.html

Organization of Mennonite conciliation practitioners who approach conflict resolution from a Christian peacemaking perspective. MCS has extensive publications, including *Conciliation Quarterly Newsletter,* an extensive mediation training manual and a book of roleplays (both cited under Books above).

NAFCM (National Association for Community Mediation)
Washington, DC
202 667-9700
www.nafcm.org

Supports the maintenance and growth of community-based mediation programs. Maintains a national directory of programs and advocates for community mediation. Extensive information on resources and publications; quarterly newsletter.

Operation Respect: Don't Laugh at Me
2 Penn Plaza, 5th Floor
New York, New York 10121
212-904-5243
www.dontlaugh.org/

A non-profit organization working to transform schools, camps and organizations focused on children and youth, into more compassionate, safe and respectful environments. Founded by Peter Yarrow of the folk group Peter, Paul & Mary, the organization disseminates educational resources that are designed to establish a climate that reduces the emotional and physical cruelty some children inflict upon each other by behaviors such as ridicule, bullying and – in extreme cases – violence.

Peace Web
Tucson, AZ
520 670-1541
www.apeacemaker.net

Links thousands of individuals and groups working for justice, peace, and conflict transformation at the community level, in academic, religious, and workplace settings, internationally, domestically, and locally. Formerly the National Conference on Peacemaking and Conflict Resolution.

Program on Negotiation at Harvard Law School
Harvard University
Cambridge MA
617 495-1684
www.pon.harvard.edu

The pioneering program that gave birth to Fisher and Ury's groundbreaking works on principled negotiation. Publishes a newsletter called *Consensus.*

Tabula Rasa Institute
Washington, D.C.
www.trinstitute.org

A nonprofit organization that promotes peace, understanding, and cooperation between people, groups, and nations by providing the resources, education, and leadership. Maintains the Conflict Resolution Education Clearinghouse and publishes the electronic journal *OJPCR: The Online Journal of Peace and Conflict Resolution.*

The Third Side
From the Global Negotiation Project at Harvard University
www.thirdside.org/

Based on William Ury's book, this site provides oral and written summaries of the book and practical suggestions for action. Includes an innovative interactive tool for mapping a conflict and identifying the third side.

Victim-Offender Mediation Association (VOMA)
c/o St. Vincent de Paul Center for Community Reconciliation
Orange, CA
714 836-8100
www.voma.org

Facilitates the exchange of information among victim-offender mediation programs around the world through its newsletter, publications, and conferences. Develops guidelines for program management and standards of practice, and advocates for victim-offender mediation. Membership includes a quarterly newsletter and a conference discount.

Victim-Offender Reconciliation Program (VORP) Information and Resource Center
Portland, OR 97220
503 255-VORP [8677]
www.vorp.com/

Aims to bring restorative justice reform to the criminal and juvenile justice systems, to empower victims, offenders, and communities to heal the effects of crime, curb recidivism and offer society a more effective and humanistic alternative to more prisons and punishment.

Appendix VI: Forms

The following forms have been used by ***Common Ground, Inc.*** Community Dispute Resolution Service.

COMMON GROUND, Inc.

Community Dispute Resolution Service

Case Record

Date ____/____/______ Case # ________

Taken by ________________________ Phone ____ Walk-in ____ Other ________________

Initiating Disputant ____________________	Other Disputant* ____________________
Address ____________________	Address ____________________
____________________	____________________
Home phone ____________________	Home phone ____________________
Work phone ____________________	Work phone ____________________
Cell phone ____________________	Cell phone ____________________

Relationship to other Disputant ____________________________________ *attach additional sheets for more Disputants

Description of the Dispute

____

____

____

____

____

____

Prompting questions: **What happened?** (What is currently wrong? What problems are you having? What don't you like about the present situation? What do you want to be different?) **Are there other persons involved in the dispute that are not mentioned above?**

How did you learn about Common Ground?

Did someone suggest that you bring this problem to Common Ground? Yes ___ No ___ If yes, who? ______________________

___ Check here if this is a reactivation of a case previously mediated by Common Ground. Explain: ______________________

Case Developer assigned ______________________ Date assigned ___/___/_____

<u>OUTCOME OF CASE DEVELOPMENT</u> Subsequent Case Developer assigned ______________________ Date ___/___/_____

Initiating Disputant Other Disputant

____ ____ Refused to participate Why refused? ______________________

____ ____ Agreed to participate

____ Case not suitable for mediation. Explain reasons and list, with date, any other referrals made: ______________________

____

Possible reasons for unsuitability: 1) one or more disputants mentally incompetent to participate; 2) Risk of physical injury to disputants or mediators; 3) legal constraints prohibit mediation)

____ Parties resolved dispute without mediation.

____ Mediation postponed or pending. Explain ______________________

Classification of dispute ____ Neighbor ____ Family ____ Business/Customer ____ Landlord/Tenant ____ Victim/Offender

____ Work-related ____ Youth ____ Agency/Client ____ Other ______________________

Mediation Panel Members ______________________, Panel Convener ______________________

______________________ ______________________

Scheduled mediation Date ___/___/_____ Time _________ Place ______________________

Mediation session #2 (if necessary) Date ___/___/_____ Time _________ Place ______________________

Agreement reached: ____ Yes ____ No If no, explain ______________________

Case closed: Date ___/___/_____ Reason: ______________________

Followup Date ___/___/_____ ____ Phone ____ Other ______________ Completed ____ Yes ____ No

If not completed, explain ______________________

COMMON GROUND, Inc.

Community Dispute Resolution Service

Agreement to Mediate

Agreement between *Common Ground, Inc.* and the Disputant named below

We understand that:

1. Common ground dispute resolution is a process by which the parties to a dispute are assisted in finding areas of agreement in order to peacefully resolve a conflict. While expressions of disagreement and sometimes anger are part of the process, all participants must treat each other with respect at all times.

2. Disputants themselves dictate and control the Agreement. There is no agreement unless all parties to the dispute agree that there is. Each disputant present at mediation must agree to all aspects of the Agreement.

3. Disputants do not forfeit any of their rights to go to Court or to other dispute resolution forums if an agreement is not reached during mediation. Any agreement reached during mediation is a good-faith agreement and is not legally binding.

4. Mediators act solely as neutrals and not as advocates for any person involved in the dispute. Mediators cannot and should not give legal advice.

The disputant agrees that:

1. I will treat all participants in the mediation process with respect.

2. I will follow the policies established by ***Common Ground, Inc.***, including the prohibition of weapons, drugs, alcohol, and tobacco at mediation sites.

3. Since confidentiality is essential to the mediation process, I agree I shall refrain from calling the mediators to testify in Court, and to refrain from subpoenaing any documents or notes taken during mediation. All information and all documents shall remain confidential except as required by law in cases of child abuse and neglect or as mutually agreed upon by all parties.

4. If an agreement is reached as a result of mediation, I will, in good faith, comply with the terms of that agreement.

5. I will not involve the mediators, the staff (paid or volunteer), or the records of ***Common Ground, Inc.*** in any Court or Administrative Hearing.

(Signed) ____________________________________ ____________________________________

Disputant or Agent — Printed Name

Date ____/____/_______

(Signed) ____________________________________ ____________________________________

Common Ground, Inc. representative — Printed Name / Position

Date ____/____/_______

COMMON GROUND, Inc.

Community Dispute Resolution Service

Agreement

Disputants: ________________________________ **Case #** __________
(printed names)

____

____

____

We the undersigned agree to the following:

We have made and signed this agreement because we believe that it settles in a satisfactory manner the issues between us raised in this mediation, and because we intend in good faith to abide by it.

Disputants (Signed):

________________________________ ________________________________

________________________________ ________________________________

Mediators (Signed):

________________________________ ________________________________

________________________________ ________________________________

Date ____/____/_______

Page ____of _____

COMMON GROUND, Inc.
Community Dispute Resolution Service

Volunteer Mediator Consent Form

Volunteer (printed name): ____

I agree that:

1. I will promote the principles of peaceful, common ground dispute resolution in my community.

2. I will volunteer at least 30 hours of time to ***COMMON GROUND, Inc.***

3. Since a volunteer organization is only as strong as the people who comprise it, I will make a good faith effort to be available for volunteer work, and to participate in a variety of tasks to maintain and build the organization, as my skills and time allow.

4. I will follow procedures set by ***COMMON GROUND, Inc.'s*** Board and will in good faith attempt to meet appropriate deadlines when I volunteer for a task.

5. The guiding principle of common ground dispute resolution is that the parties to a dispute retain ownership of that dispute and responsibility for resolving it themselves. I will not attempt to resolve people's disputes for them, but rather I will support and empower them to find their own resolutions.

6. I will treat all participants in the mediation process with respect.

7. I will maintain the confidentiality of the mediation process by not revealing any information recorded in any internal ***COMMON GROUND, Inc.*** documents or anything that is said during mediation sessions, except by written agreement or as required by law.

(Signed): ___________________________________ Date ____/____/_______

COMMON GROUND, Inc.

Community Dispute Resolution Service

Membership Application / Mediator Database

For internal use only - Please print

Name: ______________________________________

Street address: ______________________________________

City: ________________________ **State:** _____ **Zip:** _______________

Day phone: ________________________ **Evening phone:** ______________________

Cell phone: ________________________ **email address** ________________________

List any special instructions or considerations about contacting you:

____

Note: The balance of information on this form is for use within the organization only. It will be used in forming Mediation Panels and in non-identifying ways to describe this organization.

For each category, please circle the group with which you most clearly identify.

Age ≤17   18-25   26-35   36-45   46-55   56-65   65+

Gender   Female   Male

Race/Ethnicity   Hispanic   White   African American/Black   Asian

Native American   Other (specify) ______________________

Family Income per year $0 - $15,000 $16,000 - $30,000 $30,000+

Occupation/Work Experience

Clerical   Factory work   Farm work   Homemaker   Manager/Executive

Professional   Sales   Self-employed   Service   Skilled trade

Student   Unemployed   Other ____________________

Special skills or abilities (e.g., bilingual [specify languages]; know sign language)

____

____

(next page please)

Membership Application / Mediator Database (continued)

Please list any other groups for which you have specific knowledge:

____

____

____

Please state your preferences for the following roles and positions within *COMMON GROUND, Inc.* according to the scale below:

1 = I would prefer this role.
2 = not my top choice, but I would do it if needed
3 = I would prefer not to do this, but will do it if absolutely necessary
0 = Please don't ask me to do this.

____Serving on a mediation panel

____Doing case development by myself

____Doing case development with a partner

____Doing case followup (to see how the agreement is working)

____Assisting with mediator training (providing roleplay feedback, demonstrating techniques, etc.)

____Doing outreach/public relations (giving talks about Common Ground, doing demonstration mediation sessions, etc.)

____Fundraising

____Developing continuing education programs (identify additional areas and resources for training, set up practice roleplays, etc.)

Please state, as frankly as possible, any types of cases in which you would *not* be comfortable participating:

____

____

(Signed): ____________________________________ Date ____/____/_______

Thank you.

Works Cited

These are complete references to all the works cited in the text of the manual.

Becker, Howard S. 1963. *Outsiders: Studies in the Sociology of Deviance.* New York: Free Press.

Boulding, Elise. 2000. *Cultures of Peace: The Hidden Side of History.* Syracuse, NY: Syracuse University Press.

Boulding, Kenneth. 1989. *Three Faces of Power.* Newbury Park, CA: Sage.

Bush, Robert A. Baruch and Joseph Folger. 1994. *The Promise of Mediation: Responding to Conflict Through Empowerment and Recognition.* San Francisco: Jossey-Bass.

Bush, Robert A. Baruch and Joseph P. Folger. 2005. *The Promise of Mediation: The Transformative Approach to Conflict. Revised ed.* San Francisco: Jossey-Bass.

Chödrön, Pema. 1994. *Start Where You Are: A Guide to Compassionate Living*. Boston: Shambhala Publications.

Christensen, Andrew, & Neil S. Jacobson. 2000. *Reconcilable Differences*. New York: Guilford.

The Colorado Trust. 1998. *Promoting Health by Building Community Capacity: Evidence and Implications for Grantmakers.* Denver, CO: The Colorado Trust.

Deutsch, Morton and Peter T. Coleman, eds. 2000. *The Handbook of Conflict Resolution: Theory and Practice.* San Francisco: Jossey-Bass.

Diamond, Louise. 2001. *The Peace Book: 108 Simple Ways to Create a More Peaceful World. Third revised edition.* Bristol, VT: The Peace Company.

Douglass, Frederick. 1852. *What to the Slave is the Fourth of July?* Accessed at http://www.lib.rochester.edu/index.cfm?page=2945

Du Bois, W.E.B. 1903/1995. *The Souls of Black Folk.* New York: Signet Classic.

Duffy, Karen Grover et al., eds. 1991. *Community Mediation: A Handbook for Practitioners and Researchers.* New York: Guilford Press.

Durkheim, Emile. 1964. *The Division of Labor in Society.* New York: Free Press.

Elias, Robert and Jennifer Turpin, eds. 1994. *Rethinking Peace.* Boulder, CO: Lynne Riener.

Fisher, Roger and William Ury. 1983. *Getting to Yes.* New York: Penguin.

Frager, Robert, ed. 1994. *Who Am I? Personality Types for Self-Discovery.* Tarcher-Putnam.

Galtung, Johan. 1996. *Peace by Peaceful Means: Peace and Conflict, Development and Civilization.* London: Sage Publications.

Galtung, Johan, Carl G. Jacobsen and Kai Frithjof Brand-Jacobsen. 2002. *Searching for Peace: The Road to TRANSCEND.* London: Pluto Press.

Garcia, Angela. 1991. "Dispute Resolution without Disputing: How the Interactional Organization of Mediation Hearings Minimizes Argument." *American Sociological Review* 56:818-835.

Garfinkel, Harold. 1967. *Studies in Ethnomethodology.* Englewood Cliffs, NJ: Prentice-Hall.

Gilmore, Susan K. and Patrick W. Fraleigh. 2004. *The Friendly Style Profile for People at Work.* Eugene, OR: Friendly Press.

Goffman, Erving. 1959. *Presentation of Self in Everyday Life.* Garden City, NY: Anchor.

Goffman, Erving. 1967. *Interaction Ritual: Essays on Face-to-Face Behavior.* New York: Pantheon.

Goffman, Erving. 1974. *Frame Analysis: An Essay on the Organization of Experience.* Boston: Northeastern University Press.

Goodwin, Charles. 1984. "Notes on Story Structure and the Organization of Participation" in J.M. Atkinson and J. Heritage, eds., *Structures of Social Action.* Cambridge: Cambridge University Press: 225-246.

Gopin, Marc. 2005. H*ealing the Heart of Conflict: 8 Crucial Steps to Making Peace with Yourself and Others.* Emmaus, PA: Rodale Books.

Hanh, Thich Nhat. 2001. *Anger: Wisdom for Cooling the Flames.* New York: Riverhead Books.

Harris, Ian and John Synott. 2002. "Peace education for a new century." *Social Alternatives* 21:1 pp. 3-6.

Harris, Marvin. 1990. *Our Kind: Who We Are, Where We Came From, and Where We Are Going.* New York: HarperPerennial.

Harvard Negotiation Project. 2011. www.pon.harvard.edu/category/research_projects/harvard-negotiation-project/ Accessed October 10, 2011.

Katz, Neil H. and John W. Lawyer. 1994. *Resolving Conflict Successfully: Needed Knowledge and Skills.* New York: Corwin Press.

Kübler-Ross, Elisabeth. 1969. *On Death and Dying*, London: Routledge.

Lancaster, Lynne C. and David Stillman. 2002. *When Generations Collide.* New York: Harper Business.

LeBaron, Michelle. 2002. *Bridging Troubled Waters: Conflict Resolution from the Heart.* San Francisco: Jossey-Bass.

Lemert, Edwin M. 1951. *Social Pathology.* New York: McGraw-Hill.

MacBeth, Fiona and NicFine. 1995. *Playing with Fire: Creative Conflict Resolution for Young Adults*. Philadelphia: New Society Publishers.

Merton, Robert F. 1968. *Social Theory and Social Structure.* New York: The Free Press.

Merton, Robert F. 1976. "Discrimination and the American Creed," pp. 189-216 in *Sociological Ambivalence and Other Essays*. New York: The Free Press, 1976.

Payne, Ruby K. 1995. *Poverty: A Framework for Understanding and Working with Students and Adults from Poverty*. Baytown, Texas: RFT Publishing.

Ramsbotham, Oliver, Tom Woodhouse, and Hugh Miall. 2005. *Contemporary Conflict Resolution: The Prevention, Management and Transformation of Deadly Conflicts, Second Edition.* Malden, MA: Polity Press.

Reilly, Patrick M. and Michael S. Shropshire. 2002. *Anger Management for Substance Abuse and Mental Health Clients: A Cognitive Behavioral Therapy Manual.* DHHS Pub. No. (SMA) 03-3859. Rockville, MD: Center for Substance Abuse Treatment, Substance Abuse and Mental Health Services Administration.

Schellenberg, James A. 1996. *Conflict Resolution: Theory, Research, and Practice.* Albany, NY: State University of New York Press.

Sennett, Richard and Jonathan Cobb. 1972. *The Hidden Injuries of Class.* New York: Vintage.

Simmel, Georg. 1950. *The Sociology of Georg Simmel.* Trans. by Kurt Wolff. New York: Free Press.

Simmel, Georg. 1955. *Conflict and The Web of Group-Affiliations.* New York: The Free Press.

Thomas, William I. and Dorothy S. Thomas 1928. *The Child in America: Behavior Problems and Programs.* New York: Knopf.

Tutu, Desmond. 2000. *No Future Without Forgiveness.* New York: Image.

Ury, William. 1991. *Getting Past No.* New York: Bantam.

Ury, William. 2000. *The Third Side: Why We Fight and How We Can Stop.* New York: Penguin.

Weisinger, Hendrie. 1998. *Emotional Intelligence at Work.* San Francisco: Jossey-Bass.

Wilmot, William W. and Joyce L. Hocker. 2005. *Interpersonal Conflict, 7th ed.* New York: McGraw-Hill.

Winslade, John and Gerald Monk. 2000. *Narrative Mediation: A New Approach to Conflict Resolution.* San Francisco: Jossey-Bass.

Withers, Bill and Keami D. Lewis. 2003. *The Conflict and Communication Activity Book: 30 High-Impact Training Exercises for Adult Learners.* New York: AMACOM.

About the Author

Patrick J. Ashton received a Ph.D. in Sociology with a concentration in conflict and social change from Michigan State University in 1981. While at Michigan State, he also obtained a Certification in College Teaching from the Department of Sociology and received an all-university award for excellence in teaching. Pat has taught in the Department of Sociology at Indiana University Purdue University Fort Wayne (IPFW) since 1979 and has been a member of the Graduate Faculty of Indiana University since 1991. In 1998 Pat was inducted into Indiana University FACET (Faculty Colloquium on Excellence in Teaching). In 1999 he received the North Central Sociological Association's Distinguished Contributions to Teaching Award and the John P. Ulmer Outstanding Service to Minorities Award from IPFW. In 2000 Pat was honored as a Great Man by the Office of Diversity and Multicultural Services at IPFW.

In 2001 Pat received an Indiana University President's Award for teaching and the IPFW Friends of the University Teaching Award. In 2002 Pat Ashton was the IPFW nominee for U.S. Professor of the Year, sponsored by the Carnegie Foundation for the Advancement of Teaching. In 2003 he received the Indiana Purdue Student Government Association Award for contributions to student learning and development. In 2010 Pat received the IPFW CELT Luminary Award for contributions to teaching and learning and in 2011 he received an honorary P.A. Mack Award for Distinguished Service to Teaching from the Faculty Colloquium for Excellence in Teaching (FACET) at Indiana University.

Besides regularly teaching Principles of Sociology, Pat Ashton has taught courses at both the undergraduate and graduate level on urban and community studies, conflict resolution and mediation, work and occupations, industrial sociology, technology and society, women and work, social theory, social problems, and social psychology. Pat developed a course in sociological pedagogy for graduate teaching assistants and high school social studies teachers. He has developed graduate courses in social theory, program evaluation, multiculturalism, and professional development. Pat's courses have been crosslisted with Women's Studies, Peace and Conflict Studies, and with the Master of Liberal Studies program. He has also taught for the Division of Labor Studies.

Pat is the author or co-author of fifteen published research articles on urban and community development, the effects of plant closings on displaced workers, social theory, sustainability, and social change. Pat is the co-author of a recently published book on sustainability. In addition, he has more than a dozen publications on teaching and pedagogy. Pat Ashton's course materials appear in over a dozen sets of model course materials published by the American Sociological Association. He is also the author, through two successful editions, of the study guide, instructor's manual, and test bank that accompanied a leading introductory sociology textbook. Pat has made over two dozen presentations on teaching and pedagogy at the local, state, regional, and national levels. In addition, he has organized and conducted over eighty workshops ranging from a half-day to a week long on topics such as conflict resolution and mediation, sustainability, curriculum development and pedagogy.

Pat Ashton received a certificate in community mediation in 1994 and a certificate in mediation training in 1995. Pat has taken over 100 hours of additional training in advanced conflict resolution techniques. He has conducted mediations in schools and in the community between neighbors and in organizations. He has taught mediation and conflict resolution techniques to middle schoolers, neighborhood leaders, human service providers, college students, and sociological practitioners. Pat is a founding board member of *Common Ground, Inc.,* Fort Wayne, Indiana's volunteer community dispute resolution service. He wrote and designed most of the forms used by *Common Ground,* and was president of the organization from 1995-2000.

Pat is a member of many national organizations concerned with mediation, training, and teaching tolerance, including: Association for Conflict Resolution (where he holds a Practitioner/Educator certification), the National Association for Community Mediation, Educators for Social Responsibility, Association for Applied and Clinical Sociology, and the Southern Poverty Law Center (publishers of *Teaching Tolerance).* Pat has served as a member of the Coordinating Panel [Board of Directors] of the Center for Nonviolence, a Fort Wayne nonprofit agency that works to assure the safety of women, children, and men by providing opportunities to build nonviolent life skills, create nurturing homes free of violence, and develop a nonviolent community. Pat also currently serves as Director of the Indiana University Purdue University Fort Wayne Peace and Conflict Studies Program.

Index

D

E

F

G

H

I

Z